GROUNDED IN GOD

Care and Nurture in Friends Meeting

EDITED BY PATRICIA McBEE

Articles from *Pastoral Care Newsletter*

QUAKER PRESS
OF FRIENDS GENERAL CONFERENCE · PHILADELPHIA, PA

ISBN: 1-888305-71-1

Printed in the United States of America

Composition and design by David Budmen

Cover photograph by Neece

This project was sponsored by the Ministry and Nurture Committee of
Friends General Conference. Thanks to the members of the project
committee, Pat Fox, Robin Greenler and Carolyn Terrell for their thoughtful
assistance.

To order more copies of this publication or other Quaker titles call
1-800-966-4556 or on the world wide web at www.quakerbooks.org

Contents

INTRODUCTION

Help Wanted: Person with deep spiritual life, infinite patience, great wisdom, and vast knowledge of the foibles of human nature. Job requires availability 24 hours a day, 7 days a week to accompany friends and neighbors through the messes and joys that life provides.

That may be what we would like to find in a pastoral caregiver, but who could meet those requirements? Who would be willing to take on that assignment? If no applicants with those qualifications come forward, how then do we care for one another?

This book is by and for the everyday people who find themselves in the position of providing pastoral care to one another. We ordinary meeting members find ourselves faced with such matters as clearness for membership or marriage, care for the sick, and resolution of conflict in our meetings. We take the risk of reaching out, hoping that we can learn to be present to one another in a love that is grounded in God. We may fear that the job is beyond us, that there are situations that we do not have the insight, knowledge, and skills to handle.

Of course, Friends have generations of experience in caring for one another. Quaker pastoral care, like Quaker spirituality, is has as its foundation listening for the still, small voice that draws us closer to the Divine and to one another. Pastoral care is as delicate as sitting in expectant listening with someone confronting a grave life crisis and as robust as doing six loads of laundry. It is as practical as casseroles and as ephemeral as prayer. It is hard-headed questioning, and it is tender touch.

In reading *Grounded in God* you will meet hard-headed and tender Quakers who share what they have learned in providing care within their meetings. This is not a textbook for the professional, but a guidebook for those whose principle qualification is a willingness to serve. These writers recognize that sometimes the skills of a professional are called for, and they advise on when and how to seek professional support. But the real wisdom of this book lies in the recognition that there is *always* a place for the steadfast, loving support of one's community. We proceed in the faith that "they who live in love live in

God and God in them." (I John 4:17) As we open our hearts to one another in love we are grounding our care in God.

How This Book Came to Be

In 1993, after years of supporting meetings in her role as coordinator of the Friends Counseling Service, Arlene Kelly proposed a newsletter that would provide a vehicle for experienced caregivers to share their wisdom with others. With a generous grant from the Chace Fund for the first year of publication, *Pastoral Care Newsletter* was born out of her concern. Arlene drew upon her knowledge, training and experience to identify themes and contributors, and Helene Pollock assisted with the editing. Over its nine years it has grown beyond its origins in Philadelphia Yearly Meeting to circulate throughout North America and beyond. In my work as editor since 1997, I have found it to be a privilege to work with the writers in drawing out their wisdom and guidance for Friends.

The Quaker Press of Friends General Conference proposed collecting articles from *Pastoral Care Newsletter* in a volume that could serve as a reference for all those seeking to give care and nurture in Friends meetings—and for any group of loving lay people seeking to provide care to one another.

Wisdom for Giving Care

Each chapter of *Grounded in God* provides advice for addressing a specific question or challenge that faces pastoral caregivers. As you read along you will discover that underlying that specific advice are themes that come up again and again and again. I like to think of these themes as core wisdom that applies every time we undertake pastoral care.

The central element is to be grounded in faithfulness to the Divine. We seek to hold an awareness of that of God in each of our beloved meeting members, no matter how difficult or needy. We seek the guidance of the Spirit as we discern our leadings in caring for one another. In the process of giving this care we deepen our awareness of God's presence in our lives which, in turn, increases our ability to give care that is grounded in God.

Many writers lift up the importance of the meeting community. All of the delicate issues that caregivers are called upon to face become easier when the caregiver and the person cared for have come to know one another in the life of the meeting. It is easier to ask for help from someone you have learned to trust through working together to get out a mailing, sharing a meal, participating in meeting retreats, worship, and worship-sharing. By giving attention to deepening the connections in the community, we lighten our load as pastoral caregivers and make it easier for meeting members to know and respond to one another's needs.

Another recurring theme is that we must not be stopped by a sense of not knowing how to approach someone in need—or by the fear of being intrusive. As you read along you will find yourself reminded to reach out, even if you are feeling hesitant. Many of the articles refer to cases where meeting members were hurt because the meeting did not seem to notice or care when they were going through a difficult time. It is better to err in the direction of reaching out and being rebuffed than to fail to respond at all.

Our writers concur that the key tasks of pastoral caregivers are in being present and listening. It seems so simple as to go unnoticed. Can these simple gifts really help? For nearly every problem, the first step is to be there listening with loving openness. Sometimes nothing else can be done except to be with someone in her pain. Sometimes listening is *all that needs* to be done to help a person discover the needed direction. Sometimes being present and listening is the starting point for discovering more concrete next steps.

And finally, you will find yourself repeatedly reminded to know your limits as individuals and as a committee of caregivers. While some situations may be best addressed by a friendly inquiry made by a delegated member of the committee, other situations may call for the involvement two or three members of the committee rather than one. Some situations of care require the contribution of many members of the community. On the other hand, there are some matters in which the meeting's role should be a limited one. Perhaps our role is to help strengthen the family's response, or to refer the member to appropriate professional assistance, or to stand supportively by while a person finds his own inner resources. Every instance of pastoral care calls for discernment—"what is our rightly ordered response in this situation?" As Friends we believe that when we ask that question in faithfulness and openness, an answer will come sometimes in the still, small voice and sometimes in finding a path of caring opening before us.

How to Use This Book

Grounded in God is organized into six sections covering broad areas of providing care and nurture in our meetings. The chapters within each section are made up of several articles addressing a specific facet of the theme. In each chapter, a main article gives an overview of the subject, shorter articles give practical pointers. Most chapters include an account of "one meeting's experience" in addressing the issue. Additional resources for each topic are listed in the resource section beginning on page 309.

You can use *Grounded in God* as a reference book, a place to turn when an issue comes up in your meeting: How do we support marriages in our meeting? What is the best way to respond to a person who is experiencing severe depression? What special needs of single people should we be attentive to? When you are faced with a question that is new to your meeting, *Grounded in God* can help you approach it in the company of other meetings that have already encountered this concern. Each chapter has a set of questions for discussion which can help you to apply the information to your meeting's specific situation.

Grounded in God can also be part of the ongoing orientation of caregivers to this work. You might want to give a copy to each new person appointed to your committee and perhaps make it part of an orientation meeting for new committee members.

We hope that many Friends will choose to sit and read from chapter to chapter, along the way deepening the sense of the breadth and depth of the calling to pastoral care in our meetings.

There Is More to the Story

There is more to explore on the issue of care and nurture in Friends Meetings than the 34 chapters in *Grounded in God*. Four times a year, *Pastoral Care Newsletter* continues to bring the experience of seasoned Friends to questions of caregiving. For subscription information, contact Pastoral Care Newsletter, Philadelphia Yearly Meeting, 1515 Cherry Street, Philadelphia, PA 19102. (215) 241-7068.

A Word about Names

It is difficult to write about what this volume is and who it is for. The term "pastoral care" appears in almost all yearly meetings' books of *Faith and Practice*, but it is not a term commonly used in conversation by unprogrammed Friends. We tend to refer, instead, to the work of certain committees. However, those committees have different names in different yearly meetings: ministry and counsel, ministry and oversight, and overseers are most common. In recent years some African American Friends have raised concerns over the terms "overseer" and "oversight" which call up memories of how those terms were used by slaveholders. (See p. 125). This has led some meetings to creatively adopt new names for their caregiving committees such as "care and counsel," "membership care" and "listening ear."

If you serve on a committee with one of these names, this book is for you. Within the book we have opted for the terms caregiver, pastoral caregiver, and caregiving committee. We use the traditional names only in instances when it is the name of the committee in a specific meeting. We hope that you will recognize yourself in these pages, even if the names are different from what is used in your meeting.

Patricia McBee, March 2002

Acknowledgments

Thanks are due to many people whose work has converged into this volume:

Thanks to Arlene Kelly who had the vision to create a medium for experienced caregivers to share with others and to Helene Pollock who assisted her in the first three years of *Pastoral Care Newsletter*.

Thanks to the Chace Fund for providing funding for the first year so that *Pastoral Care Newsletter* could get off the ground.

Deepest appreciation to all those who have written for *Pastoral Care Newsletter* and who have allowed us to include their work in *Grounded in God*. They have worked with no compensation except for that of knowing they are part of a circle of Friends encouraging one another to be more loving and faithful. And thanks to the individuals and meetings who have allowed their stories to be told.

Great gratitude for the unsung steady service of the *Pastoral Care Newsletter* Committee. Sue Heath and Carolyn Terrell who have served on *PCN*'s committee throughout its nine years and others who have served along the way include Suzanne Day, Harriet Heath, Frank Kuehner, and Jean Robbins. Their wisdom, down-to-earth understanding of the Religious Society of Friends, and keen eyes for detail are reflected in every page.

Thanks also to the Care and Counsel for Meetings and Members Working Group of Philadelphia Yearly Meeting (formerly the Family Relations Committee) which has fostered *PCN* through the years and to Steve Gulick staff person of that committee for his many services large and small including the production and mailing of *PCN* throughout its history.

Thanks to Barbara Hirshkowitz of Quaker Press of Friends General Conference for wanting to collect this wisdom into a single volume to be available to Friends and to David Budmen at FGC for his work in reformatting the newsletters into this attractive book.

Finally thanks to all those who undertake the care of one another. May this book strengthen your service and help you to ground it in God.

THE ROLE OF PASTORAL CARE

The Ministry of Pastoral Care

Reflections of a Pastoral Caregiver

Growing into the Role
of Pastoral Caregiver

Deep Listening: Applying the Disciplines of
an Elder to Pastoral Care

Discerning Our Leadings as
Pastoral Caregivers

THE MINISTRY OF PASTORAL CARE

Pastoral Care Newsletter, Vol. 1, No. 1 • September 1993

BY ARLENE KELLY

OVER THE PAST FEW DECADES I have been grateful for opportunities to interact with both those who provide pastoral care and also with persons who are the recipients of the meeting's care. Both groups have taught me a deep respect, indeed reverence, for the ways in which the healing Spirit works among us. Both have exposed me to the wisdom of others as they have sought to meet the challenges placed in front of them in a way which is consistent with our values as Friends.

In this, the first issue of the *Pastoral Care Newsletter*, I have been asked to lift up some of the major themes which I have heard over the years as individual Friends as well as meetings have tried to understand the meaning of pastoral care and to live into that ministry in a meaningful way. Knowing that these reflections are in no way complete, it is our hope that this newsletter may stimulate discussion in meetings on the issue of pastoral care, and that you will seek ways to share the fruits of those discussions by submitting your ideas for inclusion in future issues of this newsletter.

The term "pastoral care" is not as common as some other Quaker language. Nevertheless, Philadelphia Yearly Meeting's *Faith and Practice* states that, "Pastoral care and counseling are the special responsibility of this committee." What is it that that phrase encompasses? Certainly it is the carrying out, on behalf of the meeting, of responsibilities in relation to membership and marriage. And still it is more. Pastoral care is the way in which we journey with each other in times of celebration, sadness, turmoil, transitions and along the quiet stretches. Together with our shared worship experience, it is the main glue which holds our meeting community together.

As our committees work to be more faithful and skillful in carrying out the ministry of pastoral care, I have heard the following three questions to be lifted up with regularity. Let us consider them as a starting point:

Question 1: *How can I be of help in a difficult situation when I have no experience in it? Doesn't this require help from someone with more experience or training than myself?*

It is, indeed, challenging to consider how to enter the lives of others at a time of crisis in a way that is caring and helpful. How do we journey with someone through the terminal illness or death of a loved one? How do we enter a marital crisis? What do we have to offer in situations of mental illness or substance abuse?

I have come to know that one essential ingredient is to recognize that we are not responsible for fixing the situation. Except for those few situations in which provision of some material aid is needed, we are not likely to be able to resolve the situation, but rather to be with the person or family in the midst of it. Our belief in the possibility of the Spirit being at work in this moment can be tremendously liberating if we allow ourselves to live into it. We are called to be instruments for the work of the living God; we are called to be channels through which the Spirit can move. We are not responsible for determining what the outcome will be, for making the "right" thing happen any more than we are called to make a gathered meeting happen on Sunday morning. We are not called to be perfect; we are called to be present. How do we, within our caregiving committees, corporately ground ourselves in that awareness?

It is also important for individual committee members to be aware of their particular gifts. We are all gifted in different ways. More energy needs to be put into naming what it is we have to offer and less into feeling inadequate because we are not as good at something as another. Praying, accompanying, listening, problem solving and offering relief on concrete things are all ways of caring. A lovely story I heard many years ago was told by a woman who earlier in her family life had gone through the crisis of having one of her three young children hospitalized with a critical illness over several weeks. One day a meeting member arrived at her door and told her she was there to pick up the family's laundry. She took it, washed it, ironed it and returned it. There were no words about the sick child, but there was love and caring. How do we support each other in our committees in naming and claiming our gifts?

Question 2: *What right do I have to butt into someone else's business? Won't they tell us if they want us to know there's a problem?*

Whenever I hear this question I think of the question which I have heard a multitude of times on the opposite side.

> Why, when I was having so much difficulty, did the meeting not reach out to me? Someone must have noticed that I was not coming to meeting. When I was there I would cry in worship. I couldn't ask for help. I felt so alone. Why didn't someone let me know they cared?

We need to consider seriously who we are truly protecting when we have an overly strong caution about intruding. Very often, I think, we are protecting ourselves. Because we do not feel confident of our ability to express our caring well, we hold back and tell ourselves that the other person would not want us bothering them.

An act of true caring is never intrusive. It may be awkward. It may not be fully received by the other at the time. But it is never intrusive. Admittedly, true caring, i.e., love, is something which needs to be nurtured within us. It can only flow fully when we suspend our judgment and leave judgment in God's hands. Erich Fromm put it well when he said, "It is not enough 'to love,' it is not enough 'to want the best' for another living being. . . . [U]nless I can let go of my wish to control, my love becomes destructive. Love is always an active concern for the growth and aliveness of the one we love."

How does each of us come to know ourself and to heal our own woundedness, in order that we can approach another in the time of their need, by being fully present to them? How do we witness to our trust that the Spirit can work in a healing way in their lives. Our role is to be a channel for that work rather than to control the outcome? What do we do as a committee to ensure that all we do in pastoral care springs from this place of centeredness? What are the ways in which we work to develop some of the skills in listening, opening hard subjects etc. which will give us more confidence to enter a situation of need?

Question 3: *Why don't people let us know when they're having difficulty? Why do we so often find out after the fact?*

This question is related to the previous one, but it lifts up different facets of the issue of how to discern and respond to the need for help. This question leads into another question—one which I seldom hear asked, but which I feel we need to address with a great deal more intentionality. That is: How can we deepen and strengthen our meeting as a community?

If we do not have a sense of community in our meeting—a reality which becomes the context for all else—then we can be pretty sure that we have not developed a climate of trust and safety which will allow people to acknowledge the vulnerability they feel in times of need. Pastoral care involves finding ways to nurture vital authentic relationships among our members and attenders so that when problems arise the relationships are already in place to provide a context for exploring the problems. A meeting's attention to queries such as the following may helpful.

Queries related to the sense of community in the meeting:

- How do we wish to be perceived by our members, by visitors? Do we feel satisfied that people's impressions are consistent with the way we wish to be perceived? If not, why not? How might we work toward a greater consistency?
- What does it mean to be a member of this meeting? What is the responsibility of the meeting to its members? What does an individual or family have a right to expect of their meeting? What is the responsibility of the member to the meeting? When there is disappointment of expectation on either side, what is a creative way to deal with this?
- What does it mean to be married under the care of the meeting? What is the role of the meeting and specifically of the clearness committee? What is expected of the couple? Does the meeting, through its clearness committee or some other means consider itself to have an ongoing relationship, to which it attends, with couples it marries?

It is important for our pastoral care committee to provide leadership in enabling the meeting to address queries such as these. To begin with, a sense of community is not possible without a sense of common identity, a sense of what binds us together. The meeting's answers to these queries, can, at the very least, identify common expectations for behavior that can help individuals in exercising their gifts within the life of the community. At most, the meetings' answers to these queries can serve as a mandate for those who act on behalf of the meeting. For example, if the meeting has not developed a shared understanding of what it means to be married under the care of the meeting, then a given clearness committee does not know how thorough or superficial a clearness process to undertake. Then, when a particular committee encounters an unusual or difficult situation, it will be operating in uncharted waters. In addition to the lack of experience with the particular problem, the committee will not know what the meeting expects of it. In my experience, it is the committee's lack of clarity about the expectation of the meeting which is often more immobilizing than the situation itself. That immobilization can keep the response from being full and caring. Such situations of lack of clarity often are the cause of tremendous hurt in the meeting.

Developing a sense of community within the meeting does not occur simply as a result of our working together on committees nor, indeed, simply as a result of worshiping together. If a sense of community is to be developed there must be opportunities to come to know each other outside the roles which we usually play within the meeting, and there must be opportunities for sharing in some depth. A few of the creative ways which some meetings have found to nurture the life of the meeting in this way are: (1) Friendly Eights; (2) meeting-sponsored gatherings for the discussion of common concerns of particular clusters of people, such as parents or couples; or (3) an annual "meeting weekend" in which folks come together for planned programs, meals, recreation and in-between times of being able to chat. *What are the ways which your meeting has found to be effective in developing a sense of community?*

In conclusion, in this article I have described pastoral care as a ministry offering care and support to all persons who are part of the meeting family, as well as a ministry which considers the well being of the meeting collectively. How that ministry is best carried out will vary according to factors such as the meeting size, the range and concentration of age groups, the transiency or permanency of the meeting constituency, the amount of diversity, whether the meeting is in a time of transition, a spurt of growth, etc.

There is no one right way to carry out the ministry of pastoral care. As you search for a sense of what pastoral care is for your particular meeting, we hope you will share your insights, questions and concerns with us.

Arlene Kelly has served as clerk of Philadelphia Yearly Meeting and as clerk of Central Philadelphia Monthly Meeting. She served for over 30 years on Overseers of her meeting, including as the clerk of that committee. She carries a concern for nurturing and strengthening Friends meetings as faith communities.

Questions for Reflection

1. What are the aspects of pastoral care that we carry out most effectively in our meeting?
2. Are there aspects of pastoral care discussed in the article by which we feel challenged?
3. Is there a sense that we need to deepen our understanding of pastoral care in the meeting? If so, what would help ?
4. What do I experience to be my particular gifts which I bring to the work of pastoral care?
5. What is our sense of how fully we are succeeding in being a caring community in which there is a sense of safety and trust? If I was struggling with a crisis in my life, would I be willing to share it with people in the meeting whom I trust?

Reflections of a Pastoral Caregiver

Pastoral Care Newsletter, Vol. 1, No. 3 • February 1994

by Regina Hallowell Peasley

ARLENE KELLY'S ARTICLE, "The Ministry of Pastoral Care," sparked my thinking about what it means to take seriously the calling of the Spirit and become a member of the pastoral caregiving committee, called overseers in my meeting. In my experience, taking on this service means many things. It means caring, sharing, loving, receiving, listening, praying, centering, compromising and, most importantly, following the Light as you see it. When I was first asked to serve, it was important for me to take time to pray about whether I truly felt called. Although, as a meeting member I was basically familiar with this committee's work, it was also helpful to consult *Faith and Practice*, which sees the committee's responsibility as "pastoral care and counseling of the meeting membership . . . should take a personal interest in the spiritual and physical welfare of each member of the monthly meeting. Membership on this committee calls for dedication, tact and discretion and should be entered into prayerfully, with an alert willingness to be of service."[1]

As a new member of the committee I immediately recognized that the work was extensive and varied. In my meeting, as in most, the pastoral care committee's agenda is full as we talk about ways to help people get better acquainted, plan for the newsletter, receive applications for membership, choose clearness committees, consider what to do with delinquent members, share knowledge of illnesses and other major events in the lives of members, and deal with sticky pastoral care issues centering around behavior Friends find difficult, or conflict within a family or between meeting members.

The positive aspect of the busy agenda is that a new person is quickly drawn into the work and learns by doing. The negative aspect

[1] Philadelphia Yearly Meeting, *Faith and Practice*, 1972, p. 50.

is that our very busyness sometimes keeps us from having time to step back and reflect on how we are doing and to consider which areas of either individual or corporate growth we may wish to nurture. When the reading of the *Pastoral Care Newsletter* led me to such reflection, the questions on which I found my thoughts focusing were:

> How does each of us grow into the role of care giver so that we are able to carry it with some confidence? How do we, as a committee, deepen and mature in a way which makes use of the wisdom of the group and the guidance of the Holy Spirit? How do we, as a committee, deepen and mature in a way which supports each individual in carrying out his or her ministry?

These questions are present, at least implicitly, in any of the pastoral care which we carry out. In my experience they are most likely to emerge when we are faced with a difficult, usually conflictual, situation.

It is important, I think, that we learn to blend the committee's strengths, and yes, our weaknesses. If we are both grounded in what we know, and comfortable in acknowledging what we do not know, then we are able to act not only from our strength but also to seek the skill or the information we lack. Unfortunately, when we are not confident in ourselves either individually or as a committee, a lack of experience or knowledge can become too easy a place to hide. It is a given, for example, that most of us are not professionally trained as counselors. Does that mean that we cannot reach out in a caring way when we see an individual or family in disress? I don't think so. We need to find ways to know deeply that each of us is a minister and to acknowledge our gifts. We need to know when and how to seek help if it is needed. Our meeting has discovered what an incredible resource the Philadelphia Yearly Meeting offers through the Family Relations Committee and its Friends Counseling Service. We have experienced the way in which these Friends are able to offer an objective view of a situation as well as being well trained in methods that utilize our best skills. Very often they spark the meeting caregivers to actions that are needed. They help to bring out our strengths.

Part of our growth comes through recognizing and nurturing the gifts which each caregiver brings. While newer committee members learn from more seasoned folks, those with many years' experience also gain a great deal from the newer and often younger members. This sharing happens when the meetings are safe, so that people can speak from the heart. Business should be conducted in a spirit of worshipful seeking. In the absence of that safety and spirit of seeking we are much more likely to slip into the trap of judgement, slip into the trap of saying, "this is the way we've always done it." Also, we are much more likely to be blind to the changing needs of our members in regard to pastoral care. How do we open ourselves to be responsive to our membership as it is today with all the complexities of single parent families, families with both parents filling demanding jobs, same gender couples and individuals seeking to find a spiritual home with us, as well as being open to all of the aspects of pastoral care with which we are more familiar?

Challenging Situations

As a pastoral caregiver, I find myself growing most through situations in which there are differences—where there is often more heat than Light. I wonder how this is for others. There is little which really prepares us for dealing with these problems. We truly need to turn ourselves over to the leading of the Spirit.

One example comes to mind. For the sake of confidentiality I have taken some poetic license, yet the issues as outlined are those with which we struggled. From my conversations with Friends outside my meeting, I know that these issues are not unknown in other meetings as well.

A situation which had been known or suspected by several of us came to the attention of our committee. A married member of meeting was apparently becoming involved with another member of meeting in ways that threatened the marriage. The first question with which we wrestled mightily was: "Should we even be discussing this?" It seemed simpler to follow the path that said we would be interfering. "Is it our concern?" "Is it affecting the life of the meeting?" "If we DO something, what would that be?" Yes, we went through that and more! We even tried to "escape" by questioning whether the facts were really facts. We didn't have to look far for that one, because the spouse of the married person approached our committee and asked for help.

In looking back I realize that we were scared, uncomfortable and perhaps even a little angry. The anger came from our sense that the involvement of the two people was wrong, and it also came from being placed in the position of needing to address it. We would rather it wasn't happening. Being able to admit our feelings to each other at the committee meeting helped us turn our attention to the three members of our meeting who all needed our love and understanding. We wondered how we could be present to each one, and how not to stand in judgment while still saying that the behavior of the two people was wrong within the values of our Friends community. We struggled to find an answer. We paused and worshiped. We centered our thoughts and focused on the "Query on Care for One Another:" "Does your meeting, in appropriate ways, counsel any member whose conduct or manner of living gives cause for concern?"

That phrase, "in appropriate ways," got our attention. In reflecting on some of the thoughts put forward by Arlene Kelly in her article, I can see that we would have been further helped in our consideration of what was "appropriate" if we had had fuller discussions in the meeting about the meaning of community, and had given more conscious thought to the relationship between members and their faith community. What is it that members should expect of the meeting and the meeting of them? The best time for such discussions, of course, is not when a problem arises. General discussions of such matters provide a context which can give rise to appropriate responses when problems arise.

In dealing with the situation before us, it was agreed that two caregivers would visit the person who seemed to be carrying more initiative in the relationship. It was decided beforehand that the purpose of the visit would be to clearly state the concern of the committee, and to describe the way that the meeting was being affected. The plan was to just go and talk without judging or advising. The visit was done in love, with an emphasis on listening. Unfortunately the visit did not have the outcome we had hoped for. The two people were received with defensiveness; the member was expecting to be reproached. In due course the individual chose to resign from membership.

This was a painful situation for us. The two caregivers who had made the visit had a sense of failure, particularly when the Friend who was visited was very critical of them to others in the meeting. At moments like that it is important for the committee and the meeting to be sensitive to the feelings of those who have carried out the ministry on behalf of the meeting.

Did this outcome mean that we should never have gotten involved? I don't think so. Committee members knew in their hearts that there was no other way to proceed. Those making the visit tried to prepare their hearts. Caring for one another was the focus of their vision. What this situation taught us was that there are times when the interests or needs of individual members are in conflict with the interests or needs of the community. In such instances we need to prayerfully seek the right course of action. But there may not be a way, in the short run, for the situation to be resolved so that all parties are pleased with the outcome.

In this situation, as it turned out there was, in time, a sort of healing between the member who resigned and the meeting. The behavior that had raised questions was brought to an end, and the individual re-applied and was accepted back into membership. I feel clear, though, that the action of our committee would have been rightly ordered whether or not the healing took place. Have you faced situations with similar challenges in your meetings? What has been the learning from them?

Sources of Support

I have found that prayerful seeking of the Light, either as a group or individually, is the most powerful way to gain insight, to speak to "that of God" in others and to be God-led in deliberations. Under guidance of the Light, I have come to see how the group and the individual can grow in awareness and in the ability to resolve problems according to the Divine will. Under the guidance of the Light, I have seen our meeting becoming increasingly able to pool and weigh the diverse aspirations and judgments of our members. We have been enabled to gain courage, to make decisions and to move forward while being freed from the bonds of narrowness, self-interest and prejudice.

I find it helpful to remember the ways in which earlier Friends banded together when one of them was imprisoned for reasons of conscience. The meeting cared for the family of the person in need and then took them food and clothing. The meeting supported them in their stand. The term "necessitous cases" is not often used these days but the needs go on. In the times of the underground railroad, Quakers were recognized as friends who would risk life and limb as well as reputation or imprisonment to aid those in need. These examples can guide us in considering not only the nature of our responsibility, but also the spirit in which our work should be done.

So "dear reader," when the nominating committee asks you to serve, and when you say "yes," remember that you aren't in it alone. You're working with, praying with, and helping a group of conscientious Friends who care. Help is available if needed. Give it your best and reap the rewards of knowing that you are growing in God's love.

Regina Hallowell Peasley has been part of Gwynedd Meeting all of her life. She has served the meeting in many capacities, including clerk and longtime pastoral caregiver.

One Meeting's Approach to Pastoral Care

Newtown Meeting has developed a system of pastoral care which has been successfully operating since September of 1992. A central advantage of the new system is that it utilizes the natural social networks of the meeting. Individuals in the meeting identify persons with gifts in communication and pastoral care who need not be members of particular committees, such as Worship and Ministry. One result of implementing the new system has been to increase communication in the meeting in appropriate ways, while respecting confidentiality.

Setting up the System

The new system was developed over a period of months by the Pastoral Care Committee in consultation with Worship and Ministry. It was decided to initiate the new plan for a trial period. A letter was sent to resident members and regular attenders asking them to list three persons whom they would feel comfortable going to in times of difficulty or in times of joy. The three choices allowed for a degree of flexibility in making final assignments. After the response forms had been returned, the clerks of both committees set up the list of pastoral contacts. Each person participating was assigned a pastoral care contact person. Each of the pastoral care contact persons had several people on their list, and they were consulted regarding their willingness to work with each person assigned to them. The committee also gave consideration to the needs of those who did not respond to the letter and those who indicated that they did not wish to have a pastoral care contact.

Overcoming Initial Hesitations

At first there was some discomfort with the term "pastoral care," as it seemed to denote a "professional" service for which meeting members did not feel prepared. The committee offered encouragement to the new pastoral care contact persons. Guidelines were sent out, noting that although "most of the nurture and usefulness [needed by pastoral contact persons] should not require more than a normal amount of knowledge and wisdom," there might be times of uncertainty. At such times, the pastoral care contact persons were encouraged to "get in touch with a member of the committee with whom [he or she] felt comfortable, taking great care that confidentiality be maintained." Committee members also offered to assist in making referrals to professionally-trained counselors.

A Year and a Half Later

There is a sense is that the quality of pastoral care in Newtown Meeting has been enhanced, largely because of the increased communication in the meeting. The committee seeks continual feedback as to how the system is working.

Many thanks to Pat Darenau of Reading (PA) Meeting for suggesting this article.

Questions for Reflection

1. Do we conduct our meetings in a way which allows time for reflection and creates an atmosphere in which differing points of view can be lifted up?
2. When we encounter a situation in which there are differences between members, or between the meeting and a member, do we acknowledge those in an open and constructive way? Are there obstacles within ourselves or the meeting which makes the addressing of those differences more difficult? What would help to remove those obstacles?
3. Do we as pastoral caregivers find appropriate ways to counsel any member whose conduct or manner of living gives cause for concern?
4. What could our committee do to be more supportive of my work in pastoral care?

Growing into the Role of Pastoral Caregiver

Pastoral Care Newsletter, Vol. 7, No. 3 • March 2000

By Gay Howard

Quakers think of a good meeting as a caring community. Caring for each other is laid on all members, but the meeting gives special responsibility for pastoral care to those called to our committees known as Ministry and Counsel, Membership and Care or whatever it may be called in your meeting. The work of caring for another is important in the community of the meeting—important in the lives of the one cared for and the one caring.

How do we, often equipped with no more than a willingness to serve, learn to give the care that is needed? Pastoral caregivers grow into the ability to do the work through apprenticeship and through the support of other committee members and the meeting. The outcome is God's responsibility.

How Can the Meeting Wisely Choose Persons for This Role?

Our meetings are made up of ordinary people who have some of the required gifts some of the time. The nominating committee might begin with those who already have skills and experience in caregiving and counseling. More importantly, perhaps, the nominating committee will seek those who will rely on experienced caregivers and the Inner Light to help them grow into this role.

Willingness to serve and willingness to learn the art of caregiving are primary attributes. Compassion, tact, and discretion are all needed in this work. An active personal spiritual life and participation in the spiritual life of the meeting are a good training ground. Perhaps the most essential gift is the ability to listen. Being aware, in part, of one's own brokenness, faults, and failures is a valuable attribute for pastoral caregivers; as is being aware when more support or skill is needed than you can give and being able to ask for help.

Discerning a Calling to Serve

Being asked to serve on the committee can be overwhelming. Most of us find that our own lives are full of uncertainties, messes, failures, and making do. How then can we help someone else with problems perhaps far worse than our own?

In considering an invitation to serve, a prospective pastoral caregiver might consider: how does this new commitment fit with the rest of my life? What experience and skills do I have that will be used? Am I willing to invest the time and energy in learning the art of being a good pastoral caregiver? What can I learn in this context? Will this bring me closer to my community? Will the experience of being a caregiver and listener deepen my spiritual life?

We can ask the Inward Teacher whether this is work we should undertake, wait for the answer, and do our best to discern the response. What if I say "no," how will that feel? How will "yes" feel?

What Skills Are Called For?

Pastoral care calls on us to support people as they work out practical problems: physical, psychological, emotional, financial, and medical. Below are some of the key skills a pastoral caregiver can develop in order to be responsive to these needs.

Listening skills are important. Indeed, listening skills are important in all aspects of the Quaker meeting. Meeting for worship is listening to God and listening to other Friends as they speak. Meeting for business and committee meetings are times when we listen. There are times to speak, but speaking too much is more likely to be a problem than speaking too little. One must be willing to be present to the other's distress without feeling obligated to fix it. Listening, and especially active listening, are skills which can be learned and can be honed with practice.

Plain speaking, or telling the truth with compassion, is also called for in giving pastoral care. Sometimes we have to call a member's attention to behavior which is destructive to that member, to another person, or to the community. This is very hard to do. Committee members can help one another develop the skill of knowing when and how to state an uncomfortable truth with love and compassion.

It is also important to be able stay present in difficult situations without running away. In serious circumstances it is important that the meeting and individuals in the meeting carry out their responsibilities and not just let things slide because the situation is so difficult. No action may lead to a worse situation.

An individual committee member is not expected to have the skills to deal with all of the issues that arise. We can look for resources among the other committee members, in the meeting, in the wider Quaker family, and the community. An important skill for a pastoral caregiver is to be able to recognize when a situation is too much to be handled alone and to seek appropriate assistance. The caregiving committee as a body needs to develop the discernment to know when outside professional help is required. Crucial decisions have to be made about what information should be communicated to whom and what information should be kept confidential. This, too, is a skill to be developed. Errors can be made in either direction. Often the clerk of the pastoral care committee can be helpful in making these judgments.

Developing the Needed Skills

In the past, when Quakers were born into Quaker communities they had the opportunity to absorb all aspects of being a Quaker through life experience, perceiving the models of Quaker behavior and faith around them. The teaching of how to be and behave is still best imparted by being with a person who has the desired qualities and behaviors. However, in this time, when Quakers often have joined as adults and are dispersed throughout the population, we need to be intentional about learning the skills of providing pastoral care.

In large, mature meetings experienced caregivers can mentor a new pastoral caregiver or there can be an orientation session for new committee members. Some meetings even prepare a "Pastoral Care Handbook" which explains procedures for membership and other basic work of the committee. In small or new meetings where there may not be a sense of grounding in Quaker practice, new pastoral caregivers can seek instruction from experienced Friends in the quarterly or yearly meeting. The Traveling Ministries Program at Friends General Conference or the Pendle Hill "On the Road Program"[1] might bring an experienced person to your meeting to help the whole committee or the whole meeting understand more fully the work of pastoral care.

This direct modeling can be supplemented by reading and workshops. Periodicals such as *Pastoral Care Newsletter* are intended to address just this need. Useful materials are available from Friends

[1] For detailed information about these programs see "Resources," p. 309.

General Conference Bookstore and from Philadelphia Yearly Meeting Library. Quaker retreat centers such as Quaker Center at Ben Lomond in California, Powell House in Old Chatham, New York, and Pendle Hill just outside Philadelphia, Pennslyvania periodically offer workshops to train pastoral caregivers. Some yearly meetings give workshops at their annual gatherings, or at other times, to address concerns of pastoral caregivers and impart skills. The annual Gathering of Friends General Conference often offers workshops useful in developing the skills of pastoral care.

How Can Pastoral Caregivers Support Each Other in Carrying out Their Work?

Committee members can teach each other either directly with words or indirectly by being who they are, modeling behavior. Initiative and ideas come from an individual but are affirmed or modified by the group. The variety of gifts among the members of the committee is a great asset. As we work together, we will notice each other's gifts. Naming these gifts and encouraging their growth enhances the individual and the group. Sometimes people do not recognize their own gifts. How wonderful to be affirmed by learning that I have a gift I did not know I had! The group and each person can participate in naming gifts and encouraging their growth.

Together we can assess the particular situation and pool information, insights, experience, and gifts. After a caregiver has met with a member it may be unclear how to proceed. Then it may be appropriate to share the results with other caregivers so that more insights, gifts, and experience can be used. In the group, people can give each other affirmation. Discussion (or worship sharing) may lead to a new approach. Input from a variety of people on the committee may give a better understanding of the reality of the situation. Through working together committee members help one another develop compassion, insight and courage to act.

The Spiritual Basis of Our Work

The spiritual basis of pastoral care begins in the spiritual vitality of the meeting as a whole. If the Spirit is clearly felt in and out of meeting for worship, every person knows that he/she is deeply cared for. A spiritually alive meeting can be joyfully creative in its ways of caring. Ordinary women and men will be guided by the Holy Spirit to be tender and present in caring for one another. How we treat each other demonstrates our understanding of God and how we value other people.

One's work as a pastoral caregiver will depend on his or her spiritual life, which will be tested and enriched by the work. One way to look at the work of pastoral care within a meeting is that with one hand one reaches to God and with the other hand to another person. Then God's power flows. God's power can shape the right response to a person's unique circumstances.

Love and the presence of God work together in pastoral care. Love of God, love of others, and love of oneself are all needed. We cannot grow into our whole selves, the person we were destined to be, without receiving love and learning to love. When we love and when we are loved, we are in a reciprocal relationship. This is the unseen, and often ignored, fabric of our world; God is at the center, the source of all love. Pastoral care is an activity in which all participants are learning to give and receive compassion, the fundamental skill for life.

The forerunner and companion of love is respect. In caring for another human being, one is often required to speak a truth which is so painful that the receiving person can only hear it if it is spoken with compassion and respect. It is grace that enables us to speak a painful truth with love. Learning to love comes out of a continuing relationship with God, others and oneself. These relationships are built by spending time listening to God, contemplation, listening to others, deep sharing, spiritual friendship and listening to oneself as we ask, "What do I need? What can I give? What are my behavior and words saying to others?" Working with others who have this spiritual foundation can help one to grow in love and to learn how to care for others.

Summary

To respond to a call to pastoral care, one must be willing to serve and be committed to learning the art of caregiving. The ability to listen with compassion and awareness of one's own imperfections is important. Caregiving may make it possible to become closer to the meeting community and to deepen one's spiritual life. Mentoring and reading are primary ways to learn the craft. The caregiver will find constant use for compassion, courage and clear-sighted understanding of human interactions. The support of other committee members and the meeting as a whole is important for the work. The spiritual life of the individual and of the meeting is the context for pastoral care and provides its energy and purpose.

Gay Howard, a member of Tallahassee (FL) Meeting, has served on the Worship and Ministry Committee and on the Oversight Committee. She has been clerk of her meeting and of Southeastern Yearly Meeting and has clerked the committee revising the yearly meeting's *Faith and Practice*.

Reflections on Our Role

BY NADINE HOOVER

The Religious Society of Friends calls us to a God-centered way of life. We are called to shape our outward lives to reflect the inward experience of the sacred. Early Friends claimed that the Second Coming is *now*. As each of us goes through the continuing process of conversion, the Christ Within sanctifies all that is of God and illuminates all adversaries. As experienced by early Friends, our lifelong work is the ongoing conversion of manners (change in our behavior and our very selves) as directed by the Inward Guide, submitting all relationships, habits, possessions, finances, commitments to the Living Spirit.

William Penn raised a high standard: "They were changed men themselves before they went about to change others" (1694). We pastoral caregivers can first practice being Friends ourselves: asking for clearness committees, bring our life decisions before the meeting for discernment and sharing the sufferings as well as the joys experienced in this formation. From experimenting with how to express the Divine in all that we are, do, and say and testing our discernment in the meeting, we become intimately acquainted with God, our lives speak and we bear witness to God's Truth. Witness isn't attacking the wrong; rather it is truly knowing the Seed of Life and living it as we serve in providing pastoral care in our meeting.

At our best we are convinced of the Power of the Living Spirit and experience that Living Spirit in and among us. Many Friends experience that Power just fleetingly, if at all. Perhaps we too have felt the brush of the Spirit as we have stood in a field and felt that all was well, or laughed with abandon, or fully trusted, or stood in a clean kitchen grateful for everything. As we share experiences—not just blissful mountaintop experiences, but calm, still, ordinary experiences—we find the Living Spirit there embracing and completing us even in our human condition of brokenness and separation. In our failings we see beyond ourselves to know, accept and appreciate others and the Spirit.

It is the high calling of pastoral care committees to bring forward this quality in our community.

Nadine Hoover is a member of Alfred (NY) Meeting. While living in Florida she served as clerk of Tallahassee Monthly Meeting and clerk of the Worship, Ministry and Oversight committee of both her monthly and yearly meetings. She also served as secretary of Southeastern Yearly Meeting.

Some Thoughts on Listening

BY RALPH ROUGHTON

When I ask you to listen to me and you start by giving advice, you have not done what I asked.

When I ask you to listen to me and you begin to tell me why I shouldn't feel that way, you are trampling on my feelings.

When I ask you to listen to me and you feel you have to do something to solve my problem, you have failed me, strange as it may seem.

Listen! All I ask is that you listen, not talk or do—just hear me.

When you do something for me that I can and need to do for myself, you contribute to my fear and inadequacy.

And I can do for myself. I'm not helpless. Maybe discouraged and faltering, but not helpless.

But when you accept me as simple fact, that I do feel what I feel, no matter how irrational, then I can quit trying to convince you and get about the business of understanding what's behind this irrational feeling. And when that's clear, the answers are obvious and I don't need advice.

Irrational feelings make sense when we understand what's behind them.

Perhaps that's why prayer works, sometimes, for some people—because God is mute, and He or She doesn't give advice or try to fix things. God just listens and lets you work it out yourself.

So please listen and just hear me. And if you want to talk, wait a minute for your turn, and I'll listen to you.

Ralph Roughton, quoted in Hartford (CT) Meeting newsletter, April 1981.

Questions for Reflection

1. What criteria are used by our nominating committee for appointments to the pastoral care committee? Should we communicate to them our sense of the gifts and skills that are required?

2. What do we do to orient new committee members? Would it be helpful to develop a committee handbook of practice and procedure and/or to have an orientation meeting for new members?

3. What do we do as a committee to help one another grow in the skills of pastoral care? How do we help each other deepen our listening, hone our compassionate plain speaking and discern our gifts and limitations?

4. How do we support one another in maintaining confidentiality of members' personal matters?

5. How can we arrange for some of our members to attend a workshop to inform us about other meetings' practices?

6. How do we deepen the spiritual foundation of our work?

Deep Listening: Applying the Disciplines of an Elder to Pastoral Care

Pastoral Care Newsletter, Vol. 8, No. 3 • March 2001

by Bob Schmitt

A S THE ROLE OF ELDER RE-EMERGES as a way of deepening the ministry of our Quaker meetings, its essential disciplines offer ways in which we might also deepen our ability to offer pastoral care. Friends historically used the terms "minister," "elder" and "overseer" to describe particular roles in the Religious Society. The "ministers" preached the gospel ministry, "elders" were responsible for nurturing the ministry and the minister and "overseers" gave attention to the practical needs of members. The naming of "overseers" continues in our meetings today, and many meetings still use this traditional name for the committee that gives pastoral care. The naming of ministers and elders, however, largely died out early in the twentieth century in liberal unprogrammed Quakerism.

New Interest in Ministers and Elders

Though this article is about the work of pastoral caregivers, let me begin with describing some of the new life that is emerging from the long-disused offices of minister and elder. The two forms, "minister" and "elder," which were discarded because they had become lifeless forms, are finding new life in many Quaker meetings. I have seen Friends, as individuals and as meetings, reclaim the use of the word "minister" as a way of acknowledging particular gifts of particular Friends. For example, many meetings are recognizing the "ministry" of a member to do a particular work. Other meetings are recognizing members as having gifts to travel in the ministry.

The reclaiming and naming of the gifts of being an elder have not come as easily. In fact, many Friends are not able to get past the word "elder" which, for them, holds images of a rigid, finger-shaking scold. However, many Friends who describe themselves as ministers or having a ministry are requesting "elders" to travel with them or to help draw out their ministry. In requesting an elder, these Friends are not seeking a scold, but a nurturer who can help them hear and respond to the movement of the Spirit in their ministry. This relationship of minister and nurturing elder revives a very old Quaker practice.

Elder As a Positive Role

I want to offer a positive use of the word "elder," perhaps a new understanding of that role. It has been helpful for me to consider the role of elder as similar to the role of midwife. Just as a midwife is there to care for the safe delivery of the baby while being aware of the care of the mother, so is the elder there to care for the safe delivery of the ministry while being aware of the care of the minister. Being in the role of elder, like the role of midwife, is both joyful and demanding work. The work for both is not always pretty, painless, clean or appreciated in the moment.

My own understanding of the role of elder is that at its best it is a function, not a position. Anyone may perform an eldering function without being appointed to a particular office in the meeting. For example, our nominating committees perform an eldering function in trying to discover and call out gifts of our members for certain committee assignments or meeting offices. Pastoral care committees appointed in many meetings for Friends who are traveling under a concern, provide the eldering function of helping the traveling Friend stay true to her/his leading.

The elder is responsible for clearing a space in which the ministry may come forward. This function of "clearing a space" or "creating an opening" can be applied to our pastoral care function as well. At our best we clear a space so that clarity may come forward in those who are applicants for membership or marriage. When we work with Friends who are in conflict with one another, we seek to create an opening to that deep place where unity can be found between them.

The role of elder is one of love, care and toughness. Considering some of the disciplines of the elder may help us to carry out our pastoral care role with that same love, care and toughness.

Disciplines of the Elder Applied to Pastoral Care

Discipline I: An Intentional Relationship

As I have experimented with the roles of minister and elder, I am aware that each requires certain disciplines. The core of the relationship of the minister and elder is a mutual intention to listen together to the movement of the Spirit. The minister is tuned-in to this source so that she or he can carry out the ministry. The elder pays deep attention to that same source. Similarly, pastoral care is richest when both parties enter the relationship with the intention to listen to the movement of the Spirit.

When I am in the minister role in an intentional relationship with an elder, I give a weight to the elder's words that I might not outside this relationship. I listen with the expectation that the Spirit is speaking through him or her to me.

When I am in the intentional relationship as an elder, my focus on the minister excludes my personal needs at that time. Much as clerks need to suppress opinions in the context of the meeting for business so as to be a clear vessel, so elders suppress their needs during the interactions of care for the minister.

Discipline II: Deep Listening for Discernment

Deep listening is essential in the role of the elder—to listen with your heart, not just your ears or mind. The discernment of an elder is similar to what one uses in discerning a message to speak in worship. It is from that place of Spirit within that one listens while serving as an elder, seeking to be guided by the Inner Teacher. I find it helpful to focus beneath what is actually being spoken in words, to listen to the place from which the words are coming, to sense the movement of the Spirit.

Deep listening can also be a beneficial skill to nurture in pastoral care. In offering pastoral care to a member in need, in drawing that person out, I listen to the Spirit within him or her and also to the movement of Spirit within myself. In order to be clear enough to discern, I need to clear myself of assumptions—what I think the outcomes should be, what I would do if I were in this person's shoes, the tasks that I left behind and would really rather be tending—all the chatty little voices that I hear that distract me from deep listening. When I am successful in quieting those voices of my own stuff, when I empty myself out, I often find that the other person is able listen with less defensiveness. Together we are more able to enter into faithfully seeking a creative, mutually satisfying outcome.

Difficulties in Applying the Disciplines of the Elder to Pastoral Care

There can be challenges in applying these disciplines to the pastoral care duties in our meetings. First, there may be resistance by those Friends offering the care. Many who are drawn to service on our committees of pastoral care are motivated by a healthy no-nonsense pragmatism. Such Friends may see these disciplines as awkward or irrelevant to the process of responding to the practical needs of our members. Yet, it is my experience that deep listening can enrich even the most routine service. By deep listening we may allow the couple seeking marriage to come to a richer understanding of that commitment. We may draw out the shut-in to discover the need for prayer and presence that is as important as the need for casseroles.

Secondly, there may be resistance from the person receiving pastoral care. The disciplines of the elder assume a mutual intentional relationship to listen for the movement of the Spirit. Even if you as pastoral caregiver desire that shared intention, there are occasions where the person in need of care may not share your understanding. She may not be able, willing or open to looking at it as an occasion to submit to sharing the discernment of the Spirit. She may be completely focused on her immediate problem, shut up tight from fear or grief, or he may be defensive about why someone from the meeting wants to talk with him about the matter at hand. But even with a one-sided intention, the care-giver can set a tone of safety and openness, with the hope that all those present may become open to the presence of the Spirit.

Below is a description of how the elder's discipline of deep listening might be applied to an occasion of pastoral care.

Putting This into Practice

To exercise deep listening in the context of pastoral care I find it necessary to come to the interaction as an empty vessel or as a vacuum. Beforehand I may visualize myself emptying out, letting go of all my expectations, my judgments, my predetermined sense of outcomes. I want to go into the interaction so empty that my presence acts like a vacuum—drawing the person out, helping to reveal their own truth.

When I am in a session of pastoral care, I visualize a space between myself and the person I am tending. I use this image of space as a place to put whatever comes up in the interactions. (Sometimes I visualize a chasm with no seeable bottom, other times a chalice or a hefty garbage bag.) Whatever comes up, I generally don't want to put it on my shoulders or take it home with me. I want to help draw it out into that space where it can be held in the Light.

The imagined space can also be used to empty myself of anything that is getting in the way of my listening, to continue to create a vacuum to draw out the other person.

In the time before meeting with the person, I will prayerfully hold them or ask God to hold them if I am unable. I do this with the hope that the right outcomes will emerge.

This can be exhausting work. I plan some recovery time for myself after the meeting. I am more able to give fully of myself in the moment if I know I also have planned a time, a place for myself after being in this role. (For me, one of the defining qualities of an elder is some awareness and skill in tending her or his own self care.)

When I conceive of the time spent with another in pastoral care, I listen for the progression of questions to ask. I find it helpful to begin with one that is closer to the surface, then to progress to deeper questions and finally to return to shallow ones again to end the session. In a generalized way, here's how I would anticipate that progression:

Beginning

- Putting the focus person at ease; creating a sense of comfort: (*I am awfully glad you asked for this meeting today.*)
- Opening question: (*Let's settle into the silence and when you are ready, perhaps you can speak what brings you here today.*)

Middle

- Deepening questions: (*What do you think Spirit is asking of you here?*)
- Redirecting questions: (*You have said very little about . . . can you tell us more?*)
- Keeping focused on the issue questions: (*This is important, but I would like to steer us back to . . .*)
- Coming back to the surface questions: (*I am aware of the time. Is there more that needs to be said here about that?*)

Closing

- Summarizing questions: what seemed important here? (*We've heard this, that and the other thing. You seem very easy about this, less concerned about that than when you came in and the other thing just isn't going to be resolved tonight.*)
- Regirding to reenter the world questions: (*Is there anything more you need from us tonight? Is there anything you need to say or do*

before leaving here tonight? Is there anything you want us to hold in prayer until next time?)

Advices for Practicing Deep Listening in Pastoral Care

To exercise deep listening requires a certain amount of risk taking, a certain amount of faith. Am I ever fully certain that when I speak in worship that it is truly Spirit-led? No. It is a risk I take in the context of my spiritual community. Am I ever fully certain that the questions I ask as an elder are the "right" ones? No. It is a risk I take in the context of my spiritual community. So also in pastoral care, I open myself to the guidance of the Spirit, knowing that I may not be sure that what is coming through me is rightly led.

Know that you, too, may make mistakes. You may ask the "wrong question," give half-baked advice. If you are tentative about your ability to discern, don't do this alone. Invite the experience and discernment of others to help you refine your skill.

Know that listening in this way, as an elder would, being able to be present to another and assist in the drawing out of their highest good, is a gift Divine. It is a reality in which you will sometimes be well favored and sometimes you will not. It is a gift that needs to be used humbly and with gratitude.

Bob Schmitt is a practicing Quaker and member of Twin Cities Friends Meeting in Northern Yearly Meeting. He has traveled among Friends under concerns for faith and practice, same-gender marriage, reclaiming the roles of minister and elder, and the disciplines required to nurture a monthly meeting community. He seeks a rekindling of the fire that distinguished early Friends.

One Meeting's Experience: Seeking the Support of an Elder

As told by Sharon Doyle and Elaine Emily

Sharon's Story:

Our family was in the middle of a crisis. My teenage son had been accused of a major infraction at school. He maintained, in the face of all evidence, that he had not done it. In the hearing, held at the school at the discretion of the principal, we supported him in his moral stand, but because of the nature of the evidence, it was difficult to know what had actually happened. Our son made a moral stand, denied his guilt and took the consequences.

In the days following the event, it was clear that he was furious at us. He couldn't understand how we would not believe him. We were deeply upset with him. Everything I did seemed to make things worse. I became afraid that there would be a permanent rift. Then suddenly Elaine popped into my head, and I saw us meeting with her. Elaine is a friend, a woman in our meeting with great spiritual and healing gifts. Even though my husband does not attend meeting, he knows and respects Elaine, as does our son.

Elaine:

Sharon and I joined the meeting at about the same time and have gotten to know one another well over the years. I have known her son since he was a young child. This is a good, solid family and I had confidence that they could sort themselves out and come out of this situation intact. I knew that what I needed to do was to provide a space for the Spirit to move. It is my custom to hold people in the Light before I meet with them. Usually what comes to me in prayer is where I start and what I got was for the four of us to start with silence and prayer.

Sharon:

When we arrived at Elaine's I immediately recognized it as a worshipful space. There was a calm about the room like a meetinghouse. Elaine herself seemed relaxed and centered. She invited us to begin by settling into silence. We had agreed in advance that we were not there to talk about the details of the situation at the school but to heal the damage to our family. After the silence, she asked each of us to speak of our perception of why we were there. She functioned as a gentle, centered clerk guiding our family to talk with one another, witnessing. She reassured us by observing along the way, "I see people who are listening to each other." Her presence was calming. Through her confidence that we were going to survive this experience, we began to see our situation as an immediate crisis, not a long term problem.

Elaine:

It is hard to talk about the role I played as their family sought their way. I tried to listen behind and beyond their words. I was listening to their fears, to their love, to his yearning for his parents to support him, to their absolute pride in him for not being willing to compromise his principles tempered with their awareness of what a hard life that leads to. I tried to put myself in the place of meeting for worship and wait for the words to come—it is not a process of figuring out what to say. It did feel like a meeting for worship as the family yielded to the Spirit and spoke from a deep place where they could be unguarded.

Sharon:

I knew that I needed healing and that going into a prayerful space is a preparation for healing, but I couldn't do it for myself or for my family. That's the definition of being in crisis—you can't help yourself. That's when you need pastoral care. We needed someone who was going to hold us in the Light and be solid in that prayerful state. We needed Elaine to allow the three of us to enter that healing space together. It was very moving. We got to say the things we needed to say. My son and I cried. In the end my husband and I were released to simply love and support him, and he understood that we did. As we were leaving Elaine said to me, "You know, it's OK to think the best of your children." It's something I wrote down and put on on my wall.

Sharon Doyle and Elaine Emily are members of Orange Grove Meeting, Pasadena, CA.

Quotations on Eldering: Excerpts from "Cambridge Friends Meeting Ministry and Counsel Resources"

If . . . eldering occurs within the framework of willingly conferred authority, eldering may release great energy both within the individual and within the meeting.   *Thomas Brown, in* Quaker Life, *Jan–Feb 1983.*

The elders had essentially a nurturing role, and one might say that their voice is embodied in our queries.
Brian Drayton, in "A historical note about Elders
in the Society of Friends," 1993.

An elder who has had experience with many Friends, and who has maintained an inner watchfulness, provides a powerful connection with Truth for the . . . Friend in turmoil, confusion or temptation.
Brian Drayton, ibid.

Prayer before, during and after is essential; God's presence can make all the difference in what is said and what is heard. . . . Finding some quality in the other that we genuinely appreciate or respect and giving voice to it can establish a sense of mutual search where all those involved can feel connected with God.   *Emily Sander*

The nurturing aspects of eldering as truth speaking lie in the recognition that one can be definite without being dogmatic. . . . In all cases of truth speaking, the first motion must be love. It is the power and integrity of love as it shows through one's life that must do the convincing in the end.   *Samuel Caldwell, in* Quaker Life, *Jan–Feb 1983.*

Historically . . . because the corrective action or admonition was not always loving and helpful, we first fled from exercising this function, and are only now beginning to grope our way back toward an authentic understanding of it. Our understanding of accountability as Friends rests on the premise that we are members one of another, that we are together members of a greater whole; each of us needs fellow members to enlarge our own understanding, contribute to our nurture, and to help us see what we cannot see ourselves with our own eyes.
                Frances Taber in The Conservative Friend, *Fall 1996.*

Questions for Reflection

1. Call to mind an experience you've had when another's listening to you drew out an answer you didn't know was inside you. What do you remember about the role the other person played? What kinds of questions were asked? What other factors helped this process along?
2. Call to mind an experience you've had when someone gave you some hard advice—advice that you didn't want to hear but that you knew was true for you. How did that feel at the time? What allowed you to be able to receive it?
3. How do you prepare yourself before entering into an interaction of pastoral care? How do you check yourself as you are doing it?
4. How do you care for yourself after being in the role of pastoral care? How do you address your needs for nurturance so you are able to be a clear vessel while doing this work?

Discerning Our Leadings as Pastoral Caregivers

Pastoral Care Newsletter, Vol. 5, No. 3 • March 1998

by Martha Bush

> How do I strive to maintain the integrity of my inner and outer lives—
> in my spiritual journey, my work and my family responsibilities? How
> do I manage my commitments so that overcommitment, worry and
> stress do not diminish my integrity?
>
> *Query on Integrity*, Faith and Practice
> *Philadelphia Yearly Meeting, 1997*

OUR MEETINGS APPOINT a body to be responsible for the pastoral care of a religious society that does not rely on a paid minister to meet goals, address needs, reconcile differences. This is an extraordinary calling, especially in today's stressed and overly busy culture.

I have come to believe that the quality and nature of our compassion—our expression of God's love—is deeply affected by how we view ourselves and by how we fairly balance competing needs. We are continuously called to strike a balance between consideration of ourselves and of others in our community or among constituents within the meeting. Our ability to strike these balances more fairly will be enhanced by our increased attention to taking time to listen for the leadings of the Spirit, to caring for ourselves and to setting limits with ourselves and with others.

Meeting Our Own Needs

I start with a personal examination because I am convinced that the balance we reach in our individual lives will affect the personal energy available to us for giving pastoral care in our meetings. We are obligated to care for ourselves so that we may be better able to respond to Divine guidance as we serve others.

The following questions may help us assess how we are balancing the two sometimes competing considerations: "What do I owe others?" and "What do I owe myself?"

- Do I find that I have enough time and energy for what is most important in my life?
- Do I frequently feel overwhelmed by the demands of my life?
- Do I take time to do things that give me pleasure?
- Do my loved ones and I have time to eat together, sit together and talk with each other?
- Do I show loving kindness toward strangers and others I encounter in daily life?
- Do I find that, more often than I like, I am exhausted emotionally and physically?
- Do I notice that I feel anger, resentment, pride and attachment to my own ideas more than I would like?
- Do I feel that my choices are Spirit led?

If you feel a sense of being out of balance in these areas, you may want to consider whether you are trying to do too much, whether you are attempting to answer the call of others more broadly than is realistic for you. It may be helpful to prayerfully set priorities and limit your commitments to what you can reasonably do, based on the highest priorities.

Why This Is Fair

I raise these issues because of my own history. In my 20s, 30s and even 40s, I felt no sense of my own limits nor was I very aware of the forces that were working on me, that led me to action, and that influenced my interactions. I also did not know that I had not only a right but a duty not to help in some situations.

Without conscious consideration of my values and priorities, I took on more obligations than was fair to those I served, particularly my son. I rarely experienced refusal, renewal or restoration. Perhaps I felt too heavily the burden of the world's injustices. As I reflect on it, my behavior looked like I believed I was omnipotent and could do it all.

It can help us as caregivers to acknowledge that we are to let the Spirit flow through us, discerning from moment to moment our call to action or rest, to giving or receiving, to restoration or production, to saying "no" or saying "yes," to silence or speaking. The paradoxical result may be that if we can surrender our need to act and can function more under the light of the Divine, we may be better able to serve.

Tools for Change

Many tools may help us keep in touch with the Divine call. For me, meditation, prayer, time with friends, walking, inspirational reading, music, and less radio or TV help me live more of my time each day in the Light and equip me to face these difficult ethical questions of what/when to do for others, and what/when not to do.

Each of us can consider what tools are most helpful in keeping us centered and open to the way of the Divine in our daily lives. Valuing self-restoration and limits may require that we embrace new values and a special discipline. These values may conflict with the much earlier but still powerful religious and cultural legacy that most of us carry, i.e., Puritanism and the Enlightenment.

Mindfulness As Integral to the Divine Flow

On a moment to moment basis, mindfulness of "where am I; who am I right now," and "how can I best be with others or with myself right now" can help us surrender to the Divine flow. This may contrast with our own tendencies toward a more constricted or, alternatively, inflated view of what we must accomplish.

Let's look at the hypothetical situation of an active, giving and busy caregiver who is headed out for a restorative walk. She may have been in a challenging conversation earlier or heard some disappointing news and needs time to reflect and gather herself. Just as she is leaving, the phone rings. Should she answer it? Is her ability to respond to others' needs limited in this moment in time? Would she better serve the Divine if she continued out the door and responded to the caller's phone message later, once she had restored herself? If she answers the phone, might she have too little to give?

Two deeply physiological aspects of life—body care and our emotional life—influence the quality of our compassion. I've come to know that, like cranky little kids, we are influenced in judgment, actions and ability to be kindly toward others by plain old hunger, tiredness, or lack of physical activity or fresh air. We will better serve others and allow God's love to flow through us if we recognize our physical needs before they encumber and hinder us.

Similarly, it helps us to acknowledge when we are feeling irritable, frustrated or bored. Awareness of feelings does not mean that we have to express them. Awareness involves knowing, acknowledging, tolerating and experiencing the feeling consciously, lest it unconsciously affect our behavior in ways we would regret later.

Anger or frustration with others is particularly important to give attention to. These emotions may signal that current problems or conflicts need to be faced; or the emotions may mean a current stimulus has triggered feelings from previous experiences.

Accepting Limitations in Our Corporate Life

The dilemma of limited energies also faces us in our meeting life. There are many needs and what seems like too few resources. For pastoral caregivers, the burden today is particularly heavy in light of the larger context of our community. Our culture is hectic, competitive, materialistic, violent and overly stimulating.

Further, the responsible side of ourselves must ask: "As pastoral caregivers in our religious community, when should we say 'no' to a given demand on our attention?" We are responsible for the well-being of individual members and for the life of the community as a whole. If we cut back to focus our energies, what will happen to the meeting?

It may lessen our stress to acknowledge that conflicting needs are inherent in the human condition. We simply cannot meet everyone's needs in all circumstances. By default some needs and goals are not attended to while our attention is captured by other apparently more pressing needs.

Choosing not to respond to an opportunity for caring can be painful and difficult. For example, to see a homeless person on the way to the meetinghouse and do nothing can be draining. Yet, if we stop to be present to that person, it may cause us to neglect other commitments.

Why Setting Priorities and Limits Supports the Life of the Meeting

If our meeting is faced with limited resources, we will need to consciously weigh the interests of one aspect of our community against another as well as to decide when we are called to act and when not to act. Our challenge is to make these decisions overtly, not "choice by default," that is, failing to decide and just trying to do too much.

Directly facing these conflicts helps us discover our priorities and gifts as well as God's call for us.

We cannot know fully where any decision may lead. Let's take the example of the caregiver who does opt for the walk and does not answer the phone call immediately. The caller, in some instances, may discover previously unknown inner strengths and/or other resources in her/his life. Too much help can create more dependence than is needed or healthy, and, eventually will lead to burn-out of the committee member doing the caregiving.

Similarly, we all have known new members who don't feel entitled to set limits in their meeting participation and are extremely giving. Often these members either burn out and leave, or fail to meet agreed upon obligations. That individual would better serve by committing only to what is reasonable.

If the meeting has less than enough resources, it will need to examine what it can realistically do. This examination requires a deep searching for the leading of the Spirit as to what can be laid down. The result may be a more vital community that touches more souls.

Checklist for Priority Setting

The queries below are offered as a beginning point for an assessment of how your meeting is doing with values and priorities.

Do we

- find we don't have the time, energy and/or resources to address the deeper longings and needs of the meeting community?
- frequently feel overwhelmed by the demanding details of day to day pastoral care?
- have/take/make time to enjoy each other, with fun and joyful sharing?
- have/take/make time to meaningfully share about our own life journeys and the deeper questions we face in attempting to live our lives under the Divine will?
- seek consciously to discern when to give support to someone with a difficult assignment and when to shift an assignment to another caregiver because it is beyond the limits (time, talent, energy) of a given person?
- in our committee life, productively deal with conflict, differences and high emotions during discussions? Do we address each other

directly and plainly yet without rancor, as needed? Do we look at conflict and differences as an opportunity for growth and deeper collaboration?

Lessening Our Load

Some of the above queries suggest more work and further burnout. Below are two ways to lessen the load on caregivers by the facilitation of increased member self-care within the meeting and by clearer communication about membership expectations.

Members will have greater resources and thus fewer crises if they are connected meaningfully to others in their religious community. We all need human connection which can be easily lost in today's culture. Connection is vital to our mental and physical health and to successful day to day functioning. We can encourage structures that are primarily self-operating and self-supporting. These could be small worship groups; small support groups; groups of special needs such as men's or women's groups, Christ-oriented or universalist Friends, etc.; social events like Friendly Eights, meeting weekends, etc. (For discussions of building a vital meeting life, see p. 115.)

The work of the committee can be better shared if we have more active members. We can facilitate a periodic process whereby members corporately address each other around questions of what are our obligations toward each other.

Sustaining Hope and Measuring Results

If we expect too much of ourselves or our meeting we can easily become discouraged. Or we may press for goals that are unrealistic and impractical, thus leading to burnout and disappointment. It may help to recognize that change will come in small steps and primarily from changing ourselves, not others. We will be more empowered and less burnt out if we can accept that corporate change will not come from striving to change others. It will come, however, as each individual gradually changes her/his own behaviors, beliefs and values under the meeting's loving care.

I have been amazed at how my own inner changes manifest themselves outwardly. My tendency in some conflicts is to approach the other with my negative responses to their suggestion. However, I have found that if I wait until I have processed my feelings and find the goodness in their effort, I am able to be a conduit for the life of the Spirit. I can make constructive suggestions, compassionately acknowledge our differences and affirm their contribution to the meeting.

It is the small changes that eventually lead us into the larger changes. I have been under the weight of our meeting not doing enough to greet newcomers. This burden was made heavier by the suicide, in the 1980s, of a young woman architect who visited just a few times. She told me she was too shy to come into coffee hour.

Over the last 10 years, little by little, I have seen my meeting become more gracious to newcomers. These changes occurred without more burden on pastoral caregivers. Many people made small changes that have slowly built a new vitality in our meeting. Ten years ago, we started an Attenders Committee. Over the years, that group has done more and more: from organizing a directory of attenders and easier parking, to a personal weekly welcome of visitors, including an invitation to a welcome table.

Conclusion

As leaders in our meetings we are asked to face our own strengths and limits. From this stance of self-awareness we are able to give most economically and meaningfully to our meetings.

Welcoming the Transcendent into our lives and relationships gives us strength to acknowledge our limitations and to seek clarity in recognizing where/when we are called to respond. The Spirit helps us know when we should say "no" and when we should say "yes." It helps us know when to seek support or relief in meeting responsibilities. Devotion to following Divine guidance can help us to be fair to others when perhaps we would rather blame them, find fault with their suggestions or write them off as not helpful or reliable.

We can assure ourselves with the following:

- We are not alone in this and this journey is not by our will alone.
- We can be led in discerning the timing for addressing others, to courageously and lovingly speak or refrain from speaking.
- Each of us can discern what is my "stuff" thrown into the situation and what is the reality.

The more we care for ourselves, the more we are able to give due consideration to others. The more we set limits, the more we can give. The more we surrender our desire to take on the burdens of others, the more Light we enable the other to experience. The less committed we are to our own envisioned outcome, the more we are able to make way for the experience of the Light by ourselves and by others.

The sacrifice we are called to make is not of our own well-being, or of our self, but of our ego, our power, our control, our attachment to our desired outcome or result.

Martha Bush, MA, is a family therapist and pastoral counselor working with troubled teens and their families. She is a member of Central Philadelphia Meeting.

The Challenge of Discernment

In preparing this article, the Publications Committee realized how tricky it is to discern our limits and leave space open for the movement of the Spirit. How do we know we are not just looking for excuses not to meet our obligations? "I often think," wrote one reader, "of the advice given on airplanes to the effect of 'If the oxygen mask comes down, put on your own before helping a child or another person.' But how much do you have to provide for yourself before you turn your attention to the other?"

There is a risk that we will see meeting our own needs as our highest priority and then attend to others only with the energy that is left over. Is that what we want to say? Aren't we adults who can control our behavior even though we are hungry and tired? Should the guiding question be "What *minimal* needs of mine must be met that I may serve others?"

Another reader responded that a workshop with John Calvi at Pendle Hill had a profoundly helpful impact on her life when Calvi asserted that if you want to nurture others, you have to take care of yourself. "There is such a preponderance among Friends of the give-give-give philosophy, most caregivers in our meetings need this message of discernment."

"This article really spoke to me, an all-time doer who grew up as a preacher's daughter," commented another reader. "As a Friend and currently a pastoral caregiver, I want to give more credence to the Divine who fills the space between a need and a solution. I don't want to be a fool rushing in without acknowledging that God is already at work." I appreciated the suggestion that we step back from pressing needs and set up vehicles for mutual caring in the meeting. There is enough spiritual nourishment for all, enough to receive and to give.

Membership in Our Meetings

Membership and the Clearness Process

Grounding Newcomers in Quakersim

Inactive Members:
Keeping Some and Helping Others Move On

MEMBERSHIP AND THE CLEARNESS PROCESS

Pastoral Care Newsletter, Vol. 1, No. 4 • May 1994

BY HELENE POLLOCK AND ARLENE KELLY

- What does it mean to be a member of my meeting?
- What is the responsibility of the meeting to its members, and of the members to the meeting?
- What is the difference, in my meeting, between being an attender and being a member?

These questions are at the very core of pastoral care.

Although Friends do not have a creed, we do have beliefs and commitments. Membership binds us together as a community. Our membership means something. But as we deal with inquirers or applicants, it is not easy to explain the meaning of membership.

Clearness committees can best carry out their work if the meeting as a whole has come to a sense of unity on some very important questions: What does a solid clearness for membership process consist of in our meeting? If we assume that an applicant needs to have a basic understanding of Quakerism, what are the meeting's expectations regarding that understanding? What is the breadth of beliefs which we can incorporate into our meeting and still experience ourselves as one community? Has the meeting ever said "no" to an applicant? What would be the circumstances under which our meeting would say "no"?

There is no single right answer to these questions, but it is important that a meeting reflect on what are the right answers for it as a community.

State College (PA) is one meeting which has done such reflection. It is a growing meeting with many new members. As a concern about the meaning of membership has developed, the issue has been raised at committee meetings and at meetings for business. In the fall of 1993, the committee called on the Family Relations Committee of

Philadelphia Yearly Meeting to help them organize a workshop on the clearness for membership process. The workshop was a success. All of the active committee members, along with sixteen additional meeting members, participated.

In the material that follows, direct quotations from interviews with members of State College Meeting begin each section. The quotations have been selected because they give voice to the experience of many meetings—no matter the size. This article has been developed in the hope that the experience of State College Meeting may be useful for facilitating discussion in a wide variety of meetings.

Does Our Meeting Need to Focus on the Issue of Membership?

> One of our members made it known that he felt we were not emphasizing the spiritual journey enough—that we were seen by some as a social club. I think that was true. We were too easy in the clearness process—not discussing enough, and letting people in too easily. And then problems would arise, and sometimes people were drifting away.

There are many legitimate facets of the meeting which serve as an initial attraction for attenders. For instance, people may be attracted by the sense of community in a meeting, the meeting's social testimonies, Friends style of worship, the meeting school or First Day School. It is a blessing to have differing avenues by which newcomers can find their way into our community. The challenge, thereafter, is to help the attender discover the essence of the meeting which binds it together as a faith community. As a first step, it is helpful to learn by listening to the newer members, in order to identify those things which tend to attract people. Then the meeting can ask itself:

- Have we made it apparent to new people that at the core we are a religious society? Do we share information about the wider Religious Society of Friends in order that attenders know that Quakerism is more than just this meeting?
- Can we describe to newcomers the ways in which the various meeting activities serve to deepen our life in the Spirit?
- Have we found ways to help new members become integrated into the heart of the meeting's life? Or do we find that they remain on the periphery and then drift away?

Depending on the answers to these and similar questions, a meeting will have some sense of whether the area of membership is needing the meeting's focused attention at this time.

What Does Membership Mean in Our Meeting?

> In order for the meeting to work, we need people who can take respon-
> sibility. The meeting needs some sort of commonality in terms of our
> sense of responsibility in addition to our spiritual seeking.

Like other meetings, State College developed a statement on the
meaning of membership. The statement went through several drafts
over a period of years. One of the central values of writing a statement
is that it helps make conscious, and thereby intentional, the expectations which the meeting has of its members. Once the meeting comes
to such clearness, then interpreting the meaning of membership to
attenders is much less difficult.

There is no single right answer in terms of membership expectations. They will vary according to the size of the meeting, its traditions and its needs. Some expectations, such as whether members
carry full responsibility for care of the property, are quite concrete.
Others are more subtle.

A number of years ago, for example, Central Philadelphia Monthly
Meeting was struggling with a very difficult issue—whether a person
who was an ordained minister could become a member of the meeting. No one had any doubt that the applicant, who had been active in
the life of the meeting for some time, would make a fine member. The
problem was the person's plan to retain his ordination.

It became clear during the discussion of this issue that differing
concepts of membership are rooted in different images of the nature
of the meeting community and, thereby, lead to different expectations
of members. At a critical point in one discussion, a member reflected
that "Some of us think of the meeting as a large campfire which
emanates warmth and light. People draw as close to the fire as they are
feeling a need to be at a given time, and the boundaries of membership are determined by where the outermost ring of people falls." He
went on to say that, "Others of us see the meeting as a beautiful garden for which we care and by which we are nurtured. Any who share a
sense of the specialness of what grows in the garden are welcome to
enter the gate and be a part of it, but the boundaries of the garden are
clearly established. The expectation is that those entering will join
with what is there, rather than expecting it to be redefined to incorporate them."

As the discussion continued, it became clear that those who saw the
meeting as a campfire had no trouble including in membership the

person who retained ordination status. Those who saw the meeting as a garden felt that a very basic aspect of their beliefs as Friends would be threatened by a person's maintaining his or her ordination while becoming a member.

The core issue here is diverse images of the meeting as community. How much diversity can we incorporate within the meeting and still remain a Friends meeting? If a meeting is to maintain a core—have a sense of clarity about what binds it together as a community—there must be a way of talking about this.

The Applicant's Need for Information

> When I went to my clearness committee it was the first time I knew that membership meant a financial obligation. . . . Another issue is; do we expect people to attend business meeting? We've been somewhat divided on that. Before people apply for membership, these are things they should know. So when we get to the clearness process, we can really be talking about their spiritual state. We want to be exploring what's leading them to become a member.

When State College Meeting was looking for specific ideas about how to improve their clearness process, they learned a lot by asking some newer members what the experience had been like for them. While people spoke warmly of the clearness meeting, several applicants reported that they had felt some anxiety beforehand because of a lack of clarity about what to expect. They also said they had been afraid of being asked questions for which they did not know the answer.

Too often the task of communicating clearly to attenders about the expectations of membership is not really thought about—it's left to chance. It is far friendlier to have a welcoming statement which outlines basic information such as how long a meeting would usually expect a person to attend before considering membership, what are the important elements to understand about Quakerism and where to get additional information. Such a statement could describe the steps in applying for membership, rather than leaving the person with the sense that they are on the outside, needing to guess how to proceed.

Attenders' kits, which include a copy of *Faith and Practice*, information about the particular meeting and other useful material, can be helpful. How often do we think to announce informational weekends at Pendle Hill or elsewhere? Do we think of inviting an attender to a Quaker function outside the meeting?

Elements of a Thorough and Caring Clearness Process

Several people said that during their clearness process they hadn't been challenged enough about their spiritual journey. They came through feeling as if they hadn't had a chance to discuss their deepest feelings.

I've served on a number of clearness committees and they ran very differently. We have a person, for example, who feels strongly about the peace testimony. I can think of one time when that person was on a committee and the peace testimony was a weightier issue in that particular clearness.

I think it's important that the clearness committee be a very personal and friendly/Friendly group so the person feels cherished as a person but feels that they are on a spiritual journey—that they see this as a place where they are accepted with foibles. And I think that's a pretty tall order.

In the workshop we had on membership I was struck by [the leader's skill in] talking to applicants in such a way that they would not feel that they were on a pass-fail examination, but that they were encouraged to talk about their views and feel whether we were a place that they would like to go. And not the idea that maybe we'd accept them and maybe we wouldn't or that we always accept everybody.

These observations help us to deduce the elements of a sound clearness process. The process needs to be done in a manner that communicates a sense of caring and respect. The issue of commitment to the meeting—and the level of participation which is expected—needs to be dealt with, along with the meaning of being a Quaker, and being part of the wider Religious Society of Friends. Often the applicant will be disappointed if members of a clearness committee fail to discuss their sense of the spiritual dimension of life (recognizing that different people will use different language) and do not encourage open sharing about what it means to be a Friend. Some of the richest clearness meetings can occur as we both listen deeply and share something of our own search.

Consistency is also important. While some aspects of the discussion will be affected by the particular individuals involved, variations in the clearness experience in a given meeting should not be extreme.

In summary, an application to a Friends meeting is a serious step in one's spiritual journey. We are privileged when a person finds something in our witness which leads the person to apply for membership. We honor that witness and the witness of Friends who have gone before us if we, as a meeting, are clear about what membership in our particular Friends community means, and when we find a consistent way to share that understanding with attenders. In this process we not only discover our own truth in our own time and place, but also we reaffirm our connections with the history of Friends, and with the wider world of Quakerism.

In the clearness meeting it is important to create a climate in which the applicant feels comfortable in sharing the important elements of his or her spiritual life. The focus is not on "finding the right answers" but on seeking to discover whether or not the meeting can nurture the person's spiritual development, and the applicant can enrich the life of the community. To the extent that we are able to search for clearness prayerfully and in a deep and open way, then we have, in that moment, made real our belief that the Spirit will lead us.

Many thanks to the following members of State College Meeting who assisted in the development of this article: Jane Jenks, Mary Shaw, Russell Tuttle and Kerry Wiessmann.

This article was written by Helene Pollock and Arlene Kelly, editors of *Pastoral Care Newsletter*, with help from members of the Family Relations Committee.

Three Meetings' Experience: Different Approaches to Membership

Alapocas Meeting

Alapocas, a meeting of 26 members, does not own its own property but meets in Wilmington Friends School. From the earliest days of this young meeting, which was founded in 1976, there has been a desire to limit the membership list to persons who are *currently* active and committed to the Meeting. So all memberships are terminated every three years. At the end of the three-year period, the meeting sends out a letter, asking *all* members to reaffirm their membership commitment. The letter lists the requirements of membership in terms of involvement and financial support, recognizing that exceptions can be made in light of individual circumstances. The meeting's membership roll is then made up of those persons who reaffirm their commitment.

There are various advantages to this approach. As Alden Josey, clerk of Alapocas Meeting, points out, "People are so mobile these days." Having all memberships expire "prods people to move their membership when they move out of the area. It also helps us deal with people who have a sentimental attachment but not an actual involvement in the meeting. For us, membership consists of people willing to make a commitment to the meeting."

Alapocas' approach has also had an effect on the spirituality of the meeting. While it is not always easy to find the words, writing a re-commitment letter can be a spiritually meaningful experience. The letters, which vary from simple statements to deeply searching reflections, are preserved in notebooks which become part of the meeting's permanent archives. What results is, in Aldan Josey's words, "the collective valuing of the meeting, which is affirming to every single individual. I think it's important for a back-bench Friend to read the affirmations that others make about the meeting—that is encouraging to that Friend. Otherwise, membership can become an assumed fact. It can become part of the landscape, so that the meaning gradually fades away."

Information provided by Alden Josey.

Uwchlan Meeting

Uwchlan (pronounced "U-clan"), a meeting of about 170 members located in a rural area, had a desire to bring greater consistency to their clearness for membership process. In 1981 the meeting developed a two-page compendium on membership which lifts up key passages from *Faith and Practice* on such subjects as the meeting for worship and the peace testimony, and ends with eight queries. The queries encourage applicants to consider how fully they are able to subscribe to the precepts of *Faith and Practice* and to describe how they would interpret to a non-Friend the one main reason they wish to join the Religious Society of Friends. The queries also relate to other practical aspects of membership. Uwchlan Meeting has a standing committee on Marriage and Membership, appointed by and working closely with the Overseers Committee, but its seven members do not attend Overseers meetings. Instead, the committee reports directly to monthly meeting. This approach helps eliminate an overly long agenda.

Information provided by Robert Krentel.

Questions for Reflection

1. How well do we as a meeting do in nurturing attenders' understanding of Quakerism in general and our meeting in particular? If more needs to be done in this area, how might that be carried out?
2. Do we, as a meeting, have a sense of clarity and unity about what membership means to us? If further discussion is needed, what role might a pastoral care committee play in facilitating that?
3. Do I feel that the essential elements of a good clearness process are in place in our meeting? If not, what might we do to strengthen our work in this area?

Grounding Newcomers in Quakerism
Short Essays by Five Friends

Pastoral Care Newsletter, Vol. 8, No. 4 • June 2001

A YOUNG MAN WHO HAD BEEN ATTENDING my meeting for three or four months asked, "What do people do during meeting for worship?" A friend in a small Midwestern meeting read an article on the meeting for business and wrote, "Our meeting is made up almost entirely of people new to Quakerism. I never understood why the business meeting begins with worship." So much of the richness of Quaker practice is hidden from view. Members and attenders can participate in our meetings for months and even years without experiencing the fullness of our tradition. What can we do to help those new to our meetings to ground themselves in depth of Quaker tradition and practice?

In this article we bring you the experience of three meetings: a newly forming meeting in Maryland, an established but quite small meeting in Arkansas, and a large established meeting in Massachusetts. Though each is different in its particulars, they share a desire to help newcomers discover for themselves the life of the meeting and the richness of Quakerism.

In addition, we include a description of Pendle Hill's successful series of "Inquirers' Weekends" and Philadelphia Yearly Meeting's course "Quakerism 101" which have been used by meetings large and small.

Not only do Friends have the challenge of helping people new to Quakerism. In many meetings each member brings her or his own idea of what Quakers are, or should be. There may be a lack of a common understanding of worship and vocal ministry, of meeting for business, of the basis of the testimonies, and of our history and corporate experience. We hope that this article will stimulate discussion in your meeting that may be beneficial to newcomers and established Friends alike.

Fayetteville Arkansas: Relax and Smile

BY LaDeana Mullinix

When I consider the growth of our meeting, two comments stand out. One was made by an out-of-town Friend, whose parents live locally, who was visiting after a six or eight year absence. "Thank you for still being here," he said as he left. Another was made by an attender in the process of becoming a member. She had felt since first attending, "This is such a friendly meeting."

Our meeting doubled in active membership in the last year—from four to eight. We also have several very dedicated long-term attenders, and weekly attendance varies from six to twenty. Located in Northwest Arkansas, the Fayetteville Friends Monthly Meeting's closest Quaker neighbors are in Tulsa, Oklahoma, Springfield, Missouri, and Little Rock, Arkansas—two and one half, three and three and one half hours away. We had one period in the 15 years I have attended when internal dissension caused us (then a worship group) to cease meeting. Enough of us felt it was valuable enough to try again. Later, the tragic death of a young attender cemented the bonds within our small group.

Like many meetings, we have discussed how to encourage people to attend (Do we advertise?), and then how to instruct them in the ways of Quakerism. We have talked of having a pamphlet display, suggested reading lists, periodic "Quakerism 101" sessions, assigned mentors, and regular potlucks. None of these has ever happened.

With so few people, the additional commitments seem to hint of burden and burnout. We have used a pamphlet by Mary Moehlman (1990), *The Religious Society of Friends*, which is an excellent summary and introduction. As a meeting, we have looked at different books of *Faith and Practice*, and the *Listening Spirituality* books by Patricia Loring. We have a good-sized lending library in our rented space. Newcomers are always directed there. We also have a good variety of material for children.

Newcomers are greeted before meeting and introduced following. They are invited to attend any after meeting activity. We have tried various formats for singing, worship sharing, book study. An early attempt at study led us to get through four paragraphs in four months, but we are now committed to one chapter a month. Another favorite activity is going out for coffee. Many good discussions have come from these sessions, which may seem less daunting to a newcomer than book study or meeting for business. Often, members of the meeting will offer phone numbers to be available for questions.

Our meeting responds well to special events, especially out of town visitors. Perhaps we feel honored that someone took time to be with us. We have welcomed the Friendly Folk Dancers, visiting Friends, and AFSC representatives in the last six months. In the weeks following gathering with two Friends in traveling ministry, several attenders applied for membership. Perhaps they felt assured that our meeting's problems were not uncommon and that individuals can be members without knowing everything in advance. With all these visitors we certainly felt included in the wider circle of Friends.

As an individual, I have found great joy in our quarterly meetings, with monthly meetings and worship groups from Arkansas, southern Missouri and Oklahoma. As a small quarterly meeting, our gatherings have the feel of a family reunion with attendance from 30–60. Sharing and worshiping with this group, and watching the children grow up have increased my feeling of connectedness to the larger group of Quakers. I was surprised that other Quakers consider us as "isolated," since I have never felt that way. New attenders are often hesitant to attend these weekend gatherings, perhaps from a fear of overcommitment, but are often hooked once they do.

As attenders choose to deepen their commitment with a request for membership, they are encouraged to read, especially from the books of *Faith and Practice,* and to attend meetings for business, although these are not requirements. Membership committees, appointed by pastoral care committees, meet with the attenders at least twice to decide if membership is the best choice.

With so many new attenders in the last several years, our meeting has been focused on individual spirituality and growth. Only recently have we been able to take a stand on an issue in the larger community (the death penalty). This felt good, however, as the process had a very firm spiritual base.

Our process of integrating new Friends, while far from perfect, or even organized, seems to be working. People feel welcomed, find the reading material that speaks to them, and eventually join to the extent they feel moved. We may need to try again for some structure, but in the meantime, we are still here, and smiling.

LaDeana Mullinix is a longtime member and former clerk of Fayetteville Meeting.

The *Quaker Heron* Unites Patapsco Preparative Meeting

BY DIANE REYNOLDS

Patapsco Preparative Meeting in Ellicott City, Maryland, is a new meeting that began in November of 1996 as a worship group under the care of the Sandy Spring Friends Meeting. Now a preparative meeting, it has been growing rapidly, from an average of 16–17 people at meeting for worship to 30 or more. The meeting newsletter, the *Quaker Heron*, has helped to ground not only newcomers, but everyone in the meeting.

Early on, I felt a leading to begin a newsletter for our meeting. When way opened to begin the newsletter in the fall of 1999, one of my hopes was that it would function as an outreach to infrequent attenders or those contemplating visiting our meeting. It was to be a way to keep in touch spiritually with those who are not physically present at the meetinghouse.

I was concerned (and this may be typical of new meetings) that as a meeting we were out of balance, with too much emphasis placed on the practicalities of growing a young meeting and not enough emphasis on the spiritual underpinnings of Quakerism. I asked myself the question: what makes us more than another do-gooder service organization? Where is the religious life of our meeting? How does what people are thinking and feeling drive what they are doing?

To anchor the newsletters, which come out quarterly, I felt led to have each one focus on a particular Quaker testimony. Friends are invited to submit articles on the topic we are examining in that issue. The various issues so far have covered community, simplicity, peace, and equality. Integrity will be the topic of the next issue.

I have been surprised by how gathered each issue has been. By this I mean that the articles, coming in without coordination, have spontaneously covered the important facets of a topic without any preplanning. If one person wrote about the politics of equality and slavery, the next article would discuss equality from a biblical perspective. If one person submitted an intellectually rigorous history of equality, the next person would submit a personal and introspective response to feeling unequal. It has been astonishing to see how the pieces of the newsletter have all been distinct and coordinated parts of a larger picture.

The newsletters have choreographed themselves without preplanning and have demonstrated clearly how different voices looking at the Light together can illuminate aspects of the truth far better than can a single individual. While I am open to the idea that a particular newsletter topic might engender a group of articles on a narrow aspect of the topic, and would consider this an indication of a particular concern within the meeting, so far this has not happened.

The newsletter has helped our meeting grow and define itself. It has extended our outreach, brought people to the meeting, and caused several lapsed or infrequent attenders to phone, e-mail, or send warm notes saying how much they have appreciated seeing the newsletter show up in their mailbox. In a very basic way, it has helped build community and enhance peripheral members' sense of belonging. The newsletter has allowed individuals a chance to express their thoughts and beliefs, and has helped one person clarify his understanding of Quakerism to the extent that he decided to go from being a long-term attender to a member of the Religious Society of Friends.

The *Quaker Heron* has also given us a forum for dialogue and has helped us understand each other's interior selves. In this sense it has helped build our meeting community. It has been a valuable supplement to the meeting for worship, allowing people to give longer messages to the meeting at large. It gives individuals who may not feel comfortable talking in meeting a chance to share their spiritual experiences and insights. It has helped highlight that we are spiritual beings, united because of spiritual convictions.

As a new meeting we have had to ground ourselves in Quakerism. What does it mean to be a Quaker meeting? What are our various understandings of the core of the Quaker message? By focusing the *Heron* on the testimonies we have shared deeply about those understandings. In the process we have learned from each other about Friends history and beliefs. We have shared our questions together. This has educated all of us members and attenders, long-time Friends and newcomers.

I believe it is an important tool for spiritual growth and would encourage meetings to grow and deepen their newsletters as they are led. As an editor, I have appreciated the freedom I have been given to shape the newsletter. As with anything else, a newsletter works best when it can adapt to the needs of the meeting it serves.

Diane Reynolds is editor of *Quaker Heron*. She is also part of Friends in Christ, a Christ-centered worship group based in Greenbelt, MD. Her husband, Roger, and children, Sophie, Will, and Nick, serve in Patapsco (MD) Meeting.

Making Friends Meeting at Cambridge Friendly and Accessible

BY GIL AND SHEILA JOHNSTON

Friends Meeting at Cambridge in Cambridge, Massachusetts, with a membership of approximately 500, is one of the largest meeting communities among unprogrammed Friends in the United States. Prior to 1995 the Cambridge meeting had two meetings for worship each First Day morning. Average attendance estimates varied considerably during those years, but tended to be in the 200 to 300 range. In 1995, FMC changed to one meeting each first day morning in order to enhance the unity of the meeting community. A smaller (and quieter) meeting for worship at 5 p.m. supplemented the larger morning meeting, and together they have been attracting about the same number of attenders as before. Visitors from other meetings and new attenders are welcomed at the rise of meeting. Typically there might be three or four coming to Quaker meeting for the first time as well as a sprinkling of other new attenders just recently introduced to the Quaker form of worship.

Our practice is for the person having "care of door" to make several brief announcements at the rise of meeting, calling attention to the guest book, the weekly announcement sheets available as people leave, and inviting interested persons to come to an inquirer's table where they can obtain information or ask questions. The greeter presides over the inquirer's table for ten or fifteen minutes during the social time and often has a chance to point visitors toward a useful pamphlet or provide an answer to a question. Greeters are usually members of the Fellowship and Outreach Committee which is responsible for the process of welcoming new people to the meeting. It concerns itself with the various details of that process, such as maintaining a "care of door" roster, establishing a regular First Day procedure including greeting at the door and offering name tags to visitors, handling a brief set of announcements, dealing with visitors' questions, sending welcome notes to persons signing the guest book, and maintaining supplies of handout material.

While we look to the Fellowship and Outreach Committee to perform these functions, we try to keep reminding ourselves that it is everyone's responsibility to make Cambridge Meeting seem like a friendly and accessible place. As might be expected in a meeting of this size, some people find it less than friendly, as members and long-time attenders involve themselves in conversation during the social time and often fail to engage with people they do not already know. Happily, the 5 o'clock meeting, perhaps because of its smaller attendance, has proved to be a more effective catalyst for friendly conversation with new attenders who find their way to it.

Small groups and committees are a definite aid to newcomers seeking to find a way into the large meeting community. A young adult group embraces both students and non-students, mostly in their twenties. A small men's group grapples with the varying needs of men at different stages in their lives. Other groups focus on bereavement, spiritual direction, study of the Gospels, and discussion of the relationship between science and religion.

Committees such as Garden and Landscape, Friends for Racial Justice, Peace and Social Concerns, and Friends in Unity with Nature provide opportunities for new attenders to become acquainted with others in the meeting and begin to make their own distinctive contribution.

The role of Resident Friends (now called Friends in Residence) is an important aspect of the Cambridge Meeting's outreach to newcomers. Along with other staff members—the Meeting Secretary, the Facility Manager, and the First Day School Coordinator—the Friends in Residence are expected to maintain a friendly presence both on First Day and throughout the week. In addition, we have particular responsibility for conducting occasional educational sessions on the faith and practice of Quakers. During the last five years we have been using the Philadelphia Yearly Meeting (PYM) "Quakerism 101" materials in somewhat modified form. Experience showed us that our principal goal should be to help groups of inquirers, some new to the meeting and others long time attenders, to get to know one another and learn to feel at ease discussing Quakerly questions in each other's presence. The prepared materials offered us some excellent points of departure, but we found, as time went on, that we needed a more personal and less academic approach, and one that connected more directly with our own yearly meeting. So we chose to make extensive use of the New England Yearly Meeting *Faith and Practice*, supplementing it with some of the "Quakerism 101" materials and citations from PYM and Britain Yearly Meeting *Faith and Practice* volumes. One of our most effective sessions has been the one in which we set up a simulated meeting for business and role played our own response to a challenging issue. The "Wade House Controversy" material in PYM's "Quakerism 101" was most useful for this purpose.

We have been gratified by the fact that eight or nine recent attenders at these sessions have credited the sessions with helping them come to the place of applying for membership. During this, our last year in the position of Friends in Residence, we take considerable satisfaction in knowing that these new Friends have received some of the help they needed from the hours that we have devoted together to what turned out to be, for us as well, a path of deep, inner discovery.

Gil and Sheila Johnston spent six years as Friends in Residence at Friends Meeting at Cambridge. They are retired and live in Ardentown, Delaware.

Pendle Hill Inquirers' Weekends

BY SHIRLEY DODSON

The first Inquirers' Weekend was held at Pendle Hill in 1989 as an experiment in response to "Enquirers' Weekends" held in Britain—they have been held ever since. The British Enquirers' Weekends were designed for people who might know very little about Quakerism, for those who were curious, for religious seekers and others who may never have set foot in a Friends meetinghouse. The focus here has been to help Friends meetings in their efforts to educate and integrate attenders and new members fully into the life of the local meeting and into Quakerism in general.

This description, taken from an early publicity piece for an Inquirers' Weekend, describes the basic outline:

"Would you like to find answers to your questions about Quakerism? Become more familiar with Friends faith and practice as it is lived today? This weekend is designed for anyone interested in an introduction to Quakerism. Together participants explore the basics of:

- Friends worship: what do you do with all that silence?
- Beliefs: there's no creed, but commonly held tenets.
- Practices: including the Quaker decision-making process and Friends ways of expressing their faith in daily life.
- Terminology: what all those peculiar words mean (leading, gathered meeting, testimonies and more).

- Organization: How Quakerism is (and isn't) organized.
- Quaker spiritual community and how it affects its members, plus an overview of different Quaker groups.

"In the relaxed atmosphere of Pendle Hill, there are opportunities for worship, discussion, information sharing, celebration and free time. This weekend is designed for anyone interested in an introduction to Quakerism."

There are always at least two leaders, usually different from each other in significant ways, including gender, age, yearly meeting membership and Quaker experience. The majority of leaders are unprogrammed Friends, although leaders often have experience with programmed Friends and sometimes with Quakerism internationally as well.

Recognizing that people new to Quakerism usually aren't familiar with our sources of information, Inquirers' Weekends are made known mainly through those meeting members most in contact with newcomers. In many meetings, these are the membership committee or the pastoral care committee. In this way, Pendle Hill enters into a partnership with meetings in helping to orient new members. Inquirers' Weekends are particularly useful for small meetings which don't have enough newcomers to make up an orientation class within the meeting.

The majority of participants in Inquirers' Weekends have come from the yearly meetings nearest to Pendle Hill: Philadelphia Yearly Meeting, Baltimore Yearly Meeting and New York Yearly Meeting. However, people have also come from quite a distance, including Florida, New England and California. Meetings or yearly meetings at a distance from Pendle Hill can arrange for an Inquirers' Weekend in their area through "Pendle Hill on the Road."

For Pendle Hill these weekends are opportunities to provide a needed and useful service to Friends meetings and their members and attenders. Participants often ask important questions about Quaker faith, practice and worship that they might be embarrassed to ask in their own meetings. They meet people from many different meetings and expand their perspective on what Quakers and Quakerism are like. (For information about Inquirers' Weekends, at Pendle Hill or "On the Road," contact the Outreach Coordinator at Pendle Hill, 800-742-3150, extension 137.)

Shirley Dodson is Director of Conferences and Retreats at Pendle Hill.

Quakerism 101

BY GENE HILLMAN

"Quakerism 101" was developed in the 1980s by Philadelphia Yearly Meeting. Since that time it has spread widely among Friends as a framework for introducing new members and attenders to Quakerism. A "Quakerism 101" course might also be of use to a meeting by providing a forum for long-time members to explore together what it is to be a Quaker.

"Quakerism 101" is typically a six week course with a two hour class once each week. Classes consider the experience of early Friends, Quaker beliefs (the inward Light, the teacher and guide, universalism), worship and ministry, meeting for business (community and gospel order), witness (testimonies and concerns), and the organizational structure of the Religious Society of Friends. Participants are expected to read 30 to 50 pages in preparation for each class. Teachers select their own texts but Howard Brinton's *Friends for 300 Years*, Wilmer Cooper's *A Living Faith*, John Punshon's *Encounter with Silence*, various Pendle Hill pamphlets and selections from *Faith and Practice* are often used.

Classes may be adapted to the needs of the meeting. In planning the course it is usual for the teacher to meet with the committee requesting the course to consider issues of special concern for the meeting. Typically, a class period will be divided into two parts. The first part of every class will be the transmittal of information. Following a break, the second part of the class might be anything from discussion to worship sharing out of consideration of a query.

"Quakerism 101" starts with a component that provides information as to what it has been, and is, to be a Friend. Most of all these courses provide a forum in which we can share our experiences and understandings of walking in the Light, thereby building community as we listen to and learn from one another.

Philadelphia Yearly Meeting has developed four other traveling courses. "Quakerism 201: Faith and Witness" is an exploration of the testimonies and other concerns. "Bible" is an introduction to the Bible. "Prayer" is an experimental (experiential) course designed to teach approaches and techniques, as well as build for the participants a deeper relationship with God. Last is "Quakerism 301," an advanced course to explore in greater depth a topic from one of the earlier courses or the writings of a specific Friend (e.g. Barclay, Fox, Fell), or envision and/or plan the future of the meeting.

The curricula for "Quakerism 101," Bible (Finding Our Way In the Bible) and Prayer, as well as studies of Fox, Penn and Woolman can be obtained from the Friends General Conference bookstore. It is best if the teacher is an experienced Friend familiar with the material and able to adapt it to the needs of the meeting. However, groups of Friends with little experience can build knowledge of Quakerism by following this curriculum and its readings. Within Philadelphia Yearly Meeting teachers are available to travel to meetings to teach "Quakerism 101." (For information about "Quakerism 101," contact Adult Religious Education Coordinator at 215-241-7182.)

Gene Hillman is Adult Religious Education Coordinator at Philadelphia Yearly Meeting.

Questions for Reflection

1. Has our meeting given thought to how to help those new to the meeting learn the ways of Friends?
2. What would we regard as important to be conveyed to newcomers?
3. In our process of seeking clearness for membership, what attention do we give the applicant's understanding of Friends tradition and process? Under what circumstances would we ask an applicant to learn more before proceeding with clearness for membership?
4. Are there ways in which our meeting's process shows members' lack of being well grounded in Friends traditions? How could we address this lack in a way that strengthens and deepens our community?

Inactive Members: Keeping Some and Helping Others Move On

Pastoral Care Newsletter, Vol. 3, No. 1 • September 1995

by Sue Heath

Dear Friends: I received your letter about membership, and I want to remain part of Moorestown Meeting. My wife and I have lived here [in distant state] for twenty years and we have joined the Presbyterian Church. All our financial support goes to them, which is why I have been unable to contribute to Moorestown. But both my parents were members of the meeting, they and my grandparents are buried in the Mt. Laurel graveyard, and I will always consider myself a Quaker. I want to remain a member.

• • •

I spoke with X, who lives just outside town, and told her we had missed seeing her in meeting. She said that her work has been demanding, her children growing up, and as a single parent she just doesn't have time. She told me how much meeting meant to her when she first came to this area, and that she was sure she would be back when her life slowed down a little. I told her she could always come back to meeting then, but now, we were trying to revitalize our membership. Since she had not attended or given any support to the meeting for such a long time, we wanted to help her to reconsider remaining on our list. She was not comfortable with that, but I will talk to her again and see if her feelings have changed.

These vignettes paraphrase some of the answers Friends have received in the past few years as Moorestown Meeting has struggled to strengthen its membership list. Perhaps other meetings will find them familiar. Friends find it so very hard to release members, to help them move along, or to clarify the status of longtime inactive members. As an ex-officio member of the pastoral caregiving committee at Moorestown Meeting for ten years, I have watched Friends struggle long and nobly with this dilemma, trying first one remedy and then another. In those ten years, our membership has shrunk by over 100 members, about 20% of our total, even though we have steadily gained 10–20 new members each year.

Participation Is the Key

Our meeting has struggled to define membership for ourselves, and to define the participation required or a member. As we strive for a committed, participating religious society, we have intentionally and deliberately worked to remove from our rolls those whose membership no longer seems meaningful to them. During the dialogue, absent Friends are told what is needed from members. They have a chance to discuss their concept of membership with the Friend who contacts them, and to hear the meeting's side. Finally, some resign, some transfer to a closer meeting or to another church, some are released and some become more active in meeting. Distant Friends begin to communicate, maybe just with a yearly letter, to visit meeting when they are in the area, and to increase their financial support.

Steps We Go through before Recommending Release

Releasing Friends is the hardest. Over the years, a long sequence of communications has led to a periodic list of Friends recommended for release, and following meeting for business, members sometimes continue the process of trying to contact the inactive Friends and bring them back into the meeting community. Even when it is obvious that the inactive members do not want to be contacted, when they ignore letters and messages on their answering machines, it is hard to let go. We hear stories about times in the past when that member *was* very active in meeting, or the time when the person in question came to a funeral and told how much he or she misses meeting. Or we may hear about an encounter with the absent one at a Quaker function somewhere. Friends truly grasp at straws to prove to themselves and others that the person really wants to be a Friend. Each Friend seems to take it personally that this person is being let go, and turned loose into a hostile world. At that time the caregivers who have been working with the particular Friend need to step in, both to review the steps that have been taken before release was recommended and to help the meeting accept the loss.

In Moorestown, the first alert comes from the Friend responsible for receiving contributions. That person informs a small membership committee when a member has not made any reply to appeal letters for three years. Friends inquire discreetly as to whether the Friend attends meeting or serves on a committee. If the Friend lives away from the area (and in Moorestown about 150 of our over 400 members do live out of state), we look for correspondence that may have been received. We talk to known friends and family to see whether ties are still kept with Moorestown, because we think if distant members return to the area they will come to meeting if they still feel part of our worship community.

Eventually, a letter goes to the inactive member, outlining the concept of membership and the need to be active in the meeting. The financial obligation is mentioned but not emphasized, and for both distant and local members there is a suggestion that perhaps they might want to resign or transfer to another meeting or church. Most of these letters receive no reply, and then the work begins. Personal contact is sought with each of the inactive members, and phone calls and visits are made to local Friends. Distant Friends are approached by letter or telephone. If there is any opening it is pursued with diligence. Occasionally we discover problems that the meeting knew nothing about, such as illness, marital difficulties or job loss, and we try to minister to the need. However, the break is usually too long-term. Just the fact that no one was aware of the changed circumstances is an indication that the member had been growing away from the meeting over a long period of time, and it is hard to come in at such a late date to offer understanding and support. That is not to say that we do not try, only that this situation is difficult, and it makes us freshly aware of the need to keep in contact, to notice when someone has fallen away and to follow up before too much time passes.

Over weeks and months, replies to the letters are sought. Some examples were printed at the beginning of this article. Finally, for all the ones who cannot be contacted, or for whom the contact was inconclusive, a final letter is sent. While it is not an ultimatum, it tries very hard to be clear that the inactive member must make a decision. "This is the final letter in our series of efforts to contact you regarding the future of your membership," it begins. It briefly restates the need for participation in meeting membership, both with personal contact, attendance at meeting for worship and other events, and financial support.

The it says, "We ask that you consider the following alternatives and let us know of your intentions for continuing your membership." The alternatives are as follows:

___ I value my membership, and I am enclosing a contribution.

___ I have been attending _____ meeting (or church) and would like to transfer my membership.

___ I have been out of touch with Friends for a number of years and find I am unable to meet my membership responsibilities. I request that my name (and those of my minor children) be removed from membership.

___ Although I resign my membership, I would like to stay in touch and have enclosed $20 to continue receiving the meeting newsletter for a year.

There is a space for a signature and the date, and a space for comments. Then the letter concludes:

> If we do not hear from you by _____ [date about six weeks away], you will be formally released from membership in Moorestown Meeting. We regret the finality of this communication, but you will always be welcome to reapply for membership, either here or in another meeting, whenever you feel ready to commit yourself to the responsibility of full membership.

The series of letters ending with the modified questionnaire quoted above has been very productive, with about half the members contacted returning the form as asked. For the ones who do not return it, one more attempt is made to contact them by phone or visit, and if there is still no change in their feelings, the meeting for business is asked to release them. For a release, the name is printed in the monthly meeting minutes, which go to every member every month, and the clerk sends a letter informing the member that he or she has been released. That letter tries to be warm and loving, and to leave the door open for a future return to membership in the Religious Society of Friends.

Efforts to Encourage Participation

Increasing the activity of members is the goal of the Membership Committee. During the process described above, Friends are always alert to ways to bring an absent or inactive member into fuller participation. Each year the Nominating Committee obtains a list of nearby members who do not serve on committees. These Friends are asked to join a committee. The meeting encourages members to offer rides to Friends who do not attend meeting for worship, or to invite an inactive Friend to one of the breakfasts, family nights, potluck suppers and discussion evenings, or other events to bring Friends together.

Distant members are more of a challenge. We try to contact our out of town members each year by mail, often utilizing a form letter with a personal note at the bottom. We also send a note or card at Christmas, asking for news of the member and his or her family. The monthly newsletter is mailed to all members and attenders, and is the main instrument of contact for distant members. In the newsletter we appeal for news. One somewhat effective tactic has been to ask Friends who do a Christmas letter to send a copy to the meeting, and about ten are received each year. News from them is printed in the newsletter, and the letters themselves are posted in the meeting house for others to read.

Our meeting tries to discourage full membership for members' children who were born out of state. We feel that these families should become involved where they live, and they are gently urged to do so. Nonetheless, we carry ten or fifteen children whom we do not know on the rolls as full or associate members. Children at a distance who are full members are a special problem, since they often have not learned anything about the meeting and have no idea what membership means. Usually at age 21 they begin to receive all the mailings that go to members, including requests for contributions, and within three years some begin to appear on the three year list of non-contributors. The process of contacting them, at an age when young people are often on the move and changing addresses yearly or more often, explaining the obligations of membership, trying to activate them and help them move forward, is complicated by the fact that they have never been part of the meeting in a meaningful way.

Work with New Members

In recent years, as we have become more aware of the need to involve members and keep them active. Our clearness committees have tried to include more about membership responsibilities in the process when new members apply for membership. We try to explain how committees work and the need for everyone to do something. The meeting budget is explained, including our obligations to yearly and quarterly meetings, and there is a figure that Finance Committee uses liberally, the so-called "fair share" or amount each member, adult and child, husband and wife, would need to pay to cover the budget. Often new members do not know how much is expected as a contribution, and this "fair share" is a place to begin.

In Moorestown, the person appointed to welcome a new member has a long term responsibility to that member as a "big brother/sister." Since the welcomer will be an ongoing mentor to the new member, We try to match welcomer and member by mutual interests and to do all they can to foster the long term relationship.

Membership for Friends is a commitment to a group as well as a statement of religious faith. The community's strength and vitality is only as great as the sum of what each of the individual members brings. Just as the quality of meeting for worship is dependent on what is brought by the seeker, so also in the secular life of the meeting the time and effort of each member is essential. Pastoral care committees have the calling to foster the individual commitment, helping each Friend to give to the meeting in times of plenty and also to ask from the meeting in times of need.

Sue Heath, a member of Moorestown Meeting, has worked in various meetings, responsible for the office, files and membership records, and support for the volunteers. She was a founder of a support group for paid meeting office staff, and has served as clerk of the committee for *Pastoral Care Newsletter*.

One Meeting's Experience: Differing Views on How to Deal with Inactive Members

There is real diversity in the way that Friends across the country deal with the issue of inactive members. Many meetings do not release persons from membership. The age of the meeting (and the number of inactive members who have accumulated) and the yearly meeting assessment are among the relevant factors. The following exchange of letters between Frank Kuehner and Sue Heath is intended to stimulate more dialog on this open-ended topic.

Dear Sue:

I read your article on membership with mixed feelings. My resignation from a meeting several years ago was a very painful decision. Even though I was a young adult I did not have the maturity to handle the matter properly. I had come from another religious tradition, and my attitude toward membership was completely different from that of Friends. My resignation was simply because of my inability to contribute financially. That was a very painful time for my wife and myself, and I wish that I could have been given more support. At one point I went to the meeting and gave a contribution as a token and apology. One woman was very judgmental in responding to me. I wonder now how it would have been if she had known the whole story. . . .

I am now a member of another meeting. Now, as was true earlier, I see membership as more a matter of belief than anything else, with a focus on practice rather than dogma. I wish this were more understood. . . . It is important to be very sure that when an individual becomes a member, he or she understands the obligations or responsibilities of membership. There is also the question of the responsibilities of the meeting toward the individual member. Some meetings have pastoral care visits. When I look at the examples you give, I'm concerned that such a length of time went by before the inactive person was contacted. People go through many changes and the ability to give is different at different times. Also, I wonder how much this would be different if there were not the matter of the yearly meeting assessment. Perhaps we should have an "inactive" membership category which could go into effect during those periods in which a Friend needs to sort things out or is unable to participate in a more active manner for various reasons.

Frank Kuehner, Arch Street Meeting

Dear Frank:

Thanks for your deeply felt and thoughtful response to my article. I agree with what you say about the importance of taking each person's situation into account. At Moorestown Meeting our procedures were set up to encourage more contact with inactive members to find out why they were inactive. We start with a list of 25 and end up releasing maybe 6 or 8. Contact does take place, circumstances are considered, and compassion is shown! We are very receptive when a member says "I can't contribute money at this time in my life." And, a contribution of $10 counts! We are aware, however, that when there is trouble the instinctive response is often to withdraw. The person who may need us the most is the one who is unable to respond, and our letters just go into a large pile of other things on the person's conscience, adding to the feeling of being worthless. And we are sorry about that. We do all we can to make a contact and to try to help. But also, in our society many people deal with things by not dealing. They ignore our letters and communications because they don't want to be bothered. Moorestown has decided that we do not want to retain these people indefinitely. They have to give something. At the same time, I agree with you that another category of membership would be helpful. This is something Moorestown has been asking yearly meeting for during the last five years.

Being a Quaker is a state of mind. It should not require a name on a membership list. Membership lists are for the convenience of the clerical types in the meeting, and there are people who are called to maintain them and worry about them. All our communications stress that you can still be a Quaker, and when you are ready you can join a meeting again, ours or another one. We do not excommunicate. We just take you off our list. The faith is there and the person is always welcome.

Sue Heath

Questions for Reflection

1. Are we clear about the difference between members who are prevented by personal problems or hardship from participating in the life of the meeting, and members for whom apathy or disinterest is the main obstacle?
2. How can we become more alert to signs of need, more familiar with members' friends and support networks and more willing to inquire when someone is missed?
3. Have we in the pastoral care committee and in the meeting given conscious reflection to the question of membership and what we understand to be the responsibilities of the member to the meeting and the meeting to its members?

Pastoral Care for Marriage and Divorce

Clearness Committees for Marriage or Commitment

Seeking Clearness on Same Gender Marriage

Meeting Support of Marriage and Couple Relationships

Supporting Families Through Separation and Divorce

CLEARNESS COMMITTEES FOR MARRIAGE OR COMMITMENT

Pastoral Care Newsletter, Vol. 2, No. 4 • May 1995

BY JAN HOFFMAN

OUR CLEARNESS PROCESS FOR MARRIAGE OR COMMITMENT reflects our essential belief about the way in which Friends test the religious call of two persons into a lifelong relationship, as well as our belief about the meaning of spiritual commitment within a faith community.

Early Friends were clear that marriage was essentially a religious covenant. They saw this as quite different from marriage as a legal or social relationship; when a choice was necessary, they chose to have their marriages considered illegal rather than modify their religious witness. In 1669 George Fox described it this way:

> For the right joining in marriage is the work of the Lord only, and not the priests or magistrates; for it is God's ordinance and not Man's; and therefore Friends cannot consent that they should join them together; for we mary none; it is the Lord's work, and we are but witnesses.

So early Friends held the witness that no person had the legal (magistrate) or spiritual (priest) authority to "pronounce" two people married. Marriage was accomplished when a meeting witnessed two people exchanging vows, confirming a call to lifelong commitment.

However, the call to commitment is not limited to two individuals. It involves the meeting as well, since the couple's spiritual leading occurs in the context of a faith community, and is tested in that community as any other leading would be. The question for the couple is, "Are we called to a covenant relationship with each other?" The question for the meeting is, "Are we clear to take this *marriage*—this whole relationship—under our care?" (The question is not, "Are we clear to take the *wedding* or *ceremony* under our care?") Thus the clarity reached when a meeting takes a marriage under its care is a *double* clarity—of the couple and of the meeting.

When Does the Clearness Process Begin?

For some meetings, the process begins when the couple writes a letter to the clerk requesting marriage or commitment under the care of the meeting. For others, the process begins with the couple before any letter is written. Baltimore Yearly Meeting's *Faith and Practice* contains a series of questions to be considered by the couple *before* asking the meeting to take the relationship under its care. These focus on some of the same subjects that are likely to be explored in the actual clearness process, including spiritual life and religious beliefs, gender roles, finances, jobs, children, wider family connections and conflict resolution. Baltimore then adds two additional questions to be considered by the couple before approaching the monthly meeting:

> Why are we asking the approval and oversight of the meeting? Are we aware that oversight of our marriage by the meeting involves the continuing concern for our life together and the values established in our home? Will we welcome the continuing concern of the meeting?

> How significant to us are the promises made in the presence of God and of our family and friends as stated during the meeting for marriage?

Even before a couple considers such questions, the meeting may wish to share with them any distinction made in its policies between requests for marriage "under the care of the meeting" and requests for the use of the meeting house as a setting for a wedding that is not under the care of Friends.

Who Should Serve on the Clearness Committee?

Some meetings have experienced committees focused on family life from whose membership all clearness committees come. Other meetings have committees with a larger pastoral care focus whose responsibility it is to suggest persons—from the committee itself and from the meeting at large—to serve on clearness committees. Since the reality in many of our meetings is that not all persons asked to serve on clearness committees will be experienced in this service, they can be helped by being given materials about the clearness process and the qualities needed for such service (see resources, pp. 311–12).

Clearness committee members must be committed to the spiritual and temporal energy needed to test a call to marriage. It is less than caring to fail in honoring the importance of the couple's decision by proceeding with a shallow or superficial clearness process. A clearness process carried out with integrity, under the leading of the Spirit, must draw from us a careful probing, undergirded with loving concern; a genuine desire to be of help, accompanied by a light touch; and a firm understanding of the seriousness of the joint effort we are undertaking, coupled with a relaxed, nonjudgmental atmosphere.

Once Friends are clear to serve on a given clearness committee, they may wish to discern whether to meet together first without the couple. This may be especially useful where some members of the committee have not previously served on a clearness committee, and when there are questions about the functioning of the committee. Such a meeting provides the opportunity for members of the committee to come to a common understanding of how they will work together. Will questions be given to the couple before the meeting? If so, which questions? Are there additional questions not printed anywhere that the committee feels are important? Will the committee meet with the two individuals separately as well as with the couple together? If either has children by a previous marriage, is it appropriate to include them in the clearness process? Does anyone on the clearness committee have strong feelings which may get in the way of listening to this particular couple? Finally, legal requirements differ in different states and it is necessary that the committee be clear on what these are.

Meeting with the Couple both As Individuals and Together

The clearness process can also reflect Friends' sense that commitment between two individuals is *both* the individual leading of each person *and* the couple's leading together. This is accomplished by having two members of the clearness committee meet individually with each person in the couple before the committee meets with the couple together. Historically, the two women met with the woman, and the two men met with the man, then all four met with the couple.

Only five of our North American yearly meetings *Faith and Practices* still mention this step as part of the clearness process, and I believe that without it, the clearness process is weakened. Meeting with the individuals in the couple both separately and together affirms two significant realities: first, that there are two individuals, each with his or her leading, and secondly, that there is a *joint* leading affirmed by the full committee meeting with the couple. I have spoken with couples who have met only as a couple with the clearness committee, as well as with couples who have been met with both as individuals and as a couple. In the latter case, the consciousness of themselves both as individuals and as part of a couple which emerged as a result of their clearness process was an unexpected and valuable benefit.

New England Yearly Meeting's *Living With Oneself and Others* offers an example of the way in which the focus of different questions can indicate the many paths to clearness. In the chapter "To Those Contemplating Marriage," questions are divided into three sections: (1) for the committee to ask the couple, (2) for the couple to consider together and (3) for each individual to consider. For example, questions to ask the couple include: "In the years to come, how do *you* plan to seek the Divine assistance you will invoke in *your* marriage vows?" Questions for the couple together include: "Have *we* lovingly and prayerfully considered the differences in values, needs and habits between *us*?" Some questions for individuals are: "What is *my* present image of marriage? Am *I* open to changing this image as reality indicates? What relationship does this image have to *my* parents' marriage or to an earlier marriage of *my* own?"

What Are Some Possible Questions to Be Explored?

Books and pamphlets with sample questions are available (see resources, pp. 311–12). It may be well to discover which resources the couple are already familiar with, and to draw their attention to additional resources as well. It is also necessary to establish whether the clearness committee assumes that the couple will be prepared to address a certain set of questions when the committee meets with them. It may also be that the couple has questions they wish the clearness committee to consider before meeting with them. Of course, when the committee and the couple meet, responses to given questions may engender further questions.

One question needing an affirmative response from everyone is: Are we prepared to have as many meetings as necessary to reach clearness?

It is important for the clearness committee to focus on what they believe are the essential questions for the particular couple. There can be a great difference in age, maturity and life experience among couples asking the meeting to take their relationship under its care. An essential question for one couple may be totally irrelevant to another.

Further, would the couple appreciate many questions, or might they be overwhelmed by too many questions? I know of clearness committees who have created a customized one-page list of questions for a particular couple. I have also known couples who wanted to address as many questions as they could possibly find.

New situations generate a need for new questions. In my meeting, for example, we have minuted our willingness to take same gender relationships under our care. In our considerations of what this would mean for the clearness process, we experienced a need for new questions. To the questions in a one-page foldout from North Carolina Yearly Meeting (FUM) we added the following:

> Are you seeking a spiritual union, a legal union, or both? If you cannot have or do not want a state-recognized union, are you aware of the many legal contracts which can be drawn up to provide rights similar to those that are part of a legally-recognized union?

This question recognizes that in addition to same gender couples whose unions cannot be legalized, there are some heterosexual couples who do not wish to claim a legal privilege not extended to all couples.

In minuting our willingness to take same gender relationships under our care, my meeting was not clear to use only one name for such relationships. For some in the meeting, marriage is a term that belongs only to heterosexuals. For others, marriage is a name for a corrupt institution and they wish to use a name to which a more positive meaning can be given. Some heterosexual couples do not wish to use a term that cannot be used by all. For yet others, marriage is a term which confers on same gender relationships the same spiritual weight that heterosexual relationships have and they wish to claim that spiritual equality, even when legal equality is not granted. Given the potential of different leadings about the name of the relationship, we left that spiritual naming as a question to be addressed in the clearness committee.

The reality of divorce among us may lead to another question to be addressed in the clearness process: that of changing the vows. My own New England Yearly Meeting *Faith and Practice* states that a couple's desire to change the traditional vows must be raised with the clearness committee, and I concur with this requirement. I have heard the suggestion that "as long as we both shall love" is a more reasonable vow than "as long as we both shall live," given the statistics on divorce. I disagree, believing that the marriage vows are promises made to each other in the hope that they will be kept. The people of Israel made a promise to be faithful to God—which they repeatedly broke. As an individual, I have made promises to God to be faithful, yet sometimes I have not been faithful. The fact of promises broken does not mean I promise less in the future. I do not want to say, "I make this covenant with you, God, for as long as I can keep it." I want to promise, "I will try always to be faithful," knowing that I will sometimes fall short, but wanting to affirm my deepest desire.

Possible Outcomes

The most common outcome of the clearness process is, of course, that the meeting takes the relationship under its care. However, as North Pacific Yearly Meeting (1993) says, "It may be that unity to move forward is not readily found. The committee and the couple may choose to continue seeking God's will in this matter, or they may choose to lay aside the request indefinitely or permanently." Again, the clarity is a double clarity; *either* the couple *or* the committee may be clear to proceed or not.

Sometimes the clearness process helps the couple find themselves not clear to proceed. In one meeting I know, a clearness committee was meeting with a couple composed of a woman who had grown up in that meeting and a man from another country. The committee posed the question to the woman, "Are you planning to continue working after you are married?" "Of course," she replied. The man turned to her, amazed. "You are?" he asked. Following this exchange, the clearness committee just sat and listened as the couple discovered many contrary assumptions they held about their life after their wedding, assumptions each had not known the other held. As a result of that clearness process, the couple withdrew their request.

Sometimes the clearness committee is clear that the meeting should not take the relationship under its care. In another meeting, the clearness committee met with a couple and reported to the meeting their recommendation that the meeting not take this marriage under its care, though the couple still insisted they were clear to marry. The clearness committee indicated why they felt the meeting could not promise to support this marriage. The couple's blindness to each other's reality, together with their incapacity to recognize their own lack of awareness meant that there was no common understanding which the meeting could support. The meeting's response was to say, "How can we judge other people's leadings; they know what they're doing, they want to get married. Who are we to say that it won't work?" So the meeting went ahead and approved the marriage of the couple under the care of the meeting. Three months after the wedding the marriage broke up for precisely the reasons the clearness committee had given.

In conclusion, it is important to remember our sense that the primary purpose of a meeting for worship for marriage or celebration of commitment is to witness a covenant being made between two persons, an affirmation of their spiritual call to relationship and the meeting's call to support it. We cannot *marry* anyone, but we *can* affirm the call of two individuals to marry. We do this by taking the relationship under our care, and by our witness of a covenant two people make in a meeting for worship. In this way, we can be part of a continuing search for the variety of ways we can live in faithfulness.

Jan Hoffman, a member of Mt. Toby (MA) Meeting, has served as clerk and clerk of Ministry and Counsel of New England Yearly Meeting. She is a frequent speaker and workshop leader in a wide range of Friendly settings.

Five Meetings' Experience: Meetings Take the Clearness Process Seriously

Do we believe that a thorough clearness process should be carried out with every couple seeking to be married in the manner of Friends?

That question came before Richland Meeting during a recent business meeting. A couple had asked to be married under the care of another meeting *without* a clearness process. The couple wanted the meeting to be held in Richland Meeting. "We often don't reach consensus very quickly in our meeting," noted Ellen Schroy at Richland Meeting, "but we quickly came to agreement at business meeting. Some couples spoke to the fact that the clearness process had helped them. They felt very strongly about its importance. We affirmed that anyone being married under our roof will go through clearness." This decision was a reaffirmation of Richland's usual policy. They have a lovely, historic meetinghouse, and there are many visitors and attenders. "We try to accept new people with open arms," explains Ellen, "and we try to be open to the couples who want to be married here, but we tell them that they must be willing to go through the clearness process, and that it is not unusual for the process to take three to six months." Ellen says that many couples lose interest once they discover what is involved, but some stick with it and learn about Friends in this way.

• • •

At Mullica Hill Meeting it is a tradition that at least one person in the couple should be a member of the meeting in order for the couple to be married under the care of the meeting. "We don't want to be inhospitable," explained Judy Suplee, clerk of overseers, "and we don't like to say no, but we have made only one exception to this policy in the 35–40 years of my adult membership in the meeting, and that was some years ago, for someone who was from a Quaker family that we all knew." In one recent situation, neither person was a member or attender at a meeting, but one of them had attended Friends schools and felt a close tie to Friends. They had already set a date three months hence. The clerk spent time with the couple, and although the meeting was not able to undertake pastoral care of the marriage, the couple seemed satisfied about the way the situation was handled.

• • •

If the clearness process is taken seriously, sometimes the answer will be no. Ken Cook of Exeter Meeting recalls not approving the request of a couple who wanted to be married under the care of the meeting because their relationship was very young. "We felt they needed more time," says Ken. Ken does not regret their decision. The couple ended up not marrying.

• • •

Advice from Paul Joyce Collins and Williams of Harrisburg Meeting is as follows: "Take your time. Don't feel afraid to ask for a second or even a third meeting." Paul was part of a clearness committee that met a number of times with one couple. Individual committee members (including Paul) also invited the couple to their homes for additional meetings. The committee asked to examine divorce decrees and dealt openly with legal issues as well as with personal matters. "We really wanted thoroughness, to make sure that the couple had discussed various issues, not necessarily that they had come to any particular conclusions," explains Paul. "We believe that Friends have a legitimate process, and it's worth spending time on."

• • •

Couples—even Quaker couples—may be surprised to discover that clearness is serious business. Esther Curtis of Wrightstown Meeting recalls dealing with a young Quaker couple who wanted to change the traditional wedding vows. Since they assumed that both of their meetings would let them do whatever they wanted, they were very surprised when some of their ideas were not approved. "But," recalled Esther, "they were also impressed that we cared enough to spend the time to talk it through."

Questions for Reflection

1. What concrete steps might we take so that the clearness process in our meeting could be strengthened?
2. Are we aware of resources—both printed material and "people resources"—that we can turn to in case a particular clearness process presents an unexpected challenge?
3. Are we open to the possibility that clarity might mean not to proceed in the way in which the couple expects things to go?
4. What might we do to provide more support for couples in the meeting? (See the article by Patricia McBee, "Meeting Support of Marriage and Couple Relationships," on page 92.)

Seeking Clearness on Same Gender Marriage

Pastoral Care Newsletter, Vol. 7, No. 2 • January 2000

By Karen Stewart

WITH CONTRIBUTIONS FROM MEMBERS OF THE
PASTORAL CARE NEWSLETTER EDITORIAL COMMITTEE

For the past twenty years Friends have been asking meetings to take under their care same gender couples who feel led to be married. One by one, across the nation, meetings are taking up this question, seeking to be faithful to Friends belief in the continuing revelation of Truth.

Rarely does an issue of such magnitude come our way. Rarely are we called to reconsider a practice that has been such an important part of our cultural and spiritual heritage. We are challenged to reconcile an apparent conflict between our understanding of our biblical heritage and custom on the one hand and, on the other hand, our testimony on equality and belief in that of God in everyone.

Wrestling with this question poses an opportunity to open our hearts and minds, to examine our beliefs and to use our process of discernment to find our measure of Truth today. With tenderness and care we may find that wrestling with the issue deepens and strengthens our faith and our community, regardless of where the meeting comes down on the original question.

Some Brief Background

Quakers believe that God calls and unites a couple in marriage. Traditionally we offer assistance in the form of clearness committees to help the couple carefully consider their intent to marry. We provide the worshipful setting for their marriage to occur. We serve as witnesses to the process and take the marriage under our care, providing support to the couple in their spiritual journey together. While most of us seem in unity that the spiritual authority to marry rests with the Divine, our monthly meetings do hold the awesome responsibility of deciding whether or not to take marriages under their care.

Meetings come to consider same gender marriages in many different ways with widely varying experiences. In some meetings the rightly ordered path seems quite clear. In others deep searching is required.

In some meetings, two loved and cherished members of the same gender ask to be married and the meeting simply considers the request as they would a request from a heterosexual couple. Many meetings decide to take up the concern in the absence of a formal request for marriage, in order to avoid the possibility of saying no to a specific couple or of making a couple wait while the meeting discerns the way forward. Some meetings take it up because of a request from the yearly meeting, because of epistles from Friends for Lesbian and Gay Concerns, or because a member or group of members have a leading to bring this concern forward. For some meetings the process feels comfortable and natural while others may struggle painfully for years. However, even meetings who struggle for years often find that the process has deepened and strengthened their community. Careful attention can enhance the probability that the process is one that will enrich and enliven a meeting regardless of the outcome.

Fear and anger have sometimes posed stumbling blocks in discussing this issue. Gay and lesbian Friends may feel hesitant to make themselves vulnerable to others, fearing judgement and hostility. For some Friends, even examining the question may feel like a betrayal of long held convictions. All may share the fear that considering the issue could divide the meeting or jeopardize the meeting's standing in the community. Friends may feel vulnerable and confused. Fear can lead to anger which can cause even more difficulty. Love can cast out fear and we must constantly return to that loving and tender place where Truth will be revealed. Only then will Friends feel safe enough to do this important work.

Sometimes Friends have felt led to support committed relationships of gay and lesbian members but have had difficulty reaching unity over how to name the relationship. Some Friends may feel the term marriage is reserved for the covenant between the Divine and a man and a woman. For some gay and lesbian Friends the word marriage carries unpleasant associations with a patriarchal society and they do not want to call their union by that term. For others, marriage best describes their commitment to each other. A lesbian friend who was married under the care of a meeting writes:

There was no other choice than to follow in the footsteps of my ancestors and create a sacred bond of marriage between Lori and myself. I know that to honor that of God within the other meant that we needed to reflect God's love to our community of faith. We did this through a public statement of our love, devotion and commitment to having God rest in the center of our relationship. A commitment ceremony would not have been enough for me, marriage was the only choice I would make regardless of the social and religious interpretations of God's will. After all, it was God who led us to step forward in our faith and to make our choice for marriage.

Legal issues have been of concern to some meetings. Some meetings have feared the loss of legal recognition of heterosexual marriages under their care should they sanction same gender unions. Other meetings are concerned about how to advise same gender couples to obtain as many as possible of the legal rights that are automatically afforded heterosexual couples upon marriage.

Discerning Way Forward

With such an important issue, it is of utmost importance that we maintain a spirit of worship in all that we do. We may have to continually remind ourselves that we are seeking Divine Will together, not trying to convince each other of the rightness of our particular views. One lesbian friend wrote,

> It is important to stress that all people need to let go of their agendas when they step through the doors of the meetinghouse and be willing and ready to listen to Spirit and to move from their position if called to do so by the Divine. . . . I know this was difficult for me because it felt like so much was at stake.

Only by letting go of our positions can we truly be open to the Spirit moving among us.

Meetings may find it helpful at the start to name a group of Friends who will carefully tend the process. The pastoral care committee or some other established committee might do this, or a special committee could be appointed. One seasoned Friend advises,

> I think the criteria for membership on the committee should be Friends who are widely respected in the meeting, who have a gift of discernment, who are open-minded and teachable, and who have a commitment to the loving and Spirit filled consideration of this concern.

The goal of this committee is not to recommend a policy regarding marriage, but to provide a process to assist the meeting in discerning the leading of the Spirit.

Meetings may find it helpful to make a very tentative time frame for consideration of the issue, assemble and provide resources to be used, and ensure there are ample meetings and/or retreats to consider the issue. Resource lists and written materials may be made available. Speakers, individually or in panels, might be invited to come to meetings. Some meetings have found it helpful to have Friends from outside of their meeting facilitate discussions or worship sharing. As with any important meeting process, Friends may find it helpful to have many different ways to share and discuss the issue at times that are convenient and with childcare and transportation provided when needed.

For help in structuring the discernment process, the Committee on Sexuality of Ohio Valley Yearly Meeting has published a *Guide for Discussions on Sexuality*. This very helpful publication offers advice on process as well as sets of queries that cover sexuality, moral authority, marriage/committed relationships and civil rights/discrimination. It contains references for Bible passages and queries to use in examining them. Finally, it contains an extensive reference list. It is an excellent source of help in clarifying areas of disagreement.

Attending to Your Meeting's Specific Needs

Each meeting is unique. There is no single way of threshing this issue that will work for all. Meetings vary in size and composition. It is useful to reflect on what has helped your meeting stay focused in the Spirit while considering difficult issues in the past.

Some meetings may be well steeped in biblical teachings and contemporary biblical scholarship as it pertains to marriage and homosexuality. Others may feel the need for further study to deepen their understanding.

Some meetings may have active gay and lesbian members; others may have gay and lesbian members who are unknown to them, or members may have gay or lesbian children. Some meetings may have written minutes in support of civil rights for gays and lesbians. Others may have never broached the subject. In a meeting where there is already a great deal of awareness, understanding and sensitivity to gay and lesbian issues, the process may be far different than in a meeting where there are no openly gay or lesbian members and where the subject of homosexuality has not been explored. Given the long history of misinformation and prejudice surrounding the issue of homosexuality, it may be important to provide access to the latest information about the nature of homosexuality.

Individual Friends may vary in their attachment to this issue, but it is very important that it is seen as an issue for the entire meeting. One Friend writes:

> This is a concern that affects all members, not only gay and lesbian members. Consideration of our commitment to our biblical heritage and to our testimony of equality can take us to the core of what it means to be a Friend.

The meeting may want to discuss openly the degree to which participation is expected in the discernment process. Many meetings have felt they were moving along, threshing the issues and coming to clearness, only to have a member, who had chosen not to participate in the threshing, step forward at the last minute to block the process. Good process requires that those who feel strongly find ample occasions both to speak and to listen to others. If there are Friends who seem to be avoiding the meeting's threshing of this concern, efforts can be made to engage them one on one, listening carefully to their concerns, and seeking ways to incorporate them into the meeting's process. Again, we will need to continually remind ourselves of the need to let go of our agendas and be open to the Spirit. And we will need to be ready to help others do the same.

Some meetings have found it helpful to offer committees of support for members who are feeling vulnerable, unappreciated or marginalized by this discussion. Supportive Friends can offer love and understanding as well as encourage patience and forgiveness. For gay and lesbian members these are not abstract issues being discussed; thus, even if we proceed with a loving intent, our discussions may feel hurtful. Similarly, there may be a need to support Friends who may be having difficulty with even raising the issue. Supportive Friends can offer love and understanding and can help these Friends to bring their concerns to the meeting in a loving and open way.

Sharing from the Heart

Consideration of same gender marriage usually occurs in the context of a broader consideration of both the nature of marriage and loving committed relationships. Knowledge of the history of marriage and most particularly marriage among Friends can provide a background for discussion and further discernment.

Worship sharing may provide the best medium for considering the topic. When we know we will have a chance to speak and be heard, when we are relieved of the burden of trying to convince others of our point of view, when we are aware that the Divine Spirit will tender our hearts to the Truth, we can all be our "best selves."

An essential component of this process is sharing our stories. Sharing in general about love and relationships places everyone on equal footing, and out of that experience we can come to understand our similarities as well as our differences. Of utmost importance is hearing the spiritual journeys of gay and lesbian Friends. If there are Friends in a meeting willing to share their stories it is ideal; if not, meetings can seek out speakers from the wider Quaker community. Understanding and embracing our differences can be an amazing process in and of itself.

A meeting should be sensitive to the impact of this discussion on children and teens, with awareness of the needs of the different ages. The Gay, Lesbian and Straight Education Network is an excellent organization of educators, that has a wealth of materials and resources to share. It is very important that the meeting's discussions of this issue be respectful and tender so that children may come to recognize the meeting as a safe and supportive environment as they question and grow in their own sexuality.

When Unity Is Not Found

Having followed processes such as these, some meetings will have come to a clear sense of understanding and unity on whether or not to take same gender marriages under their care. Other meetings, in spite of their most faithful efforts, may reach an impasse where way does not open for unity. If this happens, sometimes the best course is to let the consideration rest in prayer for a while with a plan to return to it at a later date. As one friend stated, "The Spirit's time is not measured by clocks or calendars."

A meeting can also call on outside resources for help. The yearly meeting may be able to offer assistance. The Traveling Ministries Program of FGC may be able to connect the meeting with a Friend skilled in dealing with this particular issue, or a seasoned Friend gifted in helping meetings process difficult issues in general.

Summary

The decision of whether or not to support gay and lesbian Friends who feel led to marry, is a sacred responsibility as well as a great opportunity to examine very important aspects of our faith. With Divine guidance and careful attention to process, consideration of this issue can become an opportunity to deepen our faith and further our understanding of Truth. May we be aware of God's blessings on us all as we go forward with this important work.

> Karen Stewart is a member of Durham (NC) Friends Meeting where she has served as clerk. She has also served as clerk of the FGC Ministry and Nurture Committee, clerk of Carolina Friends School and co-clerk of the 2001 FGC Gathering of Friends. She and her husband, David, both psychologists, have two children.
>
> She writes of her own experience of prayerful searching on same gender marriage: "Durham Friends Meeting reached clearness to support same gender marriages a number of years ago. The process deepened and strengthened our meeting and brought many unexpected blessings."

One Meeting's Experience: Finding Unity in Germantown Meeting

Germantown (PA) Meeting received a minute from the Family Relations Committee of Philadelphia Yearly Meeting in the spring of 1985 which gently urged that monthly meetings consider same-sex ceremonies of commitment. The meeting referred it to Worship and Ministry and to Overseers who took it up in their annual joint meeting in the fall of 1986.

Following that joint meeting, over a year passed until a Friend reminded Worship and Ministry that we had not responded to the yearly meeting. Immediately a group of volunteers was gathered to produce a response. They read books, pamphlets, articles, anything that they could find in order to discuss the issue knowledgeably.

Unintentionally the group included no homosexuals, although it did include one person who thought that homosexuality was evil. A lesbian member of the meeting was added when it was brought to our attention that we had not examined the composition of the group.

This was important since gay and lesbian members of the meeting had felt excluded even though the invitation to participate had been generally given and any volunteer accepted. It was a lesson in sensitivity to differing perceptions no matter what the reality.

After months of study, the group decided that the empowerment they felt from having learned so much should be shared with the meeting. This was done by a series of adult classes including a panel of meeting members of various sexual orientations and divergent views making statements on what they looked to the meeting for in support of its members; a session led by a heterosexual couple about their participation in the organization, Parents and Friends of Lesbians and Gays; and a Germantown Friends School teacher presenting his class on homosexuality. All of these were well attended and meeting members clearly felt that they had a much deeper understanding of homosexuality.

Reports to Worship & Ministry and Overseers in the late spring resulted in a minute prepared for monthly meeting to consider in October 1988.

The minutes summarize the various perspectives in the meeting:

> For a few Friends this minute recognized a change in social mores which they found difficult and even painful to contemplate. These Friends see homosexuality as an unnatural relationship without Biblical precedent or social sanction, and usually impermanent. Such a relationship, they felt should not be supported by the meeting or presented to the meeting's children as an acceptable alternative.
>
> Many Friends, however, felt that the efforts of two people to nurture each other on the soul's journey through life should be supported regardless of the sexual orientation of the two people involved. Many heterosexual Friends felt unprepared to recognize only their own sexual preference as "natural" but felt led instead to testify to their conviction that a living community must necessarily allow for a variety of ways to make love manifest.

Since some Friends seemed very troubled by the minute, it was postponed for further discussion in the December meeting. Friends were asked to share insights with one another so that we might reach clarity at that time. Gay/Lesbian Friends undertook to visit with Friends who had opposed the minute for direct but nonconfrontational discussion, which had the effect of removing their misgivings. In December, Germantown Meeting was able to unite on the minute.

In retrospect, we feel that the elements that made such acceptance possible were:

- Germantown proceeded without haste, taking three years to reach unity. The matter was studied and presented with a vast amount of factual information.
- The gay/lesbian members of the meeting, particularly those already living in committed relationships were beloved and respected elders of the meeting. Their behavior was not discernibly different from that of heterosexuals in the meeting. They were members who carried their share of the work of the meeting and they had the love and trust of the membership.
- The action of the gay and lesbian members in addressing directly but not with any hostility the reservations of the heterosexual members.

Other Meetings' Experiences

Pastoral Care Newsletter sought a first hand account of a meeting that came to unity on not taking same gender unions under its care. We did not find such a meeting, but rather found meetings in various conditions:

1. Many meetings have not felt called to consider this matter—no same gender couple has asked for marriage under the care of the meeting and the meeting has not felt led to consider it in the abstract.
2. Other meetings have considered same gender unions and failed to find unity. In these meetings, as is Friends custom, failure to find unity has meant remaining with the previous practice of not taking these relationships under the care of the meeting.
3. Some meetings have found unity in taking same gender relationships under their care, but not in naming those relationships "marriage."

We honor the deep and sincere search of all meetings who take up this matter with a desire to be responsive to the leadings of the Spirit. We invite readers to let us know of meetings that have felt a clear and unified leading not to take same gender relationships under their care so that we can make that information available to other readers.

Questions for Reflection

1. Under what circumstances might our meeting undertake consideration of same gender marriage? If the issue of same gender marriage were raised, would the meeting be prepared to attend to it in a careful, loving, worshipful manner?

2. Is consideration of same gender marriage likely to evoke strong feelings in our meeting? If so, what has been the meeting's experience of dealing with difficult issues? What groundwork can help meeting members be open to one another and the leadings of the Spirit? Might we need to consider asking for assistance from outside of meeting to help us consider this question in light and love?

3. What background information would our meeting need in order to be prepared for considering same gender marriage? Has the meeting previously discussed homosexuality and civil rights for homosexuals? Are members acquainted with gay and/or lesbian couples? Would it be helpful to have information about the lives of gay and lesbian couples in the community? What resources can we call on to help us be better informed?

4. Does the meeting have a practice of Bible study that would prepare it for reflecting on the passages relating to homosexuality? What resources can we call on to help us wrestle with these passages?

5. Are there Friends in the meeting who can give leadership to this consideration who are widely respected in the meeting, have a gift of discernment, are open-minded and teachable, and who have a commitment to the loving and Spirit filled consideration of this concern?

Meeting Support of Marriage and Couple Relationships

Pastoral Care Newsletter, Vol. 1, No. 2 • December 1993

by Patricia McBee

O N THE WHOLE, there is a great reticence among Friends to address with each other the nitty-gritty issues of what makes relationships work. Most often our pastoral care committees feel helpless and out of place in trying to reach out to couples, particularly if the couple is known or believed to be in a stressful period in their relationship.

And no wonder we are hesitant. In our culture little is regarded as more shameful than having people know that we are having struggles in our relationships. What could be more embarrassing for most couples than to have others know they are struggling? Why do we keep from each other that all of us have rough times and that they are survivable?

Here are some suggestions for overcoming the barriers and giving meaningful support.

1. Create an atmosphere in which relationships can be talked about.

The key in supporting couples is to integrate that support into the day to day life of the meeting. If you wait until a couple is in trouble and then want to help them, you may lack the connections that make it possible for your help to be accepted. If you support relationships when they are already strong, fewer problems may arise and you will be in a better position to respond when a problem arises.

- Organize on-going couples support groups that meet monthly. These groups can include a mix of couples or be established topically such as for retired couples, couples with children, couples where only one is a Quaker, etc.

- Have periodic occasions when groups of couples get together to discuss topics related to relationships, such as: how do you integrate different family holiday customs, or how do couples make time for each other in the face of busy schedules.
- One or more times a year sponsor a discussion of a book or pamphlet on strengthening relationships.
- Set up occasions to meet with couples who have been married under the care of the meeting and elicit suggestions as to how the meeting can be of continuing support.
- Sponsor a couples retreat or support couples in attending one offered by your yearly meeting or Friends General Conference.

The critical issue is to be talking frankly about the day to day workings of relationships so that couples can see other's relationships not as picture perfect, but as resilient and creative in the face of the inevitable challenges of learning to love each other well. We learn so much more from hearing other couples, see options that hadn't occurred to us before, and finding out that we are not alone in the things that are difficult.

These occasions of discussing marriage in the ordinary times create a foundation for greater willingness to have our needs known and accept support in hard times.

2. Reach out to couples in good times and bad.

The societal taboo against revealing your relationship is so strong that the meeting has to work at ways to make it easy and safe. Don't wait for couples to overcome their hesitations on their own. Call them specifically to invite them to one of the gatherings listed above and make it clear that it is an opportunity to honor marriage and committed relationships as a spiritual path and that their participation will be a support to other couples.

When the grapevine tells you times are rough for a certain couple, don't wait for them to contact you. Have someone they know and trust offer a listening ear and the meeting's support.

3. Establish channels for seeking and giving help.

Make sure everyone in the meeting knows where to turn for confidential help.

- Some meetings establish a contact person for each member when they want to tap the meeting's support systems. In my meeting it is your "Friendly contact." In other meetings, households are paired in a buddy system. When something comes up, you talk to your Friendly contact or buddy and explore whether other meeting help should be sought.
- In some meetings there is a standing committee for marriage clearness and support and it is made clear how to contact that committee.
- Meetings can designate an individual, sometimes the clerk of the pastoral care committee, who is known for being able to keep things in confidence. This person can then help the couple identify what support they need.
- In some meetings marriage clearness committees remain in contact with couples and are available for consultation.

4. Use informal as well as formal channels.

Often there are individuals in the meeting who can be supportive to a couple in need without "the meeting" having to get officially involved. Several years ago when my husband, Brad, and I were going through a very painful time, three or four couples of our friends in the meeting buoyed us up with their willingness to listen and love. I don't know if our needs were ever on the agenda of the pastoral care committee, but we got the support we needed.

Sometimes, of course, it is important to use the formal channels. I have seen cases in which members didn't recognize informal support as outreach from the meeting and felt as though "the meeting" had not responded to them even though many meeting members had. This leads to the next idea.

5. Tailor your response to the needs of the couple.

Put your focus on loving these two people in the best way they can receive.

Do you approach them together or individually? With a formal delegation from the caregiving committee or an informal call from a friend? Do you urge them to seek professional help or provide background support while they sort it out on their own? All of these approaches are useful in some cases. Hard and fast practices and procedures won't convey the caring you want to give.

Here are some things the meeting can do for couples who are in a time of trouble.

- Express the meeting's affection for them and confidence in their ability to find the best solution.
- Just listen in love.
- Staunchly regard each member of the couple as worthy of love and understanding, no matter who seems "to blame," and help their partner to do the same.
- Provide child care or other concrete support to give the couple opportunities to work on their relationship without distraction.
- Have a list of professional resources. It is often hard to choose a professional counselor, an annotated listing can be a great help.
- Facilitate the use of a counselor by helping pay the fees or by providing child care or transportation.

The meeting's delegates to a couple may not be professional counselors, but they are qualified to bring love, which is God, to people who are troubled. Let them know that they are loved and valued before, during and after a hard time, whatever the outcome. It's amazing how healing and empowering that is.

6. Build a reputation for being affirming and not judgmental.

If a relationship breaks up, find ways of reaching out in love to both individuals. They are both suffering. They wonder if the meeting disapproves or blames or rejects them.

When couples hear of practical ways in which another couple was given the meeting's loving care, it will be far less intimidating to accept an offer of help. Knowing the meeting holds its members in love even when they fail can makes it easier for couples to let it be known that they are at risk of failing or just aren't quite perfect.

7. Have literature for couples where it can be picked up anonymously.

You can make it easier for people to take the first step in seeking help by making it possible to begin without identifying themselves. Things you might have available on your literature table include:

- Information on how to tap into the meeting's support system
- Pamphlets on relationship issues
- Book lists
- Announcements of retreats and workshops

- Brochures from the yearly meeting listing of Friends counselors or a family counseling service in your area

8. Sponsor a couples retreat.

Couples Retreats are a powerful and under utilized tool available to Friends. For more than twenty years trained Quaker leader couples have been conducting retreats for couples with the result of strengthening relationships and deepening spiritual bonds within meetings.

A group of five to nine couples meet for a weekend or a series of 6–8 weekly sessions to share with each other. The power of the retreat for couples is that they can give time to focusing on their relationship without distraction. All of us get busy and take our relationships and our partners for granted. A retreat gives us an opportunity to remind ourselves how rich a resource our relationship can be if it is nurtured.

Depending on the size of the meeting, a couples retreat can be held every one to five years. It can be looked at as something that is done on a regular basis to keep support of couples alive in the meeting. And couples can be brought to regard this kind of intentional nurturing of their relationship as important to themselves, the meeting and the world around them.

9. Most importantly—create a loving, caring meeting family.

If you want to strengthen relationships and be in position to be of support in times of need, play together, work together, meet informally; talk about yourselves, your hopes, your fears. Love each other and say so.

When the meeting is alive and open, all kinds of support can flow in natural, comfortable ways to couples, singles, old folks and children.

Patricia McBee has served as pastoral caregiver and as clerk of Central Philadelphia Monthly Meeting. She and her husband Brad Sheeks have been leading couples retreats since 1975. For several years they participated in an ongoing couples support group in their meeting.

Questions for Reflection

1. Do we have an atmosphere in our meeting in which couples are able to share resources and struggles?
2. What kind of activities can we hold in our meeting to bring couples together to focus on relationship issues?
3. Can we support and sustain one or more couples support groups in the meeting? Or could we sponsor a couples retreat?
4. What can we do to reach out to couples and help them overcome hesitation to participate in these activities?
5. Do we have channels for our members to seek confidential help from the meeting? If not, can we establish these channels? How can we keep members aware of the availability of these resources?
6. Could we as caregivers be more proactive in reaching out with offers of support when we know couples to be struggling?

Supporting Families Through Separation and Divorce

Pastoral Care Newsletter, Vol. 2, No. 2 • January 1995

By Jean B. Robbins

So often a meeting is stunned by the news that an active couple in the meeting is separating. How has this happened without someone—some member of the pastoral care committee—sensing that the couple was struggling with their relationship? And, how can we be present to the family in this time of crisis in a way which is caring and constructive? One would hope that a significant relationship had begun between the couple and the meeting *before* this moment of crisis. Though it may not always be possible to have a meaningful connection prior to the crisis, our work can be eased if such is the case.

Where do we begin? Remembering that we are not responsible for "fixing" the situation, and grounding ourselves in our belief of the Spirit's presence may help to reduce the anxiety which so many of us experience when hearing of marital problems. Certainly there needs to be a readiness on the part of the pastoral caregiver to listen deeply. Listening deeply with care does not mean delving into what went wrong in the past. It involves nonjudgmental listening and moving along with the persons who are hurting, beginning with where they are at the moment.

While it may be natural for a caregiver to assume that couples have their own inner resources to work through the pain, in reality those who are hurting often cannot see beyond their own troubles. Often they do not know where or how to seek help. To have a caring meeting member who will share the journey through the separation and eventually the divorce can be very helpful.

Philadelphia Yearly Meeting's *Faith and Practice* reminds us that, "Those who are asked to give counsel should remember that often the best service is to be a good listener. When advice is given, the attitude of the counselor may be more helpful than any specific recommendations. This attitude should always be one of friendliness and love."[1]

Acknowledging the Problem

If the meeting has a sense of community, there should be a feeling of mutual responsibility for each other's welfare. Everyone needs to be thinking about pastoral care. The Advices in *Faith and Practice* (Philadelphia Yearly Meeting) speak to this when they encourage us to "live affectionately as friends, entering with sympathy into joys and sorrows of one another's daily lives. Visit one another. Be alert to give help and receive it. Bear the burdens of one another's failings; share the buoyancy of one another's strengths."[2]

When a marital crisis is recognized, it involves risk taking on the part of the pastoral care committee or trusted member of the meeting. Too often we worry that we are intruding in the crisis. The Friends in the critical situation, however, need to know that the meeting cares about them. Avoidance for fear of intrusion runs a strong risk of sending a message of not caring, particularly since our experience teaches us that those lost in the crisis often are unable to take initiative in asking for help.

A couple who have been through this painful crisis deepened my understanding of what, at least for them, had been helpful. They spoke of how they were grateful for the concern of the meeting, although they did acknowledge that, by the time anyone in the meeting learned of the problem, the condition was in the advanced stages of pain and anger. They stressed the importance of the referral made to the Friends Counseling Service. Although it took them a while to come to the decision to ask for help from the counseling service, they felt in retrospect that it had been a great help for them. They hope that pastoral caregivers in all meetings are aware of counseling resources in their community, being especially mindful of those which are offered on the basis of Friends' values.

The couple also appreciated that an effort was made on the part of the meeting to call upon them for help with meeting projects. Those requests served to keep them involved with the meeting.

---

[1] Philadelphia Yearly Meeting, *Faith and Practice*, 1972, p. 148.
[2] Ibid., p. 199.

Engaging More Deeply

At the time of separation, overwhelming feelings of pain, anger and a sense of failure often come to the surface. Also, there can be a feeling of guilt about a promise being broken, a promise that was made earnestly and with love. Because this is the end of a relationship, a grieving process ensues. Accompanying all these emotions may be a feeling of anxiety about what lies ahead. Women often seem to have the ability to communicate with a network of friends. Men hurt just as much, but frequently are inclined to be stoic and not communicative. Some of the issues that are heard among couples in crisis are these: he/she does not "hear" me; he/she pays no attention to the children; trust has broken down; another person has entered the life of one or the other; he/she is physically and/or psychologically abusive; drug or alcohol abuse is a problem.

One way to connect with troubled Friends, as they wrestle with these feelings and issues, is to suggest meeting in a neutral spot for a time to talk and listen. The meetinghouse or caregiver's home with an invitation to tea, for example, are both settings in which the folks gathered can have an awareness of safety and caring. Coming together at the meetinghouse can bring a sense of calm and a reminder of the Divine Presence.

No matter where the gathering occurs, it is essential that confidentiality be emphasized and respected. This applies not only to the way in which the caregivers will hold appropriate confidences in relation to what is shared by the couple; it also applies to the two persons who are separating.

One way of helping to stabilize the separation process is to help the couple come to agreement about what each of them will be sharing with people regarding the cause of the separation. That is: can each trust the other to hold some things confidential to the two of them, or will each, out of fear of what the other is saying, begin to tell his or her side of the story to anyone who will listen? Further, the couple should be asked about their wishes in regard to the sharing of information beyond the individual or small group of caregivers meeting with them.

At times, the pastoral care committee can be helpful in assisting the couple with the painful task of letting their faith community know of the breakdown of their marriage. Yet there are also couples who prefer that the responsibility of informing the meeting be left to them.

Different Models for Meeting Involvement

I remember particularly a struggling couple who, several years ago, asked to meet with a specific member of our caregiving committee. One of the pair was not willing to seek professional help, but agreed to meet with the spouse and the designated caregiver. The Friend labored lovingly with the couple every two weeks for many months, meeting together in a comfortable corner of the meetinghouse. In this setting one could listen deeply with a feeling of reverence. Each meeting was entered into with prayerful worship, closing the same way. Anger and disbelief were expressed by each party in the presence of the caring Friend. Certain issues needed to be addressed: How would the separation be handled when telling the children? When would they notify the meeting? Where would each one live? Who would pay the bills? This part of the separation was not easy. Money matters seemed to be more of an obstacle than some of the other issues. The one spouse hoped that everything would be "fixed up" by these sessions, but the other was determined to end the marriage. Eventually the couple came to terms of separation with the caregiver walking with them through the process.

When asked by the couple to meet with them, the caregiver felt inadequate in this role. In order to be present to them, she sought and received support from the Friends Counseling Service, through telephone consultation. While respecting the confidentiality of the couple, she was able to talk through her role in the situation, thus enabling her to be more present to them. Sadly one of the partners withdrew membership in this meeting, but did find a spiritual home within another nearby meeting. It was too painful for her to stay where her spouse was still very much in evidence.

In another instance, a couple separated largely because of the husband's alcohol abuse. That symptom signalled a problem with the relationship. Since the couple were in counseling and the husband felt that the alcohol problem was his, and not the meeting's, no specific request was made for pastoral care. Both, however, were very involved with meeting committees and projects, as were the children. This involvement kept them participating faithfully in the meeting, giving each one a sense of belonging. The wife appreciated the meeting's concern, and fortunately understood that members felt inhibited about offering help in small ways unless she specifically asked for it. Then there was a warm response. After a year of separation, during which time the husband dealt effectively with his alcoholism, the couple made the decision to reunite, and asked for a clearness committee of two Friends of their choice. The role of that committee was to help the couple examine the commitment they were making to each other as they came back into their marriage on a new basis.

In still another situation, a clearness committee of three trusted Friends was chosen by a couple who had agreed to separate. They informed the committee that their decision to separate was definite but they asked for help in working through the separation in a way consistent with their values as Friends. The committee helped them to deal with the issues of child support, responsibilities of caring for the children, distribution of property, etc. As the issues were worked out, this committee became a means of accountability for each party.

This was a situation in which the matter of property was not complicated. When the assets are more complex, the role of the committee may be that of helping the couple come to clearness about the principles they want to guide their division of property, followed by a referral to an accountant or some other person with appropriate training. That person, then, can help to ensure that their division of assets is consistent with those principles.

Supporting the Children

Through most of these struggles children are caught in the chaos of the marital crisis. They need some stability and the assurance that they are not responsible for the separation. My meeting arranged for a counselor to come for a discussion of how to nurture families through the crisis of family breakdown. It was a beneficial time for questions and constructive suggestions from a professional.

If possible, it is wise for the children to stay in the same school situation for continuity in their lives, as well as for support from those teachers and friends who know them and care about them. In the meeting, intergenerational games or discussions can enable positive interaction between children and the adults; movies for all ages can be a common denominator. Sometimes there is a special rapport between an adult and a particular child. This can grow as the adult takes the initiative by inviting that child to supper or to help set up refreshments after meeting. Children need to know that they are respected and loved by the meeting.

Having a Foundation in Place

We are much better able to meet people who are at a time of crisis if we have paid ongoing attention to the development of community in the meeting. Activities and projects can be scheduled on a regular basis to lay the foundation for friendship. Small group discussions on almost any topic can help create a sense of safety and offer a chance to know one another in a deeper sense. Meeting functions such as potluck meals can further the development of friendships. Breaking bread together is a comfortable and easy way to establish a friendly connection. "Friendly Eight" dinners and discussions are another avenue for encouraging a feeling of community. Having refreshments after meeting for worship each week is conducive to conversations among members and attenders; it creates a time for sensing joys and sorrows, struggles and needs. Intergenerational projects such as leaf raking, working on a third world craft sale or a flea market all help to build friendship and trust in one another. Working together on committees serves a dual purpose. Primarily, it accomplishes a task, such as sorting clothes for the American Friends Service Committee material aid, planning for quarterly meeting program and meal or helping with First Day School. Secondarily, a closeness is developed with those persons involved in the project.

Summary

Each situation is different; no specific formula can be given. In the examples cited, we saw several different models of the way in which the meeting, through its pastoral care committee, was involved in ways which the couples found helpful. The Spirit usually leads to a solution if the caregivers involved can discern what the couple needs and wants as well as being a presence—walking beside them through this painful time. Again, *Faith and Practice*[3] reminds us that "the affectionate care and sympathy of the meeting should continue to be given to members who have been divorced. Problems of readjustment may be very difficult. Friendliness and understanding may then be of great help."

Jean B. Robbins, a longtime pastoral caregiver, has been a member of Westfield Meeting, in Cinnaminson, NJ, since 1950. She has served as clerk of the meeting as well as on Overseers, Worship and Ministry, Religious Education Committee, Collectors, Aid to Friends in Need and Funeral Committee.

[3] Ibid., p. 25.

One Meeting's Experience: Two Friends Reflect on Their Experience of Separating

Reflections from Susan (not her real name): Before the actual breakup I mentioned to a couple of people in the meeting that things were difficult. People offered support as individuals—without judgment, without taking sides. They said "we're there for you." That meant a lot. After we had separated, and with John's awareness, I wrote a letter to the meeting saying that after a lengthy struggle and real agonizing we had both concluded that separation was the best course. Both of us wanted to continue as members of the meeting, and I didn't want Friends to be guessing or to feel divided. But after they received the letter, some committee members seemed to almost pointedly ignore me. This was so extremely painful as I felt so exposed and vulnerable. Some others—even those I don't know well—did show that they cared, and that meant a lot to me.

Later John and I ran into a real dilemma around an important issue in our separation. One day I was praying about it, and I received a message to call a clearness committee. I asked John and he agreed, and we decided together on whom to ask. It was important to me that the people on the committee be even-handed, and that they trust in the Spirit. I wasn't looking for opinions—I wanted the clearness process to be prayerful and Spirit-centered. And for the most part it was. When we talked and prayerfully sought guidance about the problem together, the negativity was lifted, and it never returned.

As for those wishing to help couples in our situation, I would ask you to trust that most people have made their decision after an enormous amount of soul searching, and with great sorrow. You can give people in this situation a great gift by suspending judgment and by extending compassion, understanding and support. Just be there for them—just a kind word is really all that's needed. And for God's sake don't ignore them! That's the most painful thing—to not even acknowledge that it's happened! I know others in the meeting who have had a similar experience.

John's reflections: We made the decision to separate on our own. We didn't tell the meeting we were thinking of it. It was too late for them to do anything about the separation. But the clearness committee did help us. When members of the committee expressed several points of view, that legitimized the points of view that Susan and I had, which were in conflict. In allowing the opposites to become clear, the committee created a space for reconciliation. But it wasn't easy. Half-way through it didn't look like there would be any solution at all. Finally one person offered a fairly simple statement of the problem and a simple solution, and everyone united behind it. It wasn't so much a new solution; it was the way that the problem was stated that made the difference. I call it the voice of the Spirit. It was sort of like wandering through a maze in a garden, but from a higher perspective it looks simple. It means moving beyond the idea that any one opinion is "right."

Although this wasn't the issue in our clearness process, one thing meetings could do with couples who are separating would be to help them make a recommitment to the kids. The meeting can provide a framework to help the couple—and their children—to affirm and accept the new situation, even though there's a lot of pain involved.

From the Perspective of the committee members: The committee members did not always find it easy to be open. As one member admitted, "Before the clearness meeting I had already come to see one side as in the right. So I realized that I would really need to be quiet, to listen and to be open during the clearness process, in order to fully hear both sides and to see the 'party in the wrong' as a person. That was my prayer. Then I was grateful when the Spirit broke through the meeting. The Spirit showed us a way that was simple and clear."

Note: Susan and John had some real differences in the way that they experienced the clearness process. Particular comments which seemed quite judgmental to one were seen as supportive by the other. Yet both John and Susan appreciated the committee members' willingness to be available to the process.

Questions for Reflection

1. Do we, as members of our meeting's pastoral care committee, ground ourselves in an awareness of God's presence?
2. How do we, as caregivers, enter a marital crisis?
3. Am I willing to take the risk of walking through this crisis with the couple, with love?
4. Can I listen nonjudgmentally? What might help me to do this still more effectively?
5. How can our meeting develop better ways for letting members know how to access confidential help when needed?

CARE OF THE MEETING COMMUNITY

NURTURING THE MEETING COMMUNITY

MOVING TOWARD WHOLENESS:
ADDRESSING RACE AMONG FRIENDS

THE CHALLENGE AND OPPORTUNITY
OF MEETINGHOUSE CHANGES

USE OF CLEARNESS COMMITTEES
IN PASTORAL CARE

SUPPORTING STANDS OF CONSCIENCE

Nurturing the Meeting Community

Pastoral Care Newsletter, Vol. 4, No. 3 • March 1997

By Arlene Kelly

MOST OFTEN WE THINK OF PASTORAL CARE within our meetings, we think of those times of special need or transition when we have offered the support of the meeting to an individual, couple or family. This essay calls attention to the need for pastoral care of the meeting as a whole. In reflecting on the question of how we nurture the meeting community, we are turning our attention to the context within which individual acts of pastoral care occur. Whether a newcomer feels led to become part of the community, whether members of the community in a period of crisis feel safe to reveal their need, or whether the meeting nurtures the gifts of each individual member depends a good deal on whether we, together, have become a caring community.

I feel that our meetings benefit when the committee charged with pastoral care is intentional in recognizing that a Friends meeting is an alive, dynamic entity that needs tending if its various parts are to be in a right harmony with each other. Some meetings intuitively care for and nurture their life as a community; other meetings go through periods of conflict and dissension by not being mindful of issues embedded in community life or in not knowing how to respond to them.

Community in the Spirit

I want to ground this article in the awareness that our Friends meetings are faith communities; i.e., communities of people who have come together out of a shared belief in a Spirit, a God, the Light. We give different names to that Spirit. Nevertheless, our joining together in a search to discern the will of that Spirit and to witness to its reality through our actions forms the glue which holds our spiritual community together.

Lloyd Lee Wilson, in his book, *Essays on the Quaker Vision of Gospel Order*, speaks compellingly of the difference there is when community is based on a belief that God can work in our lives. His comments begin to lead us toward one definition of community for Friends meetings:

> The individual whose commitment to the community is based on a sense that these comunity members are somehow special human beings, who have the right concerns and values and live the right lives, will find great difficulty when members of the community fail to live up to these standards and expectations.
>
> In contrast, the individual whose commitment is based on an acceptance of a covenant relationship with God has a different reaction to these inevitable pains and disappointments. The covenant relationship says that we are given in relationship to each other precisely in order to help one another through these painful times into a fuller relationship with God and one another. What is a centrifugal force in one case is a bonding experience among a covenant people. Our individual sins and failures become opportunities for the community to practice true loving forgiveness, to offer spiritual counsel and guidance, and to offer spiritual and emotional healing.[1]

Maintaining an awareness that our meetings are based on a covenant relationship with God can make a significant difference in our meetings and in the effectiveness of our work of pastoral care.

Developing a Vision of Community

No article can prescribe what kind of community each meeting should form. It is important, therefore, that each meeting have opportunities to share assumptions and expectations. What can our meeting expect of its members? Who are we to each other?

Do we have a shared sense of what we wish to be as a community of Friends? How are we at welcoming and integrating new persons into our meeting community? Is there, on the whole, a climate of trust and openness among us, or do we find members of the community to be cautious or angry with each other? These are just a few of the questions which can help us begin to focus on the communal life of the meeting and to identify aspects of the meeting's life which would benefit from care and attention.

The pastoral care committee can play a valuable role by creating opportunities for meeting members and attenders to come together to learn about and discuss the issue of the meeting as a community. One approach to this would be to sponsor a potluck dinner to be followed

---

[1] Lloyd Lee Wilson, *Essays on the Quaker Vision of Gospel Order*, 2001, p. 69.

by an evening of discussion and/or worship sharing. The discussion is likely to be richer if one or two members of the committee prepare some opening remarks which address the different dimensions of community. Then people can break into groups of 8 to 10 to discuss a set of questions prepared ahead of time and based on the opening remarks. Some meetings I know have approached it by having a quote, such as that by Lloyd Lee Wilson cited previously, or another found to be meaningful, and having people do worship sharing around it. Perhaps the queries included in this article would be a good beginning. The evening can be wrapped up by folks coming back together and identifying in the full group the ideas they found to be most stimulating and challenging and perhaps thinking together regarding what would be a good next step for carrying the discussion forward.

The dialogue might also take place in a series of articles and responses in the meeting's newsletter followed by discussion in adult forum or meeting for business.

Building Community

Community is built by doing it. It can grow out of the regular ebb and flow of the meeting's life: our meetings for worship and for business and our work together on committees.

Community occurs when we miss someone at meeting and call that person or family to say that they have been missed. It occurs when we reach out to the person whom we don't know well and have a substantive conversation. Not surprisingly, it occurs when we, as a meeting, rally around a family or individual who is going through a crisis or when we, as a meeting, rally around an issue in our larger community which requires our care and attention. In each of these instances we have allowed the barriers between ourselves and others to dissolve, we have found our oneness in the Spirit.

These natural community-building processes can be reinforced by intentionally creating opportunities for members of the community to get to know each other more fully. Pastoral caregivers can play a valuable role in helping the meeting develop such opportunities.

Potluck dinners are a time-honored way of bringing members together. Some meetings have elaborated the potluck dinner into Friendly Eights—groups of eight coming together for an evening of fellowship over dinner. There can be a focus for the evening or not, depending on the interest of the participants.

A meeting weekend or meeting retreat, with both a theme and opportunity for fun together is another approach which many meetings have found to be fruitful in building community.

These and other community building activities are spelled out in more detail on page 115.

In any of these efforts it is essential, I feel, to remain grounded in the reality that we are a community of seekers. We are held together as a religious society by our belief that something which is greater than ourselves is working in our lives.

The Changing Seasons of Community

Another important dimension of nurturing community is to realize that there are seasons in the life of a community. The ebb and flow in the size of the meeting and shifts in the age composition are two examples of changing seasons. Attentiveness to these cycles can help us move through them in ways that strengthen our sense of community.

Pastoral caregivers can be mindful of the needs of each season. A number of meetings across the country experienced a significant increase in meeting membership as the result of the Gulf War. Such growth is a blessing, but it also presents a challenge to a meeting if a sizable segment of people active in the meeting are newly convinced Friends. How is the tradition transmitted? How do we help new members to learn about Quaker processes? Much of our transmission of the tradition is nonverbal, by action and osmosis, but we need to ask ourselves whether that is sufficient during times of rapid growth.

Alertness by the pastoral care committee can help to avert some of the strains brought about by rapid growth. We can encourage the Adult Education Committee to provide opportunities to learn about some of the basics of Friends faith and practice. We can support and encourage the more experienced members to be mentors, particularly in Friends business processes. We can encourage the Nominating Committee to be mindful of the need for newer members to have an opportunity for seasoning before giving them responsibilities for which they may be inadequately prepared. These are but a few of the ways the pastoral care committee can be helpful at a time of rapid growth in the meeting.

One meeting's experience was that its growth was steady, but not rapid. That presented different challenges as the meeting went from 25 or 30 members to 50 members. In reflecting on the impact of this growth, the pastoral care committee of that meeting realized that the informal word of mouth communication which had served them well wasn't working now that they had become a larger meeting. Newer members were not part of the informal systems and felt left out. If the meeting wanted to keep newer members of their community from becoming discontented and dropping out, it was time to think of a newsletter or other more formalized means of letting all concerned know of what was happening.

Most meetings are feeling the impact of changes in our larger society. In the United States, people are working longer hours, we have more single parent families, children are becoming involved in team sports at younger ages. Free time has become far more precious. Pastoral care can help their meetings discern ways a faith based community can respond to these realities.

Do you find any resonance between these examples and the experience of your meeting? What other factors are affecting in your meeting's life?

Whether we consciously acknowledge these things and discuss them or not, they are at work in the life of our community and having an impact. There are serious and important value questions embedded in them such as: What does it mean, in these times, to live a life of simplicity—both individually and as a faith community? Is our Quakerism and attention to our spiritual lives to be at the center, or simply another of the myriad things to which we need to attend? If we desire it to be at the center and to be that which informs all else that we do, then what does that mean, in day to day specific terms, regarding who we are as a community? The pastoral care committee can serve the meeting by providing opportunity for these questions, and others which are relevant to your particular meeting, to be lifted up for reflection.

Finding Time in Our Committees' Agendas to Address Questions of Community

It is always a challenge for our caregiving committees to deal with all the business that comes before us. Big picture questions tend to get squeezed out by immediate needs. Yet there is the reality that tending to the community in a steady way can avert a crisis and helps the meeting be prepared to better meet immediate needs.

The pastoral care committee in my meeting has found it helpful to set aside twenty minutes of focused reflection at the start of each agenda. Though our agendas are full, we discipline ourselves to step back and look in depth at one dimension of our community's life. It is not a time for decision making, though it may lead us to issues that need further discussion and action.

Conclusion

In this article I am urging pastoral care committees to keep their finger on the pulse of the meeting in order to sense how the communal life of the meeting is ebbing and flowing. Our work in pastoral care of individuals and families is made easier when members of the community have opportunity to come to know each other in an authentic way and to dialogue with each other regarding our expectations of community.

We don't have to know all the answers ourselves. Our belief in the possibility of the Spirit being manifest in this moment calls us to be open as channels for that Spirit. Pastoral caregivers are, I believe, called to provide leadership in naming the questions to be addressed in the life of the community and in inviting other committees, and, at times, the meeting as a whole, to seek together for the answers.

> Arlene Kelly has served as clerk of Philadelphia Yearly Meeting and as clerk of Central Philadelphia Monthly Meeting. She served for over 30 years on Overseers of her meeting, including as the clerk of that committee. She carries a concern for nurturing and strengthening Friends meetings as faith communities.

Some Community Building Activities for Meetings

Family Meeting: Some meetings schedule a separate worship experience for families and others. Their sense of community has been enhanced by Quaker stories, singing, guided meditation, short periods of unprogrammed worship time and sharing of religious experience.

Members' Photos: Some meetings put together directories with photos of members or post photos of members on a bulletin board. A caption with the photo can include names, hobbies and interests. This really helps put names and faces together.

Worship Sharing: Worship sharing groups provide opportunity for members to share in depth on a topic. Some meetings have worship sharing before or after meeting on a regular basis. Others invite sign-ups for a group that will meet once a week for four to eight weeks or more.

Creative Listening (Claremont Dialogue) is a structured process for sharing based on personal experience which helps members to get to know one another more deeply. See the pamphlet Quaker Dialogue, "Creative Listening," published by Claremont Meeting, 1991. "We developed a depth of warmth, love and understanding. We had all known one another from three to ten years, had worked side-by-side on committees, yet in all those years we had never begun to reach this depth."

Friendly Eights: Members and attenders are invited to sign up to participate in potluck dinners in each others' homes. Groups of eight are assembled to meet together on a certain date. The conversation can be informal or more formal worship sharing can follow the meal.

Meeting Retreats: Retreats give an extended, relaxed time for playing and sharing together. Activities can include: workshops on topics of interest to the meeting, art projects, sports and games, folk dancing, and talent shows. Retreats can be held at a camp, a retreat center or in the meetinghouse. Some meetings schedule a retreat for the same weekend year after year.

Work Projects and Workcamps: A work day at the meetinghouse to do repairs and sprucing up can be a wonderful way to build community—especially if it is followed by sharing some food and conversation.

Questions for Reflection

1. What words or phrases describe the life of our meeting community: exciting, set in our ways, Spirit-filled, backward looking, evolving, divided?
2. What dimensions of the meeting's life as a community are rich and flourishing? Which dimensions are languishing or filled with tension?
3. What aspects of our meeting community have changed over the past few years? What impact have these changes had on the life of the meeting—in a positive way/in a negative way?
4. How can we as a committee build attention to the meeting community into our regular agendas and processes?
5. Are there particular needs of the meeting community to which our caregiving committee could be responsive at the present time? What are they?
6. How can we help the meeting and other committees to give attention to our community in the Spirit?

Moving Toward Wholeness: Addressing Race Among Friends

Pastoral Care Newsletter, Vol. 9, No. 2 • January 2002

COMPILED AND EDITED BY
VANESSA JULYE AND PATRICIA McBEE

The lead article for this issue is collected from comments and contributions of many Friends considering how to be faithful to God and one another on matters of race within the Religious Society of Friends.[1] It has been compiled by editor, Patricia McBee and guest editor, Vanessa Julye and is followed by short articles by Friends reflecting on facets of these issues.

G EORGE FOX ADMONISHED FRIENDS "to know one another in that which is eternal." In building our communities and in providing pastoral care to our members we reach toward that deep place which transcends differences including race, class, gender or other external categories. Yet we enter our meetinghouses carrying our experience of the world around us, a world deeply influenced by these categories. Sometimes unwittingly, sometimes knowingly, too often in ways that cause distress, we let assumptions based in our racial or ethnic background influence the way we relate to one another, to our world and to God. How can we help our meetings grow toward our ideal as Friends? How can we sensitively provide pastoral care to our members of color?

As we consulted with Friends of varying backgrounds about the preparation of this issue, the sense that emerged is that the first step is

---

[1] One Friend of color cautioned that many scholars question whether the concept of "race" is useful in considering the vast range of skin colors and cultural backgrounds that make up the human community. Indeed within "racial" groupings there are many differences of experience and point of view. Nonetheless, ideas of race have influenced our experience in our meetings and we find it a useful construct with which to begin to address the assumptions that we make.

for us as a Religious Society to acknowledge that we are not the ideal that we long for. If we wish to grow toward that ideal we need to help each other to open our eyes and our hearts and our minds. We need to be prepared to question our assumptions. Friends of European ancestry may not recognize how many assumptions are based in whiteness. Friends of color may too readily assume that an issue that comes up is based in race. We need to be ready to be changed as we learn from one another. We need to be prepared for the likelihood that discussing race will elicit strong emotions including frustration, sadness, guilt, anger, defensiveness, confusion, hope and longing.

We Are a Multiracial Religious Society

An amazing amount of pain is caused by the simple failure to acknowledge that Quakerism—including North American, liberal, unprogrammed Quakerism—is multiracial and multicultural. Below are a few examples of when Friends of color felt invisible or unwelcome.

A board member at Pendle Hill was escorting a prospective lecturer around the campus. As they entered the main building a workshop participant approached them and said, "There's no toilet paper in the ladies room." Since both were African-American women were they mistaken for housekeeping staff? That was how it felt.

A life-long Friend who is Asian American says that she can be "going along being just me and then be brought up short" by comments such as "You speak excellent English. Where are you from?" "New Jersey," she responds. "Where are your parents from?" "California."

The lecturer at a Quaker event spoke stirringly about white privilege. She began that part of her talk with the comment "I, like the Society of Friends, am white," and went on to discuss how white privilege benefits "us." Her audience, however, included African American, Asian American, Native American Friends and possibly others. Similarly, an African American Friend wrote about "building healthy relationships between Quakers and people of color" seemingly overlooking Quakers of color.

A Latina Friend shared with us that her meeting was hosting a series of workshops on racism. As fliers were being passed out, she noticed there were no references to Hispanic, Asian, Native American or any other ethnic group but African Americans. "I really dislike feeling like the race police. I did point out that this is not just black and white—it is everyone."

Look around your meeting. You probably will observe that most members are white and middle class. But look closely for those who do not fit those categories. How do we harm them and the Religious Society of Friends when we refer to Friends as a white, middle-class group? To the extent that we allow that inadequate self concept to persist, how does it limit us as a Religious Society?

Looking at One Another As We Really Are

As you look around your meeting or yearly meeting and see people who are different from you in race or class, what assumptions do you make about them? Do you assume that they are similar to other people of that race whom you have known? What assumptions do you make about people of your own race?

What assumptions do you make about yourself as a person with a racial identity? A European American writes, "Most of us who are white have never really thought about what it means for us to be white. We see people who are not white and want to reach out, but have no idea how because of the legacy that has kept us isolated and segregated. We are part of a white culture that does not talk about, or even notice, its own whiteness."

An African American woman writes, "Racism is part of my daily life. It affects me in everything I do. There are people of European descent everywhere I go. I am surrounded by images which are constantly reinforcing that our cultural standard is that of the middle-class European American, a standard that most meetings have adopted." Does either of these describe your experience of the world? How would you describe the effects of your race on your world view?

Assumptions about ourselves and others in our meetings affect the ways in which we interact. What assumptions do we make about why people have come to worship among Friends? Are we surprised to discover a Friend of color who is a second or third generation Friend? Do we assume that a new attender is a refugee from explicitly Christian religious expressions? Convinced Friends of various backgrounds who are spiritually nourished within the Christian tradition are shocked and saddened when they encounter Friends who feel Christian language is out of place among us. Many seekers come to Friends for the unprogrammed worship. Do we slip into the assumption that African-American convinced Friends are more likely than others to miss the music of their previous religious tradition or that Asian-Americans are more likely to like the silence? We might be surprised by what draws a specific person to our meetings. One person of color reported that she began to feel connected to her meeting not in meeting for worship or reflecting on Quaker beliefs but in the down-to-earth connection when she was removing the stuffing from the turkey for the meeting's Christmas celebration.

What assumptions do we make about people's background and interest? Friends tend to relate to each other assuming that members and attenders will have a specific base of knowledge from obtaining a college degree, that we are financially secure enough to have expendable money, that we are interested in current events and listen to *NPR* or read the *New York Times*. Look again at the members of your meeting. Would you be surprised to learn that a European American man well known among Friends does not have a college degree or that an African American woman is the fifth generation in her family to have one? Does race influence the assumptions you make about the financial resources of a Friend in your meeting?

Examining Our Corporate Assumptions

Race not only affects the way we relate as individuals. It effects our corporate life as Friends. Remembering Friends history of work for abolition and for civil rights or Friends work among relocated Japanese Americans during World War II, we may be lulled into thinking that Quakers are less racist than the general population. When Friends of color find that white Friends are not much different from the rest of the culture, it can lead to disappointment and anger. That anger can lead to defensiveness in white Friends.

A look at our history would show that Friends, both past and present, have been inconsistent in approaching matters of race. In addition to our positive history of work for racial equality, Friends participated in the slave trade, owned slaves, segregated our meetinghouses, made it difficult for African Americans to become members, and financed schools for African Americans while keeping schools for Friends children segregated. In the nineteenth century Friends worked for better treatment of Native Americans but debated whether the Native Americans should be consulted about what help they desired. Some Friends of color have found that it seems easier for white Friends to build coalitions with people of color outside of Friends than to address issue of racism with the Friends community. Knowledge of our full history, good and bad, can help us in finding our way today.

Assumptions about race and class affect our meetings for worship and for business and every part of our community life. Two European American Friends were asked by their meeting's Worship and Ministry Committee to meet with a new attender who frequently spoke in meeting, often in ways that showed a deep life in the Spirit but sometimes in ways that seemed inappropriate. As the conversation progressed she asked for a pause so that she could reflect on "the way you white people do things." The meeting members were startled, they thought they were talking about the way Quakers do things. How do we know what of our practice is based in discernment of the Spirit and what is based on cultural assumptions of the white middle class?

Our assumptions shape our messages in worship and the tone of worship itself. Our sedate meetings may be an expression of the discourse of the highly educated. Can we open ourselves to other ways the Spirit might break through among us? Might Friends of other cultural backgrounds help us see some of the ways our assumptions may block the movement of the Spirit in our meetings?

We have a custom in our meetings for business to ask for a time of reflection and re-centering when conflict or strong feelings emerge. When is this Spirit-based? When might it be an attempt to avoid facing up to something difficult? Might there be other Spirit-led ways of engaging one another around conflict?

How do the words we use reflect racial assumptions? Some African American Friends carry the memory of the term "overseer" as it was used in the days of slavery. Persons who are neither European American nor African American feel left out of discussions of race that focus on those two groups.

How does the decor or our meetinghouses reflect race? Are there photographs, paintings, or quotations on the wall? If so, do they reflect the images and thoughts of people of color as well as of European Americans? Do the books and magazines in our libraries reflect positive images of people of color? Do they address issues of race and class? Do they speak to Friends of varying educational levels?

Reaching Toward Wholeness

How can we create the Religious Society of Friends that we long for? As we identify, challenge and rid ourselves of assumptions we will grow toward our ideal as Friends. Here are some suggestions for steps you can take in helping your meeting reach toward wholeness:

1. Create a loving space within your meeting for Friends to have conversations that allow them to check out assumptions they are making about one another.
2. In providing pastoral care to individuals in your meeting remember to ask rather than to assume that race does, or does not, have a bearing on the care they need.
3. Create formal and informal settings to engage in dialogues about race and it's impact on our meetings.
4. Establish a committee or small group in your meeting to examine issues of racism and how it affects the meeting and to make recommendations on how to respond to those issues.
5. Make clearness and support committees available for Friends in your meeting who are working on the issues of racism.
6. Build a relationship with a neighborhood congregation made up of people of color. Invite speakers from those congregations to tell you about issues important to members of their congregation. Work together on a project in the community.
7. Review and update the photographs, paintings or quotations on the wall along with the books and magazines in the meeting library so that they address issues of race, class and varied educational levels.
8. Support people of color in your meeting through helping them identify and build relationships with other people of color in the Religious Society of Friends.
9. Publicize events sponsored by or specifically for people of color.
10. List your meeting in the church section of the local paper for people of color.

As you proceed, remember that discussing race elicits strong emotion and so does change. It is important to be patient with one another, to listen to and follow the Spirit as it moves among us.

Vanessa Julye has served as clerk of Friends of African Descent and as a member of the Friends General Conference Committee for Ministry on Racism. She has a minute of travel in the ministry recognizing her concern for helping the Society of Friends become a more inclusive community for people of color. Patricia McBee is editor of *Pastoral Care Newsletter* and works among Friends on discerning and responding to the leadings of the Spirit. Both are members of Central Philadelphia Monthly Meeting.

Contributors to this article include Jean Marie Barch, Monica Day, Nancy Diaz-Svalgard, Pamela Haines, Chester McCoy, Gale Rohde, Miyo Moriuchi, Trayce Peterson, Beckey Phipps, Carol Smith, Claudia Wair, and David Yamamoto.

From the Experience of an African American Friend

by Claudia Wair, Langley Hill (VA) Meeting

I am not an expert on racial issues. I'm just a Quaker who happens to be black. What you read here is from my experience and the result of a great deal of prayer. Not all Friends of color will agree with my ideas. Some of what follows is painful for me to reveal, and some of it may be difficult for white Friends to read.

I've heard that some Friends fear that people of color want to "change" Quakerism. The only thing I want to change about Quakerism is the same thing I want to change about American society as a whole: the myopia of the dominant culture. This myopia extends beyond race into economics (how many working class whites are Quakers? people on welfare?) and level of education (how many high school dropouts, of any race, are members of your meeting?). We are a denomination of privileged people, at least in this country, and privilege can blind any of us to the lives of the "other."

A question I frequently get is "What can white Friends do to be more welcoming to people of color?" While I do not doubt that this question comes from a sincere desire to do what's right, I must admit I find it a bit patronizing, even a bit amusing. The answer is so simple— be Quakers. Look back at the early Friends words and works. If you take the testimony of equality to heart, then when you see my face, you will not treat me any differently than anyone else. Yet, on more than one occasion, I've been mistaken for domestic staff among Friends. I must say that one gets tired of being "used" to it.

From my many years worshiping among Friends, I've come up with a short list of things to consider about racial issues in our meetings. The list is by no means all there is to the matter. But it's a start. Therefore, I ask you to prayerfully consider the following:

Recognize that modern Quakerism is little different from the rest of United States society. Quakerism's members bring many of the values of the dominant culture with them. We are very much influenced by society in the way we perceive others, no matter how we may protest otherwise.

Set aside your assumptions. I've been a Quaker for almost 20 years, and still Friends I've been acquainted with much of that time are surprised to find I have a post-graduate education. On more than one occasion I've been asked whether I miss the music of my Baptist upbringing. I admit I'm tired of answering, "No, I don't miss the music, and by the way, I was Methodist."

I came to Friends for the same reason as others have—to worship our God in the living silence.

Give us some space. As a person of color enters your meeting for worship, try not to overwhelm your visitor. Too much attention can be worse than no attention at all! Once that visitor becomes a regular attender, don't ask that he or she sit on every committee that might address issues of race.

Worship groups for Friends of color are not exclusive clubs, maliciously excluding white Friends. It is a time and a place to worship with others who share the debilitating experience of racism in this country. It is a place where we can, in the manner of Friends, nurture and support one another in the day-to-day difficulties people of color and our families face. It is a place where we don't have to explain ourselves or our backgrounds to well-meaning if sometimes insensitive Friends.

Appreciate the gifts we bring as individuals not as spokespersons for a monolithic "Black" or "Asian" or other community. Just because our skin is a different color than yours does not make us experts on the dynamics of race in America. Please don't ask us to be teachers. If the meeting finds itself discussing matters of race, please don't ask the few people of color to speak as representatives of their race. Rather, ask individuals if they are willing to talk about their experience, preferably one-on-one. If that person says "No," understand that such a complex and highly personal issue is extremely hard to talk about, especially with those you may not know well. If the individual says "Yes," be certain you're ready to truly listen—it may be hard to hear some of the things that might be said.

Be open to difficult truths. Modern Friends of all colors find it difficult to deal with conflict, often choosing the politically correct over plain speaking. The only way to work through racial issues, whether at the monthly meeting or global level, is to build trusting relationships with people of color. Trust takes time and work. Be patient.

Discovering a Place for Myself Among Friends

BY DAVID YAMAMOTO, ANN ARBOR (MI) MEETING

I first attended a Friends meeting nearly 20 years ago in Berkeley, California. I was invited by a friend who knew of my interest in spiritual pursuits, peace and peacemaking, conflict resolution and the environment. I had a lot of reservations about going back to organized religion, but I thought the values of Friends would be strong enough to attract me, and it turned out to be the case.

I loved the silence and simplicity, though I immediately noted that I was the only person of color in the meeting. Over nearly five years of worshiping with Friends in Berkeley I did not make close connections with any of the people there, but I continued attending because I liked the silence and many of the messages, I liked the idea of communicating directly with God without the necessity of an intermediary.

When I married and moved to Ann Arbor, Michigan, my wife and I tried out both the Unitarian Church and the Quaker meeting. We found the meeting to have much more of the spiritual quality that we were seeking. In Ann Arbor Meeting I connected to some of the people on a personal level more than I had in Berkeley, but I continued to feel racially and ethnically isolated.

Because of the sense of isolation I became sporadic in attendance at meeting. We adopted two children whom we want to raise with a spiritual background, and I found myself attending meeting as much because of wanting that exposure for the children as for myself. My wife, who is white, was comfortable in the meeting and there are more children of color than adults of color in the meeting so our children did not share my sense of isolation. They attended meeting regularly, often without me. As the children got older they questioned me about why I didn't go all the time, and I was faced with the issue of how I was going to support the spiritual values I said that I wanted them to experience.

Three years ago I committed myself to attending meeting on a regular basis. By attending consistently I came to realize that my experiences with the Friends did give me spiritual satisfaction. And thus it became easier to attend consistently. However, the issue of racial and ethnic isolation was running concurrently. I wanted to become an advocate and an activist for examining why there are so few people of color in our meeting and felt that I could not do that as an attender. After nearly twenty years of worshiping with Friends, last April I became a member of Ann Arbor Meeting. Since then I have become the convenor of an interest group on race/ethnic diversity in the meeting and attended a conference at Pendle Hill on Quakers and Racial Justice.

I feel spiritually at home in the Religious Society of Friends. However, I have felt separated culturally. It is my dream that I, along with all Friends of color, will feel as one—spiritually and culturally— with our Religious Society. While that day is not now, I am comforted that there many Friends, as agents of change, who share this dream.

What's in a Name?

BY ERNESTINE BUSCEMI, MORNINGSIDE (NY) MEETING

As an African-American member of the Religious Society of Friends and a person working on inclusion and diversity among Quakers, I find the term "overseer" off-putting and hurtful.

"Overseer" is used widely throughout our religious culture. Early Quakers used it with true meaning of watching over and directing the Religious Society of Friends. However, in our current environment the word overseer carries other meanings and a lot of pain.

For many African Americans, the connection with the term overseer begins in slavery. The overseer was the person who watched over you while you toiled for hours. That overseer held the dehumanizing power of holding a person's life in his hands. Today activists for prison reform, such as Angela Davis, use the vivid language of describing conditions in prison as plantations, with guards as overseers, and prisoners as slave labor. Just recently, I overheard a group of African American and Hispanic teenagers talking about their day in school interchanging the word overseer in the conversation for the term teacher. I asked its meaning and was told overseer was the person with the whip and chains, the power of life and death.

We in the Religious Society of Friends must continue to be sensitive and vigilant about our publications and our way of speaking because for some, our language is riddled with anguish, sorrow and pain.

Our committees, as with early Quakers, continue to have the charge of watching over and directing the Religious Society of Friends. Changing the name overseer would mean that we Quakers are allowing safe places where understanding and love come together for a shared experience, nurturing that of God in everyone. For me, the Light is the core where true healing takes place and everyone is whole.

As Quakers we can think outside the box. Here are some examples of renaming: Membership Care, Friendly Ears, Ministry and Counsel, Pastoral Care, and Ministry and Nurture. I am grateful to see that some changes are being made. In this manner we are saying, "Welcome. Be a part of our blessed community."

A White Friend Speaks to Other White Friends: Nine Suggestions for Addressing Racism

BY GALE ROHDE, TWIN CITIES (MN) MEETING

1. Acknowledge your own racism and that in the Religious Society of Friends. Acknowledge your own goodness and that of other whites, even racist ones.
2. Do not seek to distance yourself from the "bad" whites and be one of the "good" ones. We are all good ones, but all have some racism. Answer the spark of God in everyone.
3. Don't make people of color do all the work of advocating for themselves or educating whites (including you). Actively take on the issue yourself or, at minimum, be supportive.
4. Examine yourself prayerfully and honestly.
5. Be ready to listen without defenses and to create opportunities for people of color to tell you about their experiences. Even if you don't perceive something as racism, assume they are better able to recognize it than you are and be open to the possibility that their perceptions are legitimate.
6. Don't expect other groups to do all the changing to fit into our way of doing things. (A good suggestion for including young people, too.)

7. It is important to develop relationships with people of color and expose yourself to other cultures and experience being in the minority.
8. Mistakes are better than inaction, but it is important to persist and to take responsibility to clean up your mistakes.
9. You might feel dumb and awkward and like you are doing everything wrong, but it's still worth doing and at some point you will be doing more and more right.

One Meeting's Experience: Addressing Race in Red Cedar Meeting

BY THEO MACE, UNIVERSITY (WA) MEETING

In the early '90s I began attending Red Cedar Friends Meeting in East Lansing, Michigan, with my then partner Deborah, an African American. At that time we were one of two interrracial couples attending meeting and the only lesbian interracial couple.

When Deborah raised concerns about how few people of color attended Red Cedar, some in meeting responded that African Americans prefer a "livelier" service, full of music, prayer and preaching. Deborah found this stereotype offensive. She raised other concerns as well, suggesting, for example, that the meeting and its Peace and Social Justice Committee might find that issues at home, including racism, were as important to consider as traditional peace concerns in the wider world.

There was discomfort, if not anger, in meeting about these issues. Often Deborah was angry and hurt herself. And, sometimes she was alone in expressing these concerns because other Friends of color either did not feel the same way she did, or did not feel led to speak about them. Sometimes this created confusion, but provided a vivid example of the fact that just because people are of the same race doesn't mean they hold the same point of view, even on issues pertaining to race. We do not expect white Friends to be in unity on all issues, why should we expect that of others?

As a result of Deborah's raising these matters, meeting took several actions. The Peace and Social Justice Committee began to analyze how meeting could look at each of its committees to determine what actions they could take to become anti-racist and hence more welcoming to people of color. We decided to make Red Cedar's outdoor sign more welcoming by painting one of the two hands being shaken (depicted on the sign) in a darker skin tone. We joined with a predominantly African-American congregation in a community home repair program. Ministry and Pastoral Care sponsored a workshop on white privilege, as well as a worship sharing series delving into the emotional origins of racism. And meeting initiated mid-week meetings for worship at the Black Child and Family Institute, in an area of the city noted for its racial and economic diversity.

All this work certainly made meeting more aware of concerns about racism and affected many Friends deeply and permanently, but it did not increase the number of people of color who attended. Nor did it eliminate all tension regarding the issue of racism in meeting.

However, in 1998, when Deborah was diagnosed with a recurrence of cancer, most of the unresolved tensions and concerns seemed to take a back seat. Red Cedar Meeting provided both her and her immediate caretakers with the deepest spiritual and physical sustenance as they came to grips with the exacting requirements of this final illness. The meeting lifted Deborah up, and Deborah lifted the meeting up, as we all witnessed her dying. The experience of her death in the midst of this loving Quaker community makes me feel that there is hope, through love, of finding a way to overcome the barriers to truly seeing that of God in each other.

THE CHALLENGE AND OPPORTUNITY OF MEETINGHOUSE CHANGES

Pastoral Care Newsletter, Vol. 8, No. 2 • January 2001

BY BARRY ZALPH

CONSIDERING CHANGES TO A MEETING'S PHYSICAL HOME will likely cause both excitement and anxiety within the meeting. This holds true whether the meeting faces buying its first meetinghouse, renovating or expanding its current building, moving to a different site or laying down property ownership. The meeting's pastoral care committee can help members and attenders view the transition as a series of opportunities to clarify the meeting's mission, support that mission, and grow together as a spiritual community.

The pastoral care committee can help the meeting follow the Spirit's guidance from the first considerations of a change through the adaptation to a new space (or the abandonment of proposals to change the meeting's home). Usually, the meeting names a building planning committee to weigh architectural and financial issues. The pastoral care committee focuses on different questions: Do Friends approach meetinghouse issues in an attitude of humility and openness? Do Friends' words and actions reflect patience and faith that way will open? Do relationships among Friends testify to an understanding that the house and grounds exist to support the spiritual fellowship, and not vice versa? By gently reminding Friends of these (and similar) queries, the pastoral care committee can spiritually enrich the meeting throughout a potentially long and arduous process. Attention to these spiritual issues can indeed replace a sense of arduousness with one of joy and community vitality.

The Meetinghouse: Why Do We Need It?
Why Do We Want to Change It?

The incentive to move or change a meeting's home often comes from dissatisfaction with one or more aspects of its current home: excessive costs, inadequate space, poor accessibility for mobility-impaired Friends, etc. Rather than hurrying to solve the apparent problem, we often benefit by framing the issue more broadly. How to house the meeting and how much to spend on physical facilities may distract us from the question, "What does the Spirit call us to do?"

We may want to be all things to all seekers, and make unrealistic demands of ourselves and our meetinghouse in the process. Deliberations over the future of the meetinghouse provide a meeting with an important chance to examine its mission and gain new clarity and unity. In turn, clarity about mission will greatly facilitate decisions about the property changes that may be needed.

Many building projects come about to make room for growth in First Day attendance, yet we often have only vague ideas about whom we seek as new attenders. Do we intend to reach out to people of color, families with children, people with disabilities, others? How will we accommodate newcomers when they appear? A good meeting-house location and design can remove barriers to newcomers who might attend the meeting and can help them feel at home when they arrive. Even so, our attitudes and behavior towards newcomers will play a larger role in their eventual decision to join us or to move on.

If a meeting already has a meetinghouse, long-time meeting participants probably have many good associations with it. For some, this building represents the first place they truly felt at home in a religious group. For others there is a sentimental attachment to the room in which they were married or where their parent's memorial service was held. The prospect of moving to a new location or dramatically altering the feel of this building often causes not only grief but active resistance. The details of proposed changes and their many advantages have little influence on this resistance. Pastoral caregivers can help the meeting by respecting these feelings and drawing them out. (See "Roles for the Pastoral Care Committee," p. 132.) By strengthening the bonds among individuals and between each individual and the meeting, we can reassure Friends that the meeting will remain their spiritual community after any move or change.

Whether Friends feel strongly attached to changing the property or to keeping it the same, we each face the spiritual risk of seeing it as "my meeting." If we relinquish our sense of ownership, we can see ourselves as a body of seekers drawn together by and accountable to the Divine. In this attitude, we can accept the possibility of changes that might disconcert us but will serve a holy purpose of which we have only a dim awareness. Seeing the meeting and its property as a Divine trust helps to free us from squabbles over personal preferences and to open us to wise stewardship of our resources under the Spirit's guidance.

Financial Issues

To build, buy, renovate or expand a meetinghouse usually involves expenses far beyond the meeting's normal operating budget. Consultant and author, Peter Steinke, notes money as one of the issues most commonly involved in congregational conflict. Steinke's books and the Mennonite Conciliation Service *Mediation and Facilitation Training Manual* (see resources, p. 313) provide many insights into how spiritual communities can deal gracefully with potentially divisive issues, including those involving money and property.

Decades of familial and cultural conditioning and personal experiences have formed in each of us deeply ingrained attitudes toward money. These attitudes vary dramatically from person to person. This explains in part why money acts as such a flash point in many group decisions. The pastoral care committee can help Friends appreciate their differences in attitude and approach one another charitably in the midst of financial disagreements. Working through our differences gives us opportunities to know each other better and to build friendships that transcend the need for similarity of beliefs. (This can come in handy in other aspects of the life of the meeting!)

Friends often feel reluctant to "spend money on ourselves." We may feel proud of our meeting's devoting well over half of its budget to charitable giving and advocacy efforts. Considering a major capital expenditure often raises questions about the "selfishness" of such spending. Honest examination can reveal whether an expensive building project would compete with or facilitate the well-discerned work of the meeting. Carefully and prayerfully considering the mission of the meeting, and how a change in the facility might support that mission, will help the meeting to gain clarity on the expenditures required by a proposed building project.

Whether the meeting can raise the funds needed for the proposed purchase or renovation is only the tip of the iceberg of financial concerns. The meeting, under the guidance of the building committee, should also weigh the long-term balance of likely income and expenses (including the meeting's charitable giving) after completing the building project. Financing, legal issues, and many other practical matters are discussed in *A Friendly Meeting Place* (see resources, p. 313).

Roles for the Pastoral Care Committee

Several matters deserve the attention of the pastoral care committee throughout the process:

Help Friends stay patient and realistic. Three times in fifteen years Rochester (NY) Friends Meeting considered moving, each time deciding that the benefits of staying put outweighed the disadvantages. After another 15 years, the meeting again considered moving and reached clarity to do so. Even then, the planning, acquisition and renovation of their new meetinghouse took six years. (See "Rochester Friends New Meeting House, *FGConnections*, Fall 1999.)

See to the openness and inclusiveness of every element of the process. Communicate to a fault. Give everyone (including infrequent attenders) multiple opportunities to learn about every committee meeting, threshing session, etc. Actively solicit participation, rather than leaving it to individual initiative. Seek to ensure that the process does not inadvertently exclude or marginalize any group (e.g., young adults, people who work on weeknights, people not fond of intellectual debates, etc.). Encourage less vocal Friends to speak and more vocal Friends to listen.

Help Friends recognize the value of both rational analysis and spiritual discernment. Neither by itself will likely lead to good decisions about a meetinghouse. Help Friends grow in appreciation of each others' complementary gifts of analysis and spiritual receptiveness, rather than seeking to homogenize the meeting into one or the other approach.

As Friends direct attention to the building, we sometimes lose sight of ourselves. Sometimes we imagine ourselves in an unrealistically favorable light. Conversely, sometimes we underestimate skills and gifts at our disposal. The pastoral care committee can serve as a spiritual mirror. Perhaps the plans for greatly expanded First Day School space call for an examination of our chronic shortage of First Day School teachers.

Perhaps the consistent participation of 20 Friends in meetinghouse planning events indicates that we need not fear a lack of volunteer commitment for the next phase of the work. In observing and reflecting the meeting's lapses in self-awareness, the pastoral care committee must maintain a humble and loving attitude. This is not a work of finding faults, but rather of noting opportunities for us all to grow in the Light.

In all of this, share your faith that the meeting is not alone in this work. As did ancient Friends, I have experienced the Spirit that draws us into unity and empowers us to follow our leadings, if only we attend to it. When we center in the Light, "way opens."

The Meetinghouse As Lightening Rod

Many meetings have experienced difficulties, or even grievous schisms, over property concerns. The related issues of mission, stewardship of resources and inclusiveness call forth a wide range of thoughts and feelings. Conflict is an inevitable, and potentially constructive, result. Healthy meetings consider conflict as an opportunity to learn from one another and draw closer in the Spirit. They acknowledge conflicting viewpoints openly, and the people in disagreement continue to treat each other with love and respect. Apparent absence of disagreement (especially during the early stages of exploring and planning) usually means that someone is holding back from expressing a dissenting opinion. The books by Mennonite Conciliation Service and Steinke (see resources, p. 313) give excellent guidance on transforming conflict into opportunities for growth in the Spirit.

Beware of Friends looking to a building change as a panacea. Identify and address unresolved issues (e.g., racial homogeneity, inadequate hospitality to newcomers, poor planning for the needs of disabled members, etc.). Remind Friends that a physical move or change will not, by itself, fix the problems. Unless the meeting has worked in its current home to address the problems, an improvement in the facility or location is not likely to resolve them.

Summary

The right meetinghouse can enrich the life of a meeting in many ways. Even apart from this end result, the process of coming to unity on and bringing to fruition a building project can deepen the spiritual fellowship of the meeting. The risks and rewards of a building project extend beyond the financial and physical to the spiritual realm. The prayers and diligent work of a meeting's Pastoral Care Committee can help the meeting navigate the risks and reap the rewards of this transition in a meeting's life.

Barry Zalph is a member of Louisville (KY) Friends Meeting, where he has served as recording clerk and as a member of several committees including the Adult Religious Education Committee. From 1995–2000 he served as part-time field secretary of Illinois Yearly Meeting. Outside of Quaker circles, Barry nurtures his spirit through long distance bicycling and vegetarian cooking.

Exploring and Choosing among Property Options

1. Examine the need or leading to change the status quo. What do we hope to accomplish by changing the meeting space? How can we come to know if we are so led?

2. Consider the meeting's cherished features and its inadequacies. Envision the meeting maintaining its current virtues while improving on its current weaknesses. Identify how changes in the property could foster the desired improvements.

3. Identify misgivings and resistance to change (or resistance to participating in the discussion of prospective change). Provide safe space for individuals to explore and express their negative thoughts and feelings. Help the meeting to respect minority voices, which often make a crucial contribution to discerning truth. Give Friends private opportunities to tell their stories and share their misgivings. Then, encourage them to participate in the group discussions. Discourage people from presenting their misgivings by proxy, as this creates many chances for miscommunication and undermines group discernment. (Of course, it is appropriate to make allowances for someone who cannot participate in person due to illness, disability or other unalterable circumstance.)

Resistance to participating in a discussion of options may indicate a sense of disempowerment ("It doesn't matter what I say, *they'll* just go ahead and decide what *they* want anyway") or alienation ("This isn't really my meeting, so I shouldn't stick my nose in"). It could also stem from bad associations with past moves, whether involving family, work or church. Personal invitations may help bring these Friends into the discussions. Stay alert to interpersonal tensions that may have a bearing on a person's or group's unwillingness to take part. Address these tensions separately from the meetinghouse discussions. Unresolved interpersonal grievances can avalanche as disaffected individuals stay aloof from the deliberations until the eleventh hour and then seek to veto a plan that they associate with their antagonist(s).

4. *Open the floodgates for visions*, big and small, of how to make the meeting more like the envisioned ideal. In the early phase, Friends should feel encouraged to bring forth all attractive ideas, independent of their apparent practicality. Ideas need not assume a change in the building. For example, a meeting facing overcrowding during First Day worship might consider holding two meetings for worship each week rather than moving to a larger space.

5. *Winnow the options*. Usually this involves a building planning committee. The committee arranges a number of opportunities for Friends to question and comment on the many suggestions, and to discern the key attributes of the meeting's new or expanded home. The committee then fleshes out the most promising ideas, and considers their (roughly estimated) costs and benefits. This is not yet the time to hire an architect to prepare drawings or otherwise commit financial resources to any one option.

Committee meetings should be open. The committee will probably choose to schedule a series of large group meetings to present particular options and receive feedback from anyone in the meeting community. This stage culminates in the committee bringing to meeting for business a handful of options, any one of which the committee feels would serve the meeting well. It is, of course, possible that the committee will unite in recommending a particular plan. In this instance, the committee must take special care to stay open to the discernment of the meeting for business, which may not find unity with the committee's favored proposal.

6. *Discern*. Wait upon the Lord. Don't rush. Do not let the time pressures of the real estate market drive your process. If the meeting minds the Light, external circumstances will fall into place to enable the meeting to do as the Spirit leads. The discernment phase will probably take a period of months. During this time, the meeting will probably decide to seek architectural and financial details about one or more of the proposed options. Usually, the building planning committee will remain active during this phase.

7. *Act.* Taking care of the myriad details of a building project (whether moving, renovating or building) requires good organizational skills and consistent diligence. Consider the possibility of laying down the committee that led the search process and naming another committee to implement the project. Even if the people on the former committee have the skills to oversee implementation, it may be time to give them a well-earned rest and give others a chance to play a major role. It serves the meeting best if the project is always seen as a collective effort and not mainly the initiative of one or a few Friends.

8. *Reflect.* How do we use this new space to best serve the Divine? Help the meeting redirect its focus from the physical and financial issues of a building to the interpersonal and spiritual issues that determine the health of a spiritual community.

One Meeting's Experience: New Meetinghouse for St. Louis Meeting

St. Louis Meeting may not be a textbook case of how to proceed on nurturing the meeting through making a change in the meetinghouse. It took a long time, with going down some blind alleys, and now that we're moved we are faced with high mortgage payments and expensive repairs. But we have come through it intact as a meeting and with a sense of rightness to where we have ended up. We love our new meetinghouse. It is a wonderful place.

Our meeting is relatively young; it was founded a little over 60 years ago. For 40 years we worshiped in a small church building in a suburban neighborhood. We liked it there. But it had become too small. When we explored remodeling our First Day School space it turned out not to meet the building code and we were ordered to stop using it. We had to do *something*.

Early on we put up big sheets of paper in the meeting asking members to write "What you like about where we are now," "What you don't like about where we are now," and "What you hope for in a new meetinghouse." We had threshing sessions and an open meeting with an architect to talk about what we really cared about. We were clear that we wanted a serene, simple place for adult worship, green outdoor space and good space for the children. We wanted to buy an existing building and we preferred staying in the suburbs.

Things did not fall in place. We didn't find any churches for sale that we could afford in the suburban areas where we were looking. We had an offer of land and considered again whether to build, but things didn't fall in place for that either. Time went on. We seemed to bounce from one thing to another. Some older, long time members were reluctant to move. One confided that she was not sure she could adjust to a new place. As impatience and frustration became obvious, we widened the search to a broader geographical area including inside the city of St. Louis.

Then somebody found a building in the city on the border between a gentrifying neighborhood and low income housing projects. The first people who visited it fell in love with it. They brought some more people who fell in love. It had good space for First Day School and a library and beautiful worship space. *But* the price was too high. The purchase price was more than the total purchase and remodeling amount recommended by the Finance Committee. In our meetings for business people said "This is the space we need." "Way will open." "We'll manage it." Some members of the Finance Committee were doubtful.

There were several meetings. There were called meetings. There were people calling for no more called meetings. There were times when we were not our best selves. Often when we were losing track someone would remind us that it is not important how this turns out; it is important how we treat each other, that we all still need to be friends when this is over. We didn't remember it all the time—just often enough so we didn't completely lose sight of these principles.

We followed our hearts instead of the Finance Committee's minds. We came to clarity to buy the building in the city. Three people stood aside from the decision, though all three supported the decision after it was made.

It hasn't been easy since then. We had to do a lot of the renovations with our volunteer labor. The costs are very high. Yet somehow we always have enough money to pay our bills.

In the struggle to find a place and set it up we had let go of many of the activities that are the core of the life of the meeting. We're getting back to being a meeting again. There is new vitality. As the tension and stress is released we have energy to greet newcomers and get to know them and draw them in.

Based on interview with Margaret Katranides, clerk of St. Louis Meeting.

Questions for Reflection

1. What is our pastoral care role in helping the meeting stay centered as we consider changes to our place of worship?
2. How can we contribute to keeping a proper balance between rational analysis and spiritual discernment?
3. What special role can we play in reaching out to those who hold minority opinions and may fear that their thoughts are irrelevant or unwelcome? What can we do to draw those on the margins of the deliberations more fully into the life of the meeting?
4. If tensions develop between individuals or groups in the meeting, how can we facilitate the healthy resolution of those tensions?
5. How can we help Friends stay patient and not be rushed by the world's time?
6. When the decision is made and the change is complete, how can we help the Friends let go of the tensions of the process, settle into the new space and open to new guidance for the life of the meeting?

USE OF CLEARNESS COMMITTEES IN PASTORAL CARE

Pastoral Care Newsletter, Vol. 7, No. 4 • June 2000

BY PATRICIA McBEE

DOES YOUR MEETING USE CLEARNESS COMMITTEES other than for membership or marriage? Many meetings are only beginning to discover the clearness process as a rich resource for the pastoral care role of helping our members discern how to order their lives more in keeping with the movements of the Spirit.

The members of our meetings are constantly engaging in processes of discernment—large and small. Sometimes there is obvious spiritual significance such as "do I have a leading to undertake a special concern?" or "how can I bring my way of living more into line with the testimonies and practices of Friends and the movements of the Spirit?" At other times members are discerning leadings about more everyday matters such as "what can I do about this job in which I feel increasingly uneasy?" or "should we add another child to our family?" Sometimes members bring to the meeting questions of clearness for divorce or separation.

Meetings often have hesitated to get involved at this level of members' lives, feeling that it is not the meeting's business—and it is not our business to tell people what job to hold or how many children to have. The object of clearness committees is not to tell someone what to do, but to lovingly support a person in opening to the guidance of the Inward Teacher.

The Meeting's Role

Discernment of one's life course is ultimately between an individual and that person's experience of the Inward Guide. However, for many it is not always easy to hear clearly what the Inward Guide may be saying. A person may wonder, "Is this a leading or am I being self-serving?"

"Am I projecting my desires or my fears into this situation?" There are often conflicting voices—the voice of habit, the voice of prudence, the voice of social acceptability. Where in all this is harmony with the Divine?

A clearness committee can help a Friend sort out the different voices and enter into a prayerful space that helps the voice of the Inward Teacher to come through. As a person becomes clear about a leading, the clearness committee gives support in addressing fears and obstacles that may stand in the way of responding to the leading. A clearness committee may also help a member refrain from acting precipitously, giving time for seasoning a perceived leading. In the end, it remains the responsibility of the individual to discern the next step. But the meeting can play a major role in helping that person take the step with confidence and peacefulness and an unconflicted sense of right ordering.

If the matter at hand is one on which action of the meeting is being requested, a further process is required after the individual has achieved a sense of clearness. Just because the individual feels clear, it does not mean that the other members of the meeting are called to take the action being requested. Jan Hoffman of Mt. Toby Meeting in New England refers to it as "double clarity" when the meeting is called on to discern its clarity about accepting a person's application for membership or about taking a marriage under its care.[1] Double clarity is also needed when the member is exploring clearness about undertaking action and desires a minute of religious service or other support from the meeting.

The Benefits to the Meeting

When a meeting assists a member in the process of discernment, the meeting is enriched as well. Direct results may come from deepening the relationship of the meeting with the person who was seeking clearness. As a result of a clearness process that person may participate in the meeting in a more spiritually grounded way. Or the clearness process may have helped the person avoid an error that would have negative ramifications for the community.

More broadly the meeting is deepened by the increased sense of connection and caring among members. Prayerful support for one

[1] "Seeking Clarity both Personally and Corporately" in *Companions Along the Way*, ed. Florence Ruth Kline, Philadelphia Yearly Meeting, 2000, pp. 119–125.

another binds members to one another. When future issues of pastoral care arise, a connection is already established from having worked together in a clearness process. The meeting for business can also benefit from Friends feeling a deeper understanding of one another.

History of Clearness Committees

Contrary to popular assumption, the clearness committee for discernment of personal gifts and leadings is a relatively new procedure among Friends. Prior to this century, Friends had the office of "elder" whose role it was to help with the discernment of leadings to public ministry. In the nineteenth century elders tended take on the role of assuring conformity to external standards from how many horses one could hitch to one's buggy to the appropriate length of bonnet strings. "Clearance" committees for marriage were concerned with ascertaining that there were no legal or other obstructions to the marriage, not so much the spiritual or emotional right-ordering of the proposed marriage.

The current form of the clearness committee for discerning leadings and other questions of spiritual import evolved within Young Friends of North America during the 1960s and has gained increasing currency.[2] Concurrently, clearness committees for membership and marriage have taken on a deeper, more personal dimension. They now explore more fully the individual's sense of leading to commit to membership or marriage and the meeting's clarity in taking the applicant under its care.[3]

Creating an Atmosphere of Acceptance of Clearness Committees

When my meeting began talking about clearness processes several years ago, a member stated bluntly that she certainly wouldn't lay any important personal decisions before the meeting. For some, there is the legitimate fear that the meeting will want to take over and direct what members regard as their personal lives. Some may fear a lack of confidentiality if they were to share about deeply personal matters.

---

[2] Patricia Loring, *Spiritual Discernment*, p. 19.
[3] See, Helene Pollock & Arlene Kelly, "Membership and the Clearness Process," see p. 43; and Jan Hoffman, "Clearness Committees for Marriage or Commitment," see p. 73.

For others, there may be a lack of understanding or trust as to how such a process could be useful.

The best way for a meeting to overcome such hesitations is to have a successful clearness process or two and have others hear how helpful they were. My meeting's experience was that after a few successful clearness committees had taken place, many Friends came forward with requests for such support.

To jump-start interest in clearness for pastoral care, the meeting might have a forum to discuss some of the information in the books and pamphlets on clearness and discernment listed in the resources section. Or you may choose to have an article about clearness in the meeting's newsletter. A testimonial in the newsletter from a member who has experienced a clearness process in the meeting or elsewhere would be a good place to start.

When to Set Up a Clearness Committee

A clearness committee is most often set up at the request of an individual. However, the pastoral care committee could suggest a clearness process to someone who is wrestling with a decision. It can be a formal process established by the meeting or an informal one set up entirely by the person who is seeking help with discernment.

When an individual becomes aware of a need or desire for help in coming to clarity on a personal decision she or he may simply ask a few friends to listen and accompany the process of sorting through the factors in the decision. This can happen without the meeting's ever officially knowing that it has taken place. In many instances such a clearness committee is sufficient for helping the person come to clarity.

The meeting as a body becomes involved when a member approaches the meeting for business seeking the meeting's formal involvement. It is helpful to approach the meeting when the individual wants or needs a broader perspective than can be provided by her/his personal contacts or when the outcome may require the support of the meeting.

The pastoral care committee may also take the initiative in suggesting a clearness process in response to concern about a member of the meeting. For example, the committee may be aware of a member who is overwhelmed by responsibilities and may suggest a clearness committee to help sort through what can be laid aside. A family dealing with the needs of an aging parent may welcome a clearness committee to look at how they can best respond. A clearness committee may be a helpful way for the meeting to be present to a young man considering whether to register for the draft at his eighteenth birthday.

Who Should Serve on a Clearness Committee?

The best persons to serve on a clearness committee are those with the ability to listen well, to feed back clearly without adding their own point of view, to assist in deeply seeking the guidance of the Spirit and to hold the process in confidence. It is helpful if at least one member of the clearness committee has served previously on a clearness committee or has studied what has been written about clearness processes. Obviously, the more members of the committee who are gifted, experienced and knowledgeable, the deeper and richer the process will be.

It is usually helpful to have one or two persons on the clearness committee who are well known to the person seeking clearness (sometimes called the "focus person" or "seeker") and who enjoy that person's trust and confidence. A good clearness committee asks hard questions, and it is useful to be reassured that one is in the presence of loving friends.

On the other hand, it is also important to have participants who are not close friends of the focus person and who may, therefore, be able to take a more objective point of view. It is very important that none of the clearness committee members have a personal interest in the outcome that may color their objectivity in helping the focus person come to her or his own clarity.

Persons knowledgeable about the subject at hand can also be an asset. If the focus person is dealing with how to care for an aging parent, it would be helpful to have someone present who knows what the options may be. For a young man considering whether to register for the draft, it would help to have people present who understand the legal, practical and spiritual consequences of nonregistration.

The usual number of persons on a clearness committee is three to five. It is generally possible to combine all of the above criteria in those three to five persons. Not all of the members of the clearness committee have to be members of the pastoral care committee, though if it is a concern raised by the committee, it is helpful to have at least one member who can report back to the larger committee.

Effectively and faithfully assisting a member in achieving clearness is an exacting discipline. There are wonderful resources available giving step-by-step guidance for clearness committees; several of them are listed in the resource section of this book. I strongly recommend that members of a clearness committee read from those resources before undertaking this service. Jan Hoffman's "Clearness Committees and Their Use in Personal Discernment" which is only four pages long and may be photocopied, can provide a basic grounding for all committee members. Even Friends who have previously served on a clearness committee can benefit from refreshing themselves on the depth and subtleties of an effective clearness process.

A Need for Openness

Great discipline is required when the individual already feels clear and seeks a clearness committee to gain support or endorsement for a proposed action. I have participated in clearness processes in which the individual, feeling clear in him or her self, resists entering openly into a process of discernment. Some committee members may be reluctant to raise any serious questions about whether the meeting should accede to what the focus person is requesting. I have seen conflict arise among committee members about how thoroughgoing a clearness process is required, as though they felt they had to choose sides. When action of the meeting is requested, it is often helpful for the members of the clearness committee to meet first without the focus person to arrive at a common sense of their purpose and their responsibility to the meeting.

Clearness committees can also be hindered by committee members who come with a preconceived idea of what the outcome should be and mistake the clearness committee for an occasion to express their opinion or to guide the individual in a particular direction.

A clearness process works when all participants are willing to question assumptions and open themselves to new light. John Woolman waited three years for Mt. Holly Meeting to support his travel among slaveholding Friends. This kind of deep seeking, when carried out with faith and trust in the guidance of the Spirit, has the potential of leading to deeper clarity and understanding both on the part of the meeting and on the part of the person seeking the meeting's support.

What Clearness Committees Are Not

Clearness committees are not a substitute for professional counseling. Great caution is needed when an individual, couple or family is in distress. Pacific Yearly Meeting's *Faith and Practice* advises that pastoral caregivers have preliminary talks with the seeker on the nature of the problem. If the committee believes that professional counseling is called for they are to advise the seeker accordingly rather than to institute a clearness process. If a clearness process is instituted its focus should be on where and how to seek professional assistance.[4]

Clearness committees are not the same as "support committees" or "pastoral care committees." Clearness committees are a short-term process for seeking clarity on a question. If the clearness process indicates a need for an ongoing support committee this can be recommended to the meeting and a support committee appointed. A support committee may assist an individual in carrying out a project or may be a liaison for the meeting when a person needs ongoing care. A pastoral care committee may be appointed when an individual is carrying out an action with the meeting's endorsement. The committee's charge is to help the individual stay true to their Guide as they carry forward. Canadian Yearly Meeting's *Organization and Procedure*[5] illuminates the distinction among the functions of clearness, support and pastoral care committees.

Summary

Clearness committees can be powerful tools of pastoral care of members who are facing important decisions in their lives. But these powerful outcomes are not automatic. They require trust and a sense of expectancy on the part of the seeker; and they require faithfulness and discipline on the part of the committee. That faithfulness and discipline includes educating oneself through study of the literature on clearness, remaining focused on the purpose for which the clearness committee is called together, and opening in trust to the guidance of the Spirit.

At its richest, the clearness process is a meeting for worship, deeply gathered in openness to new light and surprising outcomes.

Patricia McBee has served as a pastoral caregiver and as clerk of Central Philadelphia Meeting where she has been a member since 1971. She is the editor of *Pastoral Care Newsletter*.

[4] *Pastoral Care Newsletter*, "Helping Friends Seek Professional Help," p. 217.
[5] Canadian Yearly Meeting, *Organization and Procedure*, chapter X, pp. 101–102.

Two Clearness Committees at Work

To Graduate School or Not?

A few years ago, I felt a leading to enroll in the Earlham School of Religion and asked Friends in my meeting (Newtown Square, PA) to meet with me and help me to explore this leading.

Each member of the clearness committee had a unique gift to bring: one is an ESR graduate and very widely experienced among Friends and in Friends' processes, another is a deeply spiritual person and a deep listener to God's movement in our lives, a third is a practical person and who could bring balance if any of the rest of us got too far off the ground.

I expected that the answer would be "yes, you're led to go," or "no, you're not led to go." Instead, the clearness seemed to be: maybe you're led to go, but this fall doesn't seem the right time, and you should investigate some possibilities and test the leading first. This "maybe" was a surprise to me, especially since ESR grad on the committee had promoted it enthusiastically. She was the first to say "this is not a clear leading." Coming from her, this held great weight for me. The suggestion that it might be the right course but the wrong time and to wait and test it further was a relief. Particularly helpful were the specific suggestions that came from the gathering as to how to test it—as it turned out, they were just right. By the time the next spring came the obstacles to my leaving the area fell away and it was clear that I was to go to ESR in the fall.

Beth Lawn, Newtown Square (PA) Meeting

Looking Out for the Children in a Divorce

In the 1970s, Newark (Delaware) Meeting found two of its stalwart founders, with children aged 9 and 11, anticipating divorce. The meeting took the initiative, announcing to each spouse that a clearness committee was prepared to meet as often as necessary to listen and help shape practical plans.

I was as broken-hearted and bewildered by this mid-life split as my husband was angry and sure he was making the right decision. Although we could not be together without tears and bitter words, each of us welcomed the meeting's focus on our children and their future security. Members of the committee appealed to each of us parents to prepare carefully for the children's welfare before we took on lawyers. Their assumption was that lawyers would emphasize each spouse's rights and claims, and the children would fall through the cracks.

After much sweat by the committee and spouses, we forged a written plan for support and visitation and long-in-the-future educational costs which went beyond what the law required. Those basic guidelines outlasted in usefulness and spiritual weight the ensuing legal separation agreement.

What a gift to receive the caring attention of a meeting committee in a time so emotionally charged! Each family member maintains warm associations with members of Newark Meeting although our life paths have taken us far from that original home.

Suzanne Day, Westfield Monthly Meeting, Cinnaminson NJ

Questions for Reflection

1. In what recent pastoral care matters in our meeting might we have beneficially used a clearness process? How can we be attentive to possibilities in the future?

2. Are Friends in our meeting well acquainted with the clearness process and receptive to its use? What can we do to help the meeting become better acquainted with this form of service to one another?

3. How can we help one another to more fully develop the knowledge, skills and spiritual discipline required to carry out an effective clearness process?

Supporting Stands
of Conscience

Pastoral Care Newsletter, Vol. 5, No. 4 • June 1998

by Priscilla Adams and Steve Gulick

Stands of conscience are a visible sign of our living faith as Friends. As the old joke tells it, when meeting for worship was just beginning, a visitor whispered to the Friend sitting near, "When does the service begin?" The Friend responded, "When worship is over, then service begins." Our very practice of Quaker worship opens us to movements of the Spirit that lead us into service in the world.

It is common for Friends to take relatively small, everyday stands of conscience: choosing an environmentally friendly action, reaching out to help someone in need, creating a welcoming environment for children, or participating in a service project. By appreciating and nurturing such everyday acts, our meetings can deepen the basis of our faith in the Spirit and its leadings.

Sometimes these leadings bring Friends into conflict with laws and social customs. Feeling led through worship to belief in the equality of all in the eyes of God, early Friends refused to practice "hat honor" or to use the plural "you" in addressing individuals of higher social rank. This refusal to acknowledge inferior and superior status led to the persecution and imprisonment of Friends.

In response to this persecution, the essential structures of meetings were set up to help address the consequences of taking stands of conscience. Throughout Friends history, monthly, quarterly and yearly meetings, committees of Overseers or Ministry and Counsel, and funds for sufferings have addressed the physical, material, emotional, communal and spiritual needs of Friends who suffer for conscience sake.

How should contemporary meetings respond when a member is called to take a stand of conscience that carries a risk of social, legal or economic consequences?

- young men who refuse to register with Selective Service risking jail sentences, fines, loss of student loans and exclusion from government training and employment;
- people who refuse to pay war taxes risking seizure of money and property, fines and possible (but rare) jail sentences;
- Friends who participate in protest sit-ins and other such acts of civil disobedience risking possible jail and fines;
- those who leave jobs or choose not to take them for reasons of conscience risking unemployment or even loss of career;
- Friends who try to live in certain places or to send their children to certain schools in order to address social and institutional racism risking personal sacrifice and struggle;
- those who seek to live with minimal impact on the environment risking difficulties in this hyper-consumer society.

When a Friend is taking a stand of conscience, the most important support comes from the Spirit. Without that, no stand of conscience is long tenable. But even with Divine support, taking a stand of conscience can be difficult. The support of the meeting can make an important difference to a Friend's ability to stay true to a leading and ease the difficulties and dilemmas along the way.

Different meetings will have different ways of providing care for their members. Often pastoral care committees are asked to take the lead on behalf of the meeting in responding to these Friends.

Perhaps the most important specific action a meeting can take is to set up a clearness process to help the individual discern the clarity of the leading, the path of the witness and ways for others to be of assistance. A clearness committee provides perspectives which can focus and deepen the witness, indeed which can help discern if it is rightly ordered—a true calling. Often the course of the witness is altered by deeply searching, with the support of loving Friends, for the guidance of the Spirit.

When clearness is found, the clearness committee can assist the individual to identify what support is wanted or needed. In addition, the gathering for clearness can provide a means of thinking through what support can realistically be offered by the meeting.

Once the clearness committee has come to recognize that the individual is responding to a genuine call, they report back to the meeting for business both their findings and their recommendations about actions the meeting might take. Sometimes, the meeting quickly comes to unity on the recommendation of the committee.

At other times deep questions are raised. There may be Friends who disagree with the proposed action and feel the meeting should not support it. There may be concerns about the level of energy the meeting can or should invest in supporting the stand of conscience. There may be fears about the motives, skill, or even the personality of the person seeking the meeting's support. Some Friends may recognize the clarity of the individual's call, but not be called themselves to provide active support. Lovingly and prayerfully considering these concerns can bring the meeting to a deeper sense of oneness in the Spirit. In fact, coming to unity too quickly may deprive the meeting and the individual of that deep sense of being together under the Spirit's care.

In this wonderful Quaker process, the individual called to the stand of conscience receives the gift of having Friends come together in her or his behalf. The members of the clearness committee also receive the gift of trust and openness shown by the person seeking clearness. It is a privilege to be involved in important decisions of another's life and to be present to the movement of the Spirit in the life of one of our members.

The meeting as a whole also receives a gift. Discernment of the truth of a leading and the ways in which the meeting and its members might be supportive leads us all to seek the guidance of the Spirit. Following a discernment process, the stand of conscience and the support of the meeting are more deeply shared and, thus, Friends are more ready to respond to the demands that evolve during the stand of conscience.

Of course, not all situations neatly fit this process. Sometimes a Friend does not approach the meeting for clearness at the beginning of a witness, but may seek support when problems arise. In other cases a person may come into membership when they are already actively carrying out a stand of conscience. In these instances, the meeting has to come to unity on what is its proper role and how fully it is willing or able to become involved in supporting this stand.

Once the meeting is under the weight of supporting a witness, it needs to discern what kinds of support are most appropriate. These can vary quite a lot from case to case. The list below is suggestive of types of support the meeting can consider:

Form a support or pastoral care group.

This group can meet with the person as needed to assist with discerning, planning and implementing. The support committee can encourage the person in maintaining the regular spiritual disciplines that sustain the witness. It is helpful for the meeting when an individual or group of Friends coordinate the meeting's response.

Write a minute of support for the individual's stand of conscience.

This is a clear statement that the meeting has considered the concern and is united in recognizing that the Friend is following a leading of the Spirit. The purpose of the meeting's minute is to acknowledge publicly that the individual is taking an action which springs from spiritual leadings and which is in line with Friends beliefs. It is not a statement saying that all Friends feel led to the same action. The minute can be sent on to the quarterly meeting and yearly meeting for endorsement.

Help the Friend identify and contact other Friends about the concern.

This can range from helping to find others interested in the concern, to writing to other meetings, perhaps asking for their own minutes of support or to writing to editors of Friends publications. Priscilla has found that receiving minutes from numerous meetings has been tremendously supportive in her witness against payment of taxes for war. Most importantly it has provided spiritual support—knowing that other Friends feel that her actions are holding up fundamental issues of conscience for Friends.

Help with fundraising.

Some stands of conscience may lead to little or no financial expense. Others may have expenses for getting the word out, for legal counsel or to help cover loss of property or loss of employment. The pastoral care committee or the support committee can help identify where funds might be available and how to go about raising them.

Help with reaching out to other denominations and the broader community.

The concern can be brought to a church council meeting, to specific ministers, to congregations which might be interested and to community groups. The meeting can provide ideas or help with making the contacts.

Support Friends if they face antagonism or attacks for their stand or if their stand leads to personal difficulties.

This is a crucial time for the meeting to stand by them by listening, helping discern appropriate responses, being a presence if needed and helping to respond to the feedback.

For example, Friends joined with Steve at the IRS for worship when he faced seizure of property to satisfy his tax debt. Friends gathered in worship for Priscilla while others accompanied her into a hearing in tax court.

Become a clearing house for support or outreach.

If a person begins to be overwhelmed by the demands of the stand and by offers of support, others can offer to receive some of the calls or to do some of the reaching out.

Provide support for the needs of the family.

This could come in the form of helping with childcare, meals, transportation, visiting with family members troubled by the action or responses to it or other possibilities. It can also include support for the spouse, especially one who is not involved in or perhaps not even in harmony with the witness. Steve found that his spouse felt very alone in a way that he did not: he had the comradeship of other resisters while she did not have the support of other spouses. For a time there was an effort in the monthly meeting to have a support group for resisters and their nonresisting spouses. Although this did not last very long, it gave his spouse others to talk to and a sense of not being alone.

Support the children.

If there is a lot of media attention, strong reactions from others, or if there are particularly busy times with the witness, the children may need support. This could include letting the children know that other people feel the witness is important, helping them think about their responses to the reactions of others or providing additional loving adults to do things with them during times when their parents need to focus on the witness.

Find people with specialized skills.

The witness may come to a point when lawyers, doctors or people who work with the media are needed. There may be members of the meeting community who can fill these roles, the meeting may help discover others who would provide their services *pro bono* and/or funds may be required to hire someone with the needed skills.

The meeting should establish its own expectations for the means and frequency of reporting to the meeting as a whole. There also should be a process, agreed upon in advance, for how to discern the meeting's response to changing needs for support.

Because the support of one individual living out a stand of conscience can take a great deal of time and spiritual, emotional and other energy, it is important to keep it in balance with the other responsibilities of the meeting. Indeed, there may be more than one member taking stands of conscience on the same or varied concerns. Care for such stands of conscience is only one aspect of the pastoral care of our members that we Friends must address as we try faithfully to live in the world but not of it.

> Priscilla Adams is a member of Haddonfield (NJ) Meeting and has been supported by her meeting and many other Friends in a stand against payment of war taxes. She has served as Philadelphia Yearly Meeting's regional Peace and Social Concerns staff person for Haddonfield Quarter.

> Steve Gulick is a member of Central Philadelphia Monthly Meeting where he has served as clerk, a member of Overseers, and on Peace and Social Concerns. He also served on Philadelphia Yearly Meeting's War Tax Concerns Support Committee and for 25 years he was a war tax resister.

Winter Park Meeting Supports a Stand of Conscience

Three years ago, Winter Park Meeting in Florida welcomed a new attender with a strong concern for human rights abuse. Rita Lucey's interest in Quakerism grew simultaneously with her commitment to closing the School of the Americas in Ft. Benning, Georgia.

Demonstrating against abuses perpetrated by Latin American military graduates of the school, Rita twice trespassed onto the military property. She was one of 25 "repeat offenders" sentenced to six months in prison and $3,000 fines. On March 23, 1998, she reported to federal prison camp to begin her sentence.

As her concern grew, she kept the meeting informed of her activities on this concern. At the same time, Rita came into membership in the meeting. The spiritual leadings which had transformed her life began to work their way through the rest of us, like yeast in dough.

We felt a strong desire to stand with Rita on the eve of her imprisonment, which lead to a meeting for worship followed by a candlelight vigil. We sang to live guitar music and heard Rita talk. As suggested by Rita we participated in a responsive reading calling on the strength of such heroes as Martin Luther King, Jr., Mary Dyer and our meeting's own World War II conscientious objector. About 100 people came, many from other groups Rita has touched. Orlando Meeting joined us, as did Rita's husband of 46 years, their children and grandchildren. The evening ended with tears and hugs.

The meeting prepared a taped interview with Rita and an exhibit to show Southeastern Yearly Meeting after her incarceration. SEYM was moved to establish a meeting for sufferings and a fund to receive donations for Rita's books, fine and other needs.

Winter Park Meeting has recorded three ministers to visit her, to report on her needs and to maintain contact with her husband. One writes periodic reports to all concerned with Rita's condition. The rest of us are not permitted to visit her, but we write individually. After meeting for worship, we contribute to a weekly group letter. We send books and journal subscriptions. We tell her story to others. We hold her in the Light. Rita has stirred us deeply and drawn us together. We are grateful for her presence in our midst.

Martha Morris, Winter Park Meeting, FL

Questions for Reflection

1. Are there noticeable ways, great or small, in which worship has led to action in our meeting?
2. How does the meeting encourage small, everyday acts of witness?
3. How does our meeting communicate to its members that it is available to provide clearness and support for stands of conscience?
4. Are we prepared to provide a loving and Spirit-based clearness process for those seeking support? If not, how can we prepare ourselves and our meeting?
5. In what ways can we help the meeting when it is clear that a member is led to a witness that others in the meeting disagree with?
6. How can we balance the meeting's support for a stand of conscience with other demands on the meeting's care?

PASTORAL CARE FOR ILLNESS AND DEATH

CARING FOR THE TERMINALLY ILL
AND THEIR CAREGIVERS

FACING DEATH: HELPING PEOPLE GRIEVE

PREPARING FOR MEMORIAL SERVICES

CARING FOR THE TERMINALLY ILL AND THEIR CAREGIVERS

Pastoral Care Newsletter, Vol. 8, No. 1 • September 2000

BY LUCY MCIVER

RESPONDING TO THE NEEDS OF SOMEONE WHO IS DYING can seem like an overwhelming task. Most of us are not experts, only human beings who carry our own fears about facing death. Mostly we learn how to do as we go along by listening to one another. But we need not face these times unprepared if we are aware and respect the gifts of those within our spiritual communities. Responding to the terminally ill and their caregivers can be an opportunity to grow together.

Like many meetings, my meeting in Eugene, Oregon, has many elders who are getting closer to their time of dying. And we knew that not only these cherished souls but any one of us could immanently face death. We recognized that many of our responses to the dying and bereaved were unorganized. Many felt a growing concern to respond in a more intentional way. What follows is a report on what we have learned along the way.

Eugene Meeting's Story

A concern for supporting one another came to the surface through our social concerns committee which requested that the meeting look into long-term care insurance. Several people came forward to consider how we might address this concern. Through several discussions and research into insurance availability, we came to feel that the insurance issue was more an individual one. But underlying was the larger concern of how we can respond and help one another in times of health crises, including death and dying.

This resulted in the formation of Friends' Care Co-op within Eugene Friends Meeting. The co-op, an outreach arm of the meeting's pastoral care committee, responds to the needs of those within the meeting facing end-of-life and health needs and makes a monthly report. Our goal is to develop an organized way of responding to health crises.

A survey was developed to determine who within our meeting community could provide practical support. From the responses we created a skills bank of volunteers within the meeting who could be called upon to provide meals, transportation, personal care, companionship, house cleaning and lawn care, clearness committee and support committee involvement and financial support.

The original committee members became the "care team." Their responsibility is to take the initial call for help and assess what needs are apparent. Two members of the care team visit with the individual and family to determine what support is needed, what the family can provide for themselves and how the meeting can best respond to their request. From here a plan of response is developed. The team then turns to the skills bank to organize volunteers.

We have recognized that not everyone who volunteers has the experience or skills to be with the terminally ill person. Some training is needed to help those "compassionate hearts" do their work with sensitivity. To meet this need we offer verbal suggestions in our initial contact with each volunteer as we organize the contact schedule. We stress becoming aware of our body language and to show that we are attentively listening by making eye contact. We remind each volunteer that our greatest gift is offering a time of silence or worship out of which often comes space for people to speak of their concerns. In other words, we stress compassionate listening skills.

Secondly, we initiated quarterly training sessions for volunteers. The first one was centered on the topic of the rights of the terminally ill. We identified these rights as:

- The right to be in control
- The right to have a sense of purpose
- The right to be touched if they wanted
- The right for individuals to live their spiritual beliefs as they are dying
- The right to hear the truth
- The right to reminisce
- The right to laugh

We encouraged dialogue among our volunteers as we discussed these rights through sharing personal stories and experiences. Those who participated in this discussion found commonality in their fears, positive reinforcement for their gifts and an eagerness to work together.

We rely on the professionals from within our group or invited from outside the meeting to educate us in matters of pain and symptom relief as we educate our volunteers. We support our families and caregivers through education about the final rights of the dying including information on advance directives, do-not-resuscitate directives and practical matters. We do not make recommendations about medical care but attempt to strengthen communication between the family and the medical community. And we know that there is often a certain chaos for those facing death and those providing care. To address the needs that arise out of this time our goal is to develop open lines of communication, friendships and a close ability to work together. From that foundation we offer our prayer that peace will enter and create the sacredness that we all seek.

Spiritual Aspects

We continually address the spiritual aspects of our work by deepening our own spiritual life. We encourage our volunteers to read Quaker literature available to them on the subject of death and dying (see resources, pp. 314–15). Included in those readings is my Pendle Hill Pamphlet on research into seventeenth-century Quaker attitudes towards death and dying. The stories of early Friends deaths remind us that their attitude toward life and death did not so concretely separate living from dying as we do today. Seventeenth-century Friends shared the belief that they were to live every day as if it were their last. Living their faith daily was understood to strengthen their personal relationship with the Divine. Early Friends regarded death to be the climax of their spiritual journey, a final goal for which they needed to spiritually prepare.

In other words, life was not separate from death, only a part of the greater journey. Because of this belief, when someone finally came to their time of dying, early Friends saw that person to possess a spiritual authority that no other person had. At death's door a person was seen to be firmly in God's light but still among the living. One was expected to minister or witness from that liminal place. Often, the whole family along with visitors from the meeting, including children, would gather around the dying person who, in this time of close relationship to God, would preach to them.

Such an attitude toward death as a spiritual experience can create a sacred attitude towards life. Friends and family within the support circle thus can witness and affirm the one who is dying. Holding one who is dying in a sacred manner can gather us together with the Divine. We might say this experience is like birthing into the Divine love of God. Death can be experienced as a spiritual birth. The physical pains along with the emotional surrender in dying are the labor of that sacred transition.

Four Friends Who Have Received Our Care

Eugene Friends Care Co-op (FCC) has now responded to four elders within the meeting as they faced terminal illness. In each response we have found differing needs of the dying persons and their caregivers. Families vary in their structures. We try to remain open to these differences. Our aim is to fit each scenario and respect individual needs. We begin by offering simple practical suggestions that are not invasive to their family relationships. We present several options to their questions leaving the decision making to them. Truly common among caregivers is a reluctance to ask for help. We try to empower the caregivers to acknowledge their own needs and ask when they need help.

One family needed companionship for their mother as she learned to live with congestive heart failure. At the time of our involvement she was quite weak and the family unprepared for the amount of care she required. Her primary caregiver was her elderly husband. Volunteers stayed with her while family members found professional in-home care. Friends provided food and helped with its serving. We worshiped with her twice a week. Others went to read to her and/or helped with correspondence. Over the last few months this woman has gained strength and is now able to attend women's meeting and sometimes attends worship.

Another elder was dying from cancer. FCC provided support and clearness as she attempted to deal with the material accumulation of her life. Over the winter it became apparent she could no longer live alone. The FCC team worked with her family in finding 24-hour care by providing contacts and phone numbers for several eldercare agencies. Her son made the decision as to which one was best for his mother and workable for his budget. Volunteers continued to visit and monitor the care since the son lived out of town. When she neared death the son was called and supported as he witnessed his mother's dying. Because of FCC's involvement with the family, the planning for the memorial felt easier and more natural for members of the committee.

A third elder has been experiencing a slow physical decline. His wife has congestive heart failure. They very much want to remain in their home. Pastoral care organized a clearness/support committee that has met with this family for over a year. How to empower this loving wife to ask for help and to take care of her own needs has been the primary clearness task. Individuals from this committee visit regularly, and the committee meets with the couple once a month. We also keep lines of communication open with children who live away from Eugene. Close spiritual friendships have grown from this long-term commitment.

A fourth elder came to the attention of FCC from concerned members within the meeting. When the initial contact was made no additional help was being requested. Nonetheless we stressed what we could offer in specific things, like shopping, picking up prescriptions, etc. We ended the contact with letting that individual know he could call us anytime with small needs. A week later it became apparent that this elder's time of death was close when he was moved to a nursing home. Only then did he ask FCC to invite a few long-time friends to come and visit. He also asked that his wife be contacted to help with practical matters. She had not lived with him for some time, and we thought of him as divorced. Our job was to respect her coming and connect her with his children. We supported the family lines of communication as they learned to trust one another.

Always at the center of our work is the spiritual care of individuals and families. We want to strengthen the ties of meeting friendships, offer times of worship and worship sharing, and pray together for those who come to us. Volunteers are coached in ways of listening and how to open opportunities for personal sharing and worship. When our fourth elder was dying such an opportunity came to one of our FCC volunteers. As only grace can provide, minutes after this elder died our volunteer arrived to play the harp at his bedside. She felt called to stay with his spirit and play while the family gathered around him. This time grounded their family as it began to work together again.

Each volunteer is encouraged to report back to the FCC care team any concerns, joys or needs that might have come from their work.

These conversations help us to learn from one another. Volunteers are always thanked for their gifts of friendship and support. And in the sharing of these times we grow closer together in community.

In the greater meeting picture, we have come to recognize our responsibility for education of our volunteers and the community as a whole. To meet those needs, we have offered quarterly evening gatherings for anyone in the meeting to explore specific topics. Such topics include discussion around needs in senior housing, developing conversations around financial needs and support, and bringing in an attorney to speak of end-of-life topics of advance directives, wills and estate planing.

A second method of education is currently being initiated to reach more people within the meeting. We are asking individuals to write personal essays from their own experience of facing the transitions in life, health issues, etc. These essays will be printed and circulated in the monthly newsletter. It is hoped that these essays will bring into the open issues that are commonly shared but not often talked about.

Reflecting on Our Experience

As we reflect on the work that FCC is doing within Eugene Meeting, we realize that there are many kinds of situations we have not had to deal with in the short time we have been organized. We have not faced a sudden or traumatic death nor the death of a young person. We pray that if that these situations arise we will have the spiritual foundation to respond together. We know there are resources within the wider professional community to help us and perhaps that will be the topic of another quarterly training session.

As a care team we regularly must ask, "Are we meeting the needs of the terminally ill and their caregivers?" We recognize that we are learning as we go along this path. Sometimes we may bumble and fall short, only because of human weakness not from lack of love. We try to let our organization help us to evaluate each response individually rather than shape it into a patterned response. We aim to give fully and wholly to all within the meeting whether the call comes from a beloved elder or a sometimes attender. We know that as we respond we will come closer together, grow into new friendships and see one another's strengths. Most of all, we know we are not alone and that others will walk with us as we face death ourselves or within our families.

In helping others who are facing death we have come to know that we must prepare for our own death by living our faith each day. When we are then called to be with one who is dying we can support them by opening ourselves to the commonality of death and assuring the dying one of their final human rights. To prepare the sacred ground where the greatest spiritual work can be done by all within the circle, we must do this work worshipfully. We must move beyond "self" allowing all to become gathered into a larger purpose, beyond time. In those moments we feel God's presence working upon us. We truly come to know the fullness of living—the whole cycle of life and death and life.

> Lucy McIver and her partner, Karen Lundblad, are supported by Eugene (OR) Friends Meeting in their ministry to lead workshops on opening our spirits as we face death. She authored the Pendle Hill pamphlet, *Song of Death, Our Spiritual Birth: A Quaker Way of Dying.*

Visiting Friends Who Are Very Ill

1. Check in advance to see if the patient wishes to see you at this time.
2. Plan to stay just a few minutes; longer if you are sure the patient wants you to stay.
3. If others are already visiting, return some other time.
4. Your friend may be shockingly changed in appearance. It is good to be aware of your reaction, but it is generally not helpful to comment on it.
5. What you talk about is less important than the way you listen. Allow the patient to choose the subject. You might start with a noncommittal statement such as "How goes it?"
6. If the patient wants to tell you about the illness, be receptive even if it makes you feel uncomfortable. Be careful about quizzing for details or matching the account with tales of your own. Suffering is not a contest. Avoid false reassurance.
7. If you are left with choosing the subject, try to connect with what you know of the patient's interest. Some may welcome talk about the world outside: your trip to the city or some world event. Others may find that distressing. Take your cues from the patient's response.
8. Some people enjoy hearing a poem, story or article read aloud. Let the patient help choose what is to be read.
9. Others may find that reminiscing makes for good conversation.
10. When death is imminent, it is likely to be in both your minds even if neither of you can speak of it. If the patient wants to talk about it, be receptive in your listening. Just let your friend talk, if you can.

11. With some, sharing deep silence is most is the best way to communicate caring.
12. Be sensitive to how touch is received by the patient. Some people do not like to touch or be touched, while others crave direct contact. Be aware that for some touch, though desired, is physically painful.
13. "Anything I can do to help" is often meaningless, but a concrete offer like "Could I water your garden?" or "Can I fill your bird feeder?" may be really appreciated.
14. Some would-be visitors are so worried about the visit that the patient has to do the reassuring. If that includes you, perhaps a card would be more helpful.

Based on guidelines prepared by the Mental Health Committee at Medford Leas Retirement Community.

One Meeting's Experience: A Care Committee in Salem Quarter

BY MARY WADDINGTON

Salem Monthly Meeting is a small meeting nestled in the farmlands and wetlands of rural southern New Jersey. It has held meetings for worship and business continuously since its beginnings in 1676. When Bill, one of its elderly members, was stricken with a massive, paralyzing stroke, his family knew the meeting would be there for them. His one request was that he be discharged from the hospital to his home rather than to a nursing home. Forming a care committee made this possible. Other members from the quarterly meeting eagerly joined in—he had been a quarterly meeting clerk for 25 years.

The circumstances of Bill's condition were such that although mentally alert, he could not speak or move, and swallowing was both difficult and dangerous. The committee had met and their tasks had been identified and assigned by the day of Bill's discharge. A telephone tree message was sent to meeting members stating he was home and that his care committee was ready to receive volunteers.

Since Bill's body had to be turned every two hours, four-hour shifts of two persons each were created. One committee member who works at home took phone calls, filled shifts, and coordinated visits. Another organized food donations. Another took responsibility for errands and chores. Yet another created a log book into which each shift worker recorded the time and position of body turnings, fluid intake and output, and medications given. The log included a section for journaling observations, ideas, feelings and thoughts.

A peace settled over Bill once he was home and surrounded by loved ones. It was then that he quietly refused all offers of food and water. He was lucid and receptive, clearly spiritually prepared for his transition, and his decision was honored. He lived another ten days without food or water. These final days were a series of centered, mindful interactions among a meeting community that tenderly upheld one another. Anyone who wished had private time at bedside, and this sharing was intimate and often profound. Bill's spirit transitioned effortlessly. Each gift along the way, offered so generously by so many, had been an act of love.

One year later Bill's widow Mabel was diagnosed with terminal cancer. The care committee claimed it had never officially laid itself down and so was in place for Mabel when she was discharged to her daughter's home for her final four months. Again, food and visits were coordinated, bedside meetings for worship were organized, respite for the family was provided. Bill's care had been intense whereas Mabel's was protracted, but the level of commitment was the same. To this day the care committee remains attentive to the family.

In Salem Meeting, and in Salem Quarter, if ye ask, ye shall receive.

Mary Waddington is a lifelong member of Salem (NJ) Meeting where she has served in the areas of pastoral care, ministry and social concerns.

Questions for Reflection

1. How can we help members of the meeting reflect together on the challenges that will face each of us at the end of life?
2. What plans do we have in place for responding to the needs of members with terminal illness?
3. Who in our meeting has a particular gift for being with those who are sick or dying? Who has professional experience?
4. Who among the meeting might be willing to provide simple, practical help for families caring for a person who is near death?
5. What resources are available in the yearly meeting or our community to help us respond sensitively and knowledgeably?

FACING DEATH:
HELPING PEOPLE GRIEVE

Pastoral Care Newsletter, Vol. 3, No. 2 • January 1996

AN INTERVIEW WITH ANNE AND TOM MOORE

O N AUGUST 14, 1994, Lydia Moore, age 38, died in an automobile accident. What follows is an interview with Tom and Anne Moore, her parents, who describe their experience of grieving and healing. Tom and Anne emphasize that when any of us experience the loss of a loved one, our experience is unique. At the same time, the experience of grieving can point to broader, more universal truths.

Following the interview is an article by Linda Lyman, Clerk of Ministry and Counsel at Bellingham Preparative Meeting in Bellingham, Washington, which offers reflections on ways of becoming more effective in offering support to members and attenders who have lost loved ones.

Tom: It was on a Sunday evening, shortly after Mother and I had taken Anne to the airport to go to New Mexico for the Friends World Committee for Consultation Triennial. I received a phone call from Jim Clendenin, the father of Lydia's spouse, Ann Clendenin, who told me that Lydia had died in a car accident in Kansas. He was in tears, and soon I was in tears. In a way we had a great conversation. Soon afterwards I talked to the doctor, who told me that Lydia must have died instantly; she had been crushed in the accident. I also talked to the highway patrolman and learned that it was an accident for which there wasn't anyone to blame. It was something that happened. And now, as I'm telling you about it, I find myself kind of living through it again.

Anne: Tom and I had very different experiences. I was in Albuquerque, on my way to the FWCC Triennial, and I learned of Lydia's death in a phone call from Tom. Fortunately I had taken with me a whole handful of family pictures to share with the cousins with whom I was staying overnight. Going ahead and looking at the pictures was very helpful.

Then I had a time of being by myself. I chose to be by myself for a day, in the security of my cousin's home. And that was really a very precious gift. I didn't have to deal with anybody else's anguish. It would have been very different if I had been at home. At the same time, I didn't have the details to work with, so in a way I felt cheated because Tom was doing it all.

As I reflected alone there in Albuquerque, one of the very first things that came to my mind was something I learned years ago from Marjorie Sykes. "What is needful?" The only thing I could think of was "I can keep loving Lydia." And that's been very helpful to me, because that's all one can do.

Tom: One of the reasons that the people in Kansas needed to phone me was that although Ann and Lydia had been married under the care of Penn Valley Meeting, that marriage had no legal standing. So as her father I was Lydia's nearest kin. Ann, who also had been in the accident, was under sedation and wouldn't be available in any real sense until the next day. There were questions about whether Lydia's remains would be cremated or buried, and many other kinds of questions. So to each of the people to whom I spoke, I had to say, "well, you know this is a couple, and they were married under the care of the meeting, and what I want to do in my legal role is whatever Ann wants to do in her real role as Lydia's spouse." I was talking to people in southwestern Kansas, in a relatively isolated, rural area, but everyone could immediately understand the situation. They didn't in any way have any difficulty with this lesbian relationship.

Anne: A little more than 48 hours after Lydia's death, Tom and I met in Kansas City, at Lydia and Ann's house. Our friends, John and Reva Griffith, mobilized things there. (It was Reva who wrote the article about Lydia in the January 1995, issue of *Friends Journal*). We all began contacting people hither and yon. We also asked the recording clerk of our home meeting to include a note about Lydia's death in a mailing that was scheduled to be sent out to all our members.

Tom: While it's a unique experience for us, we learned that the family across the street lost a child, and so did the person down the street, a new resident, and so did many others—all parents whose young adult children died under various circumstances.

Anne: The meeting for worship the following Sunday, at Valley, our home meeting, was set aside to hold the Moore family in the Light. And I recommend that. A single red rose was up on the piano, and we had in hand the editorial about Lydia that had appeared in the *Kansas City Star*. We walked in and received hugs from everybody, which was the warmest welcome we could have had. And Tom spoke during meeting for worship. He had been reading the Bible that morning, and had found something about "let everything you do be done in love." It seemed that that was really what Lydia's life was all about.

Then we went back to Kansas City for the memorial service, which was preceded by morning worship at Penn Valley. Many dear friends were there for us. All the surviving family was present for the memorial service, including Lydia's two brothers and sister-in-law and her spouse Ann Clendenin, who attended in a wheel chair. All of Ann's family had come from Oklahoma City. Lydia had been a doctor, and many of her patients, the other doctors, the children from the Penn Valley Meeting, and Lydia's high school classmates, along with a number of our friends from Lawrence were there. It was just very amazing—there were some 1100 people there. It was a Quaker meeting, opened by the clerk of Penn Valley Meeting, with microphones up front, and people standing in line to speak. It went on for almost two hours. Six weeks later the AFSC Board, of which Lydia had been a member, had a meeting for worship in her memory.

Clearly, in helping us along this unknown path on which we had suddenly found ourselves, those meetings for worship were important. Valley Meeting helped in other ways as well. The rhythm of events in the meeting helped me recover a sense of continuity—it gave me an important focus as I continued carrying out my responsibilities as clerk. Often at the point of death people may feel disconnected. So what they need is to get reconnected. Well we've been connected this whole time. That sense of being held—that's what has carried us through.

Another way in which the meeting has supported us (certainly unplanned) was to provide the opportunity for both of us to talk with others in similar circumstances. There were a number of deaths, and we were each able to minister in various ways. In one situation I was asked to offer the opening remarks for a memorial service for the brother of a dear friend and meeting member. That was a challenge, but one that I was glad to be able to do. In another instance I declined that role, feeling I just couldn't do it.

Through this experience, I've learned how important it is to not get too tired. That takes a little extra effort. One note I received said, "be sure to pay attention to your own health because this makes more demands on your health than you realize." That was one of the cards that I valued most.

Tom: The expanded family of Friends has reached out to me in many ways as well. In my committee involvements in Philadelphia Yearly Meeting, everybody has been so considerate and supportive. Every meeting I attended, people would come up and say something to me about Lydia's death. Months later people who had just found out would say "I hope this won't upset you but I just need to say how sorry I feel." What I found, thanks to those people, was that such late commiserations were wonderful. They helped me to discover where I was. And often I found myself shedding a tear, but I was also able to say "Thank you very much. I guess I had another round of tears to shed."

One of the things Anne and I have discovered through this whole experience is the value of living one's life in touch with other people. We've felt very much surrounded by love, and upheld. We've wanted people, particularly those acquainted with Lydia, to know that we know this is not just our private grief. We wanted to let friends and acquaintances know that it's all right to talk about it. It turns out that many people want to talk about their own losses. Sam Snipes helped us to see how we could benefit from lending a sympathetic ear. That means we've needed to have time to listen. And if one's life is going on at a pace that allows one to hear people, then it's possible to offer this kind of mutual service.

Anne: It's been important to listen, even though it hasn't always been easy, particularly when Lydia's death seemed only to trigger a flood of memories about their loved one's death told in great detail. But even so, I wouldn't call that a negative. It's just been part of the process. It's been helpful for me to recognize that this process is really a lifetime process.

Tom: Anne and I have also discovered how different our feelings have been. For some time, even before Lydia's death, we've had the practice of setting aside time to talk with each other about our feelings. After Lydia's death we would check in with each other, saying "well how are you doing?" and we would find ourselves experiencing everything from crying to needing to know more information, to having different levels of need to get all the details. We kept rediscovering that each of us was at a different place. And we also found that we were able to support each other in our differences, by keeping in touch with them.

It wasn't a matter of saying "well at last you're catching up with me." It was just helping each other to be able to talk about where each of us was, to do whatever we needed to do, to recognize that whatever we each were doing was legitimate.

> Tom and Anne Moore are members of Valley Monthly Meeting, Wayne, PA. Each has served on Worship and Ministry and on Overseers as well as other monthly, quarterly and yearly meeting committees. They lived in Lawrence, Kansas for 23 years where they were active members of Oread Meeting. Anne has been clerk of Missouri Valley Conference and of AFSC's North Central Region Board. In retirement they are experiencing community living at The Hickman, a Quaker run boarding house.

Facing Death and Loss in the Meeting

BY LINDA LYMAN

Tom and Anne Moore have given us a gift. Through their awareness of the love that surrounded them when their daughter was killed, they experienced Friends as instruments of God's healing grace. By sharing the interweaving of their grief and healing, they help us examine ways Friends can respond when death touches the meeting community.

Death often surprises us. If we have done our own inner work to prepare ourselves and our meetings, we will be able to provide more effective support when someone in our meeting suffers the loss of a loved one. Here are a few thoughts to keep in mind.

Preparation Ahead of Time

One important way to prepare is to arrange a practical workshop for the meeting so that Friends can think about the areas in which decisions will need to be made. The workshop could include information about relevant issues such as wills, living wills, appointment of executor, organ contribution programs, donation of the body to a medical school and issues relating to cremation and/or burial arrangements. The workshop could also provide an opportunity for Friends to become clear about their ethical choices and how they want those choices carried out during the dying process and after death. Single members of the meeting need to make their wishes and arrangements known as to where to contact relatives, how to care for pets, etc. Same gender couples in particular need to have signed medical power of attorney forms.

Sometimes people want to write their own death notices and plan their own celebration of life or memorial meeting for worship. Providing opportunities for Friends to give consideration to such personal issues is another important step in preparation.

The other significant area of preparation is the spiritual. Pastoral caregivers need to be sensitive to their own unresolved grief and loss. It is an emotional, psychological, and ultimately spiritual journey that everyone must undergo in one form or another or they will find it difficult to be present to someone else's grief without tapping into their own hidden pain. People who have not faced their own losses frequently cannot acknowledge another person's grief; they may avoid a grieving person because they don't know what to say or do. Although that is understandable, it means that the grieving person experiences a double loss—the loss of their loved one and the loss of supportive friends.

Practical Ways to Help

During the first few days after the death, the pastoral care committee can provide the following:

- Information about burial procedures, options for cremation, etc.
- Opportunity for meeting with a small clearness committee for help with immediate decisions.
- Help with communication when many people need to be told about the death and hospitality for persons arriving from out of town.
- Help with the memorial service.
- Help with writing notices for newspapers, *Friends Journal*, or other publications.
- Organization around meals to be delivered to the person or family experiencing the loss during the first week or two. Organization is important to avoid what one Friend experienced as an overabundance of sweet desserts and no substantive food.

Often, in the case of someone who has died after an extended illness, the grieving person has been the primary caregiver. At the time of death, the caregiver may be utterly exhausted. Pastoral care committee members need to be sensitive to the need for rest before healing, or even grieving, can begin. Committee members can also mark their calendars to remember to send cards and words of encouragement at various times during the year, particularly on the anniversary of the death. Committee members can also encourage Friends to extend supper and holiday dinner invitations to the grieving person, particularly on the anniversary of the death. They can also encourage Friends to stay available to the person or family suffering the loss, to call if only to say, "You are in my thoughts and prayers. I'm here when you need me," or to stop by just for a moment, unless encouraged to stay longer.

Sometimes a meeting for worship for healing is helpful, when Friends gather together to provide an opportunity for the grieving person to share the pain and loss and to be held in the Light. This is different from the memorial meeting for worship to celebrate the dead person's life, because the focus is on the reality of the grief of the living and not on the person who has died.

Understanding Grief and Loss

Tom and Anne emphasize the importance of accepting the uniqueness of each individual's response to grief. What the grieving person needs is a listening ear and a caring presence. The pastoral care committee can be most effective by asking how they can be helpful, and by listening without making judgments. It is important not to offer advice or assume one knows what the grieving person needs.

At the time of loss, feelings are often irrational, out of control and contradictory. People generally grieve in the same way they have lived their lives. The time of loss is not the time to expect people to change their mode of emotional expression, or to act according to someone else's expectation. For instance, it's important not to have expectations about how long it's permissible to cry. ("You've cried long enough. Now stop crying. It's not going to bring your husband back.")

Each individual's experience and needs are unique. Some people need the safety of someone to express tears with, other people will cry only in private. Some people want physical contact, a time for hugs and being held; others are uncomfortable with that much closeness. For most grieving people, loneliness is felt intensely. Some people are afraid to be alone. They want someone in the house with them, someone to be present but not demanding, until a relative or close friend arrives. Some people want time to themselves—a time to think, to come to grips with the reality of their loss, to be with memories, to be reflective about what to do next, to scream or slam doors. Some people will be in a state of denial, perhaps even philosophical about the death. Others will express anger and rage or a sense of anxiety and fear, and some will blame others or blame themselves.

People going through the normal grieving process can experience a lack of energy, loss of appetite, inability to sleep or increased irritability. Sometimes people in the throes of grief will experience the physical symptoms of the person who has died. It is important not to make assumptions about physical symptoms but to encourage the grieving person to see a physician.

Some people will become depressed. Others will be accepting, relieved that the death of their loved one has brought release from pain and suffering. Sometimes people who are grieving feel like they are going crazy; they may be reassured to hear that strong feelings are a normal part of the grieving process. While most people have experienced all those feelings to some extent at different periods of their lives, the intensity of feeling will be amplified during a period of grief.

Often grieving people need to tell their story in detail many times, particularly if their loss was a sudden death. Listening without judgment, using the name of the person who has died and asking gentle questions to indicate your caring helps the grieving person to stay in contact with the meeting. If the griever seems stuck in his or her story, sometimes people get tired of hearing the same story repeated. They say "You're dwelling too much on the past, you've got to live in the present; you have to get on with life." But for many people going through the grieving process, it is that repetitive telling of the story that is very healing.

The pastoral caregiving committee can organize a number of people to make home visits to spread the repetitiveness among Friends. Other members of the meeting who have experienced similar losses may come forward to offer support. It is also helpful to suggest appropriate support groups. A committee member may even offer to attend a support group meeting with the grieving person and provide transportation, especially at first.

At the time of terminal illness and death people often find comfort in using religious language and talking about their relationship to the Divine. Friends who are comfortable articulating their own spirituality (and being silent about it) will be best able to get the sense of the person and will not assume their own language or relationship to God is the same as the grieving person's or anyone else's.

Caring for the Meeting Community

The pastoral care committee need to keep their collective thumbs on the pulse of the meeting community if a beloved member has died. Many Friends may feel the loss deeply and the whole meeting may go into a state of mourning at the loss of a vital member of their faith community. In one meeting after a clerk was murdered the whole meeting gradually descended into a state of depression, with many members experiencing unspoken feelings of anger and guilt. The meeting felt spiritually depleted. It was only after the meeting's loss was named a year later and their corporate experience shared and honored that real healing for the members and for the meeting itself could begin.

Those who have the care of the meeting have a privileged opportunity in helping Friends in the meeting face death and loss. They share not only in the suffering and pain but in the healing presence of the Holy Spirit as expressed through the human spirit.

Linda Lyman has been very active both in her meeting and in the wider Friends community, where she has given numerous workshops focused on living with grief. In addition, she presented the Sunderland P. Gardner Lecture at Canadian Yearly Meeting in 1996.

Preparing for Memorial Services

Pastoral Care Newsletter, Vol. 6, No. 1 • September 1998

By Sue Heath

OVER THE YEARS I have taken part in many Friends memorial services, and the hand of God can be seen in these meaningful times. They are often true miracles, as people come even when not expected and share wonderful celebrations of the person's life. There is that of God in each of us, and memorial services bring out the very best.

The Role of the Pastoral Care Committee

The death of a member is a time for pastoral care committee to minister to the family and friends of the deceased and to the meeting membership as a whole. When meeting members assist with some of the routine details, family and friends can concentrate on their feelings, on other mourners and on the way the deceased wanted to be remembered and memorialized.

The caregiving committee will find it very helpful to be prepared in advance with information about local funeral homes, burial grounds, cremation, funds available to assist families with funeral expenses and so on. They should know state laws and local regulations regarding embalming, burial, scattering of ashes, etc., as well as local funeral directors' understanding of Quaker simplicity. In most states, a mortuary needs to be involved no matter how simple the desired arrangement may be.

In some meetings the pastoral care committee encourages Friends to plan in advance what they would want for themselves or loved ones regarding the disposition of their body, what to include in a memorial service and facts to be included in an obituary. We need to help Friends record facts about schooling, progress of a career, volunteer work and outside interests, which will document their lives. It is also helpful to have Friends compile in advance a list of friends and relatives who should be informed in case of death. Some meetings keep this information on file for their members. (See "Sample Form for Members' Wishes for Their Memorial," p. 182).

When the Meeting Learns of a Death

The meeting is usually informed by a family member soon after a death. It is helpful for meetings to designate someone as the contact person in times of death or other emergencies. This often is the clerk of the meeting, clerk of pastoral care, or the clerk of worship and ministry. This person can make the necessary contacts to put into motion the meeting's process for support and for preparing for the memorial service.

One of the first things to do is to listen closely to what the family wants and needs and then to explain what the meeting is prepared to do for the family. This is usually a time of grief and shock for those close to the dead person, and often the Friend dealing with them needs to be sensitive to feelings of sadness and tremendous new responsibility. The Friend working with the family needs to avoid overwhelming the survivors with too much information and to listen for what is actually being asked. In one situation, a member had died suddenly far away from home. The spouse could not even begin to deal with what kind of memorial service there should be—she was totally engrossed in the mountain of details of getting the body brought across the country. The pastoral caregiver could only join in that concern and begin taking steps to help.

When it is time to discuss a memorial service, the pastoral caregiver may find that the caller has very little idea what a Friends memorial service actually is. Your yearly meeting's *Faith and Practice* may be useful in explaining Friends process. A Friends memorial service is typically held in the manner of Friends unprogrammed worship but sometimes includes introduction, readings, meditations, music and other prepared material as requested by the family and friends.

Once the family decides a memorial service is appropriate, the date and time need to be settled. Sometimes the family wishes to have the memorial service within a few days. In other cases they prefer to hold the service weeks, or even a month or two, later at a time convenient for family and friends who live at a distance. Pastoral care or memorial committee members will be able to advise the family about convenient times to use the meetinghouse. In some cases, meetinghouses are located near Friends schools, or in busy parts of a city or town and traffic considerations are important. If light or heat are insufficient in the meetinghouse, a daylight service may be advisable, or the caregiver may need to recommend alternate sites for the service.

In some cases meeting members may find it appropriate to offer to help with telephone calls to friends and acquaintances. Some meetings send postcards out to inform members and others about the death and to announce plans for service. The family provides additional names of persons to receive the notice.

Many meetings encourage families to suggest memorial gifts instead of flowers. The contact person may be helpful to the family in identifying causes that were important to the person being memorialized. An announcement of where to direct memorial gifts is usually included in the death notice or obituary. If the meeting sends out a postcard announcement, it can also include information about memorial gifts, flowers, etc.

Sometimes people ask about the obituary or notices in the newspapers. Local newspapers have different policies about accepting death notices from private parties, and the meeting will need to know the requirements of area newspapers. It is helpful if information for obituaries has been gathered in advance.

Planning the Memorial Service

In planning for the memorial service, pastoral caregivers will consult the family about their wishes and refer to any wishes expressed in advance by the deceased person. In most Friends services, the casket is not present and the service does not coincide with the burial or cremation, but these are matters of individual preference.

In some services, especially if many of those attending may not be Friends, a Friend is asked to explain the memorial service to the guests. The family may want to be consulted about who this Friend should be and what will be said. Usually the same person breaks the meeting. He or she may also explain that the family will leave and the meeting continue for a short time after which the family will be available to speak to their friends. (See "Introductory Words for a Memorial Service," p. 181).

Close friends of the person who has died are often asked to sit on the facing bench, and pastoral caregivers can help contact those people. If the family has no preferences for the facing benches, the members of pastoral care or worship and ministry can be asked.

The family usually waits until almost the time scheduled to begin before they enter together, and often they also leave before the very end of the meeting for worship. Find out if the family wishes to do this, and designate a place in the meetinghouse where they can wait before the memorial service.

If the family wants music before or during the memorial service, the memorial committee can inform them of what is available in terms of piano or electronic equipment including amplifiers and microphones. If the meeting does not have the necessary equipment, someone from the pastoral care committee may be helpful in identifying local sources. Some meetings have equipment to record memorial services, and this can be especially meaningful to a family with distant members who cannot attend.

Will the family want a printed program or short sketch of the person's life? A committee member can help them find printers and give guidance about programs, remembering that time may be limited and there may be a lot of information to compile. If programs are provided, decide if they will be distributed at the door or put on the seats in the meetinghouse.

Practical Arrangements

Often the family will be very unrealistic about how many people will attend the service, and experience shows that often more people come than were expected. It is better to plan for more rather than fewer.

The committee will want to have ushers to seat people, especially late-comers. Find out if the family wishes to designate a special place for family to sit. Be sure to have an idea of how many family members are expected, so enough seats are saved. Simple weighted white ribbons can be laid across the benches to be saved for family, so that the ushers will not have to ask people to move from those special seats.

It is very helpful to designate a family member or someone who knows the family to be at the doors with the ushers, to guide other relatives to their gathering place before the service or to seat them in the family section. If many of the guests are likely to be hard of hearing, ushers can direct them to the sections of the meetinghouse where it is easiest to hear or to listening devices if they are available.

The memorial committee should determine if child care is likely to be needed during the service or the reception. They can suggest names of teens or other people in the meeting who do child care and help arrange a place for small children—perhaps a First Day School room or a near-by playground.

Are there enough places to put coats, or do you expect people to keep coats with them? For a memorial service, where a meeting may expect many more people than usually come on a First Day, a simple rented coat rack will free up seats and people's arms and make the experience more pleasant for all.

You may expect flowers to arrive at the meetinghouse. Plan how you will place arrangements and how you will handle overflow. Be sure the family takes the flowers with them when they go, or provides for their disposal. If no flowers are to be sent, the memorial committee may decide some flowers are needed and arrange to have them contributed or ordered.

Many families like to have a guest book which helps them to remember the friends who were present. Sometimes the funeral home will provide books and pens. If there will be a guest book, plan where to place it. If it is at the entrance, people will line up to sign it and cause some delay in getting seated. Guests may be asked to sign the book at the rise of meeting or directed to sign at the reception if there is to be one. A member of the memorial committee should be place in charge of the book to encourage people to sign it and to be sure the family receives it. If needed, plans should be made for designating parking areas and to have someone in front of the meetinghouse to direct people to the parking area.

The Reception

Many meetings provide a reception following a memorial service, and it is important to establish at the beginning whether the family wants a reception and whether they have any preference about food, beverage, arrangement of the room, etc. Memorial committees often provide hot or cold drinks and either light refreshment like cookies, or more substantial food including sandwiches, finger food or a hot buffet. Sometimes the family will prefer to hire a caterer and will look to the committee for advice about local caterers.

Often the memorial committee takes full responsibility for setting up and cleaning up a reception. If a meeting does not have a ready crew of volunteers available during the day, they may need to contact members who will be coming to the service and ask if they will be willing to help out.

Some families will want a table of pictures and other remembrances, and the committee can help set that up before hand, supplying a table or other place for a display. Someone should be assigned to keep track at the end to make sure that these precious items are returned to the family.

During the reception the family often has an informal receiving line. Committee members should think of the family at this time, by bringing a drink or possibly a plate of food for them and being sure that they can sit down if they wish.

On the Day of the Memorial Service

A memorial service attracts people who have never been to a meetinghouse before, so they are unsure how to proceed and what to expect. We want to do all we can to make them comfortable. This includes attending to basic physical details such as:

- Has the building been cleaned and is the room set up for the reception?
- If the family plans a display of pictures or other mementos, are they in place?
- What lights will be used?
- Will the heat or air conditioning be needed?
- Are the rest rooms open and fully supplied with paper, soap, cups, etc.?
- Are the doors open so guests can enter the building? Are there enough seats, both in the room where the service will be held and in the room for the reception afterward? Keep in mind the needs of persons who are infirm and may not be able to stand for extended periods.
- Have arrangements been made for where coats should be put?
- Ushers, people helping with parking, and those setting up the reception should arrive at least one hour before the appointed time of the memorial service.

Friends are notoriously early, and even more so for memorial services. I have had more than one experience of all the seats being filled 15 minutes before the service was set to begin.

Ushers should be asked to seat early arrivals toward front of the meetinghouse, leaving seats in the back for those who arrive late so that they won't disrupt the meeting by walking to the front of the room.

People who come from far away may need some refreshment before the service begins, so ushers should be ready to help them find rest rooms and a place to get a drink of water if needed. In a large meetinghouse, signs to the rest rooms are helpful. Ushers should inform those with children about the child care arrangements.

At one time, a person in our meeting who died was very old, with no friends and almost no family remaining: he had also been rather difficult in the years that I had known him. I remember worrying that nothing would be said, or, worse, that people's messages would be too candid and perhaps hurtful. The miracle occurred! Meaningful messages were shared from people who remembered what their parents had said about the deceased, people who remembered him from their school days, and Friends who could see beyond his testy exterior to the warm and loving spirit within. There has never been a Friends memorial service that failed to inspire me and make me a true believer.

Sue Heath, a member of Moorestown Meeting, has worked in various meetings, responsible for the office, files and membership records, and support for the volunteers. She was a founder of a support group for paid meeting office staff, and has served as clerk of the committee for the *Pastoral Care Newsletter*.

Introductory Words for a Memorial Service

The sample remarks below are compiled from the experience of two Friends. Feel free to expand and modify them to suit the needs of your meeting and of the family.

When the family has entered the room and is seated, the person who has care of the memorial service rises and speaks as follows:

This is a called meeting of [name of meeting] Meeting of the Religious Society of Friends to celebrate the life of our member [name].

[You may insert some comments about the life of the member and his or her contributions to the meeting.]

For those of you who are not familiar with the Quaker memorial service, we sit in silence, opening ourselves to the movements of the Divine within us. Anyone who feels so led may rise in place and speak to the meeting. Share with us some facet of [name's] life which has touched your life or give some words of comfort to those of us who are left behind.

At the appropriate time, the person who has care of the service rises up and says:

> This would seem a suitable time for the family to withdraw. After the family withdraws, the meeting will continue until broken by the shaking of hands.

After the meeting has broken:

> The family will be in [name of room] to receive Friends. Please visit with them and join us for refreshments. In [room] there is a guest book which the family would like each of you to sign before leaving.

Sample Form for Members Wishes for Their Memorial

The meeting asks each of our members to complete this information and update it from time to time. Since we know not when death might visit, having this information will help the meeting to provide support to your loved one.

1. If the meeting is the first to learn of your death, whom should we notify? Who should be contacted to learn of your wishes or to make decisions respecting arrangements? Please give the full name, address and telephone number.
2. Do you have a will or other document that speaks to the matters of funeral, burial or memorial meeting? If so, where is this document kept?
3. Do you have death benefits (veteran, insurance, etc.) meant to pay funeral expenses? If so, where is this document kept?
4. Do you wish to have a memorial meeting under the care of the monthly meeting?
5. Do you have any special requests of, or instructions for, the monthly meeting at the time of your death? Do you want flowers at your memorial? Any special music or readings?
6. If persons desire to make memorial gifts, to whom or what group should such gifts be made?
7. Please provide basic information that can be used in preparing an obituary: date and place of birth, when you became a Friend, when you joined this meeting, education, profession, volunteer and professional accomplishments, names of parents and closest relatives.

Questions for Reflection

1. How can our meeting prepare itself to be sensitively responsive at the time of the death of a member?
2. Has our meeting designated someone to be the contact person in case of death in the meeting? If not, whom should we designate? How can we make sure that members know whom to contact?
3. Are we prepared with up-to-date information about funeral directors in our area? Do we know the basic requirements of the state regarding embalming, cremation, and disposal of remains?
4. Are we knowledgeable about requirements of the local papers regarding obituaries? What is our meeting's practice regarding preparing obituaries for local papers, *Friends Journal* or other publications?
5. Does our meeting keep on file information about a member's wishes at the time of death? How could we establish such a system that would not be cumbersome to maintain?

FACING CONFLICT IN THE MEETING

DEALING WITH DIFFICULT SITUATIONS

ONE MEETING'S RESPONSE
TO CONFLICT AND ABUSE

A CHALLENGE TO BE CLEAR AND CARING:
CHILD SEXUAL ABUSE

Dealing With Difficult Situations

Pastoral Care Newsletter, Vol. 2, No. 1 • October 1994

by Arlene Kelly

Situation A: I don't know what we're going to do with Friend A. It happened again this Sunday when she got so angry at Karen during social hour because Karen used the tablecloth we usually save for special occasions. She acts like she owns the kitchen. People get offended, but nobody has the courage to stand up to her.

Situation B: I'm concerned about our meeting for worship. There's so much tension, and it all seems to focus on Friend B whose messages upset people.

Situation C: Our First Day School Committee is falling apart. Nominating Committee told me that everyone they've asked to serve has said, "no," and several regular committee members aren't coming to the meetings. People are really turned off by the way Friend C goes off on her own tangents, dominating the time with concerns that are not shared by others. If we don't reappoint her to the committee, after all of these years of faithful service, I know she would be deeply hurt, particularly with the other changes she is going through in her life.

Do these anecdotes have a familiar ring? While none of them is intended to describe a specific person, they do represent recurring themes. The main goal of this article is to offer suggestions for responding in a constructive and caring way to situations such as those described above.

Because of space constraints and because they require a different strategy, two types of situations are *not* considered in this article: 1) situations of significant mental illness in which the person is out of touch with reality, and 2) situations in which the person's behavior verges on, if not crosses over into, criminal behavior, i.e., sexual harassment, child molestation, embezzlement of funds, etc. These topics are discussed in articles on pages 224 and 195, 205.

Understanding the Problem

Although it may be tempting to try to formulate an immediate response, it is much better to take time for a process of understanding and discernment in order to pinpoint the nature of the challenge. Of course every situation is unique, but one common characteristic of these situations is that they elicit strong emotions. These are situations in which a person's behavior is contrary to the expectations of the community. We know intuitively that there is the possibility of disagreement or conflict. Depending on how we deal with conflict we are likely to find ourselves frustrated, angry, confused, scared, upset and/or uncomfortable. A few of us are energized and ready to do battle.

To operate from a place of centeredness, to open ourselves deeply to the leading of the Spirit, to truly witness to our belief that God can be present in this moment as we seek a solution—this is what we are reaching toward. Experience has taught me, however, that before this can happen we must be clear about the feelings that have been elicited by the troublesome behavior. If we do not sort through and take responsibility for the emotions which have been stirred up, then it is likely that the issue is being clouded by another motivation—the desire to reduce our own level of discomfort. Let's be honest. People who exhibit behavior which we describe as "difficult" make us uncomfortable, and it is a very normal human response to want a lessening of discomfort. But as a faith community that should not be the main motive impelling us to action.

Our discomfort is useful in letting us know that something is wrong, that something needs attention—but what?

- Is the person identified as "difficult" bringing a message that we need to hear, but don't want to listen to?
- Is it what the person is saying which is troubling to us, or is it the manner in which it is being said? Is there a message (in words or actions), or is the behavior irrational and not rooted in the reality in which most of us are grounded?
- Individually and collectively, how might we be causing, or at the very least contributing to, the behavior we find unacceptable?
- Are we giving a consistent message to the person whose behavior is troubling that we find the behavior unacceptable, or do some of us directly or indirectly affirm the behavior?

These questions, and others that you could add to the list, can help us to begin the process of hopefully finding common ground which can serve as a meeting place with the person whose behavior is troubling us.

I lift up the importance of starting with our own response to and participation in behavior because of knowing my own shortcomings and because of my experience in talking with people in a number of meetings as they wrestle with these issues. We need, I think, to recognize our own propensity for turning a deaf ear to a message which is legitimate, but which makes us uncomfortable. We need to recognize how our avoiding of people with unrealistic expectations for emotional support, rather than finding a way to let them know of our limits, exacerbates their behavior. And yes, we need to recognize how we take advantage of qualities which make a person well suited to a committee assignment, such as being meticulous in the care of property, and then become impatient with them when they carry that to an extreme. I am not saying that we cause difficult behavior, but I am clear that there are ways in which we inadvertently intensify it.

Seeking a Constructive Solution

If we are to be faithful as pastoral caregivers to our commitment to address problems in our community, and to face honestly and openly differences which exist, then I think we need to be clear about what our expectations are for the outcome. Ideally, of course, we hope that the person whose behavior is causing difficulty will receive us openly when we go to talk, that the person will share with us his or her perspective, and that behavior will change in a positive direction, thereby reducing the tension between us.

Sometimes, however, even though we approach a difficult situation in a centered and skilled way, the person becomes angry with us for daring to open the subject, and we are unable to move the exchange beyond that level of defensiveness and anger. Have we failed in that instance? Surely we have failed in terms of finding a mutually satisfactory solution. Should we have avoided the meeting in the first place? I don't think so.

There are two things which are within our control as we enter a situation: 1) The spirit that guides our actions. Are we centered? Have we been open to considering what might be our part in the problem? 2) Our sense of clarity in communicating a clear definition of the limits regarding acceptable and unacceptable behavior in our meeting.

Then the other person has control over the way in which he or she will receive our concerns, and whether or not to join with us in seeking a mutual solution.

In addition to preparing inwardly for the visit and going in a prayerful spirit, what else can we do to help create a climate of trust and mutual searching? The following occur to me. What others would you add?

Assembling the visiting team. Try to have the visit carried out by people with whom the person causing the difficulty already has some relationship of trust and affection. Pay attention to the balance of energy in the group. If the person being visited is assertive and even controlling it is important to have folks who can meet that energy and not be overwhelmed by it. Conversely, if the person being visited is quieter or meeker, it is important that that person not be overwhelmed.

Fostering trust. We need to trust that, despite how difficult their behavior is, it is not the person's intention to be causing distress. (If we can't trust that, and sometimes it's appropriate that we can't, then we need to wrestle with the implications of that lack of trust).

Honoring the other's light. Try to find ways to discover how the person is experiencing the tension with the meeting. Let them know that their perspective matters to us, that we care and that we want, *with them*, to seek a solution that will work for all parties.

If I were part of a visiting team, I think that I would try to describe my distress with the way in which my relationship with the person had gotten off track. For example,

> I've been feeling really troubled about the way in which our interactions in the First Day School Committee have gone recently. I've come to realize that there are times when I've been very troubled by some of your participation, and I think that I've handled my feelings in a way which is very unfair to you. I'm sorry for that. It's not helpful to you that I and others on the committee just tune you out. I want to find a better way for us to deal with this. Does what I'm saying make any sense, when I talk about things being off track?

Then try to truly remain open and nondefensive in listening to the person.

Honoring *both* the other's perspective *and* your perspective. It's quite likely that you and the person being visited have different perceptions. There is nothing to be gained from debating whose perception is right. If you do that it is guaranteed that you'll each go away with the experience of not feeling heard by the other. This is *not* to say you need to agree with the person, or pretend that there isn't a difference. It means really trying to discover why it feels the way it does to them, and then trying to get them to hear how things are feeling to you.

For example, suppose our Friend who blew up on Sunday morning at social hour because the tablecloth was used says, "Nobody cares about the meeting house any more. Everybody is so busy running around with their own life. They know how to get tablecloths dirty, but they don't seem to know how to wash them," we can try to get them to sympathize with the busier schedules of young families (which is true), we can try to point out that meeting members really do care about the meeting house (which is true in varying degrees), etc., etc. *or*, we can say something like this: "Wow, it sounds as if you're feeling that a lot of the care for the meeting house is falling to you, and that others don't care about that, or are not respectful of all that you're doing. Is that how it seems?" My speculation would be that in one measure or another the Friend in question would say, "Yes," and we could even add, "I'd be upset too if I felt I was being taken for granted."

Now that the Friend has truly been heard, perhaps she is ready to hear our perspective. We could describe how her anger scares us, make us steer clear of property issues since we aren't sure we can meet her standards, and we realize that *a situation has developed* (not that she has caused it) which is very counterproductive for both of us. She is feeling put upon, which we don't want; and we are feeling we can't do things well enough to suit her, which is, hopefully, a situation she doesn't want. What can *we* do together to plan for *future* situations to help things be different?

Taking practical steps. Develop, in collaboration with the person, specific ways of dealing with the problem, trying to avert its recurrence. For example, a cabinet could be labeled "supplies reserved for special occasions." Think about how the problem can be addressed in a more caring manner by both sides when it does recur in some fashion.

Keeping at it. Deeply entrenched behavior patterns are *not* going to change overnight, even if the parties involved truly are trying to do things differently. Once there is an acknowledgment with the person that all parties want to find better ways of addressing the problem, a good question to raise is: What would be supportive to all parties as they try to develop different behavior? Suggest that people check in with each other in a few months to get a sense of how things are feeling to all the parties involved.

If, after all your efforts, there's no progress, then I think that the meeting has to decide what best serves the needs of the community. In following through on that it is important to be direct, caring and respectful in letting the person involved know of the decision, and to let them know of continued openness, if it is there, to seeking a mutual solution. "Nominating Committee will not be including your name on the slate for First Day School for next year. We truly value what you have to offer, but the difficulties we mentioned about your dominating the meeting are a real problem. We're not saying that the problem is all you, but your refusal to look at it with us creates a real dilemma."

In summary, our prayer should be for *humility*, which allows us to look at our possible contribution to the problem, and for *simplicity*, to speak the truth in gentle and straightforward ways. We can pray for a *rootedness* which will allow us to be mindful of the values binding us together as a community, and for *patience*, remembering that things will not change overnight. And always, we need a sense of humor.

> Arlene Kelly has served as clerk of Philadelphia Yearly Meeting and as clerk of Central Philadelphia Monthly Meeting. She served for over 30 years on Overseers of her meeting, including as the clerk of that committee. She carries a concern for nurturing and strengthening Friends meetings as faith communities.

One Meeting's Response to a Difficult Situation

This summary of an actual situation was written by a pastoral caregiver who was centrally involved. For reasons of confidentiality, details which might serve to identify the meeting have been deleted.

"John" (not his real name), a long-time member of our meeting, is very brusque—harshly spoken. His negativity has gradually gotten worse over the years, to the point where the whole meeting has been upset with him. John is very involved with a particular Quaker concern, and if the meeting doesn't support that concern in exactly the way he sees fit, he takes it personally and becomes very hostile. He says things like "I have five organizations supporting me on this issue, but nobody in the meeting is doing anything." In our committee life as a meeting, John is very, very critical if something doesn't go exactly the way he wants it to go, and he is verbally abusive at times. Much of John's problem is not a problem to him. He sees it as people being antagonistic to him. He doesn't stop to think why. His negativity goes far back into his childhood; I don't think it will ever change.

The reaction of meeting members has been to stay away from John. His anger and judgmentalism frighten people. We can't absorb all of his negativity. We're a small meeting, and we only have so much energy. Fortunately there are a few people who care about John, and I think that's very important. Somehow I've been able to maintain a positive relationship with him, because I've been able to talk straight to him, suggesting reasons why some of the things that annoy him are happening. I also try to help John with his personal problems.

Ministry and Counsel has discussed the problems with John. Virtually nothing has come of those discussions, except a sense of clarity on the need to try to maintain some kind of friendly connection with him. We will never desert him. On one occasion, Ministry and Counsel set up a meeting with John. We named a small, a carefully chosen group that we felt could talk to him on friendly terms. It was at a time when he was very, very angry with the meeting. Before we went I wrote him a letter explaining that we four wanted to understand him and work with him. But when the meeting took place, he was like a school child being taken before the principal. He just said "yes yes yes" to everything. I think he blocked things out because of embarrassment or anger. Through that experience we learned not to expect too much. Since then, our strategy has been for me to reach out on a one-on-one basis. This has worked well because I can be perfectly frank with John, and he knows I'll be there next time for him. And now I think he knows deep down that the meeting is there for him, even though it's hard for him to accept the caring.

My advice to other meetings would be to always see the other person as a human being. You can never force anything on a person. The interaction has to be grounded in the person's feeling of respect for you, and your respect for the person. Greet the person with friendliness. Respect the fact that there are always two sides to every conflict. Try to discover whether or not the person is aware of the conflict. (In this situation, if John was aware, he covered it up.) Try to understand the person's reasons for the stance that he takes. (In this case, we needed to ask the question: "Why does he feel so negative about us?") Remember that difficult behavior in an adult is almost always part of a long-standing behavioral pattern. It is never easy to change, but we must try, giving the person ample opportunity to get angry or even hurt, working through the feelings in positive ways of working together.

Remind the person that the group is a community, extending its warmth and love to all members. Because Quakers see love as an inclusive thing, he, too, is part of that caring. There is that of God in every person. At the same time there are expectations. No member or attender is given the freedom to disrupt the circle of love.

Questions for Reflection

1. In caring for the life of our community, are we, as those responsible for pastoral care, attentive to situations which may be causing tension among our members and attenders?
2. When the actions of a person in meeting are causing difficulty, do we find caring and constructive ways to address the situation? What are the things, if any, which would help us to be more effective in carrying this aspect of our committee's responsibilities?
3. What do I experience to be the gifts that I bring to the situation of dealing with a person causing difficulty? What are the areas of growth which I would like to achieve relative to this type of situation?

ONE MEETING'S RESPONSE TO CONFLICT AND ABUSE

Pastoral Care Newsletter, Vol. 6, No. 2 • January 1999

BY FRIENDS IN PORTLAND (MAINE) MEETING

Portland Friends have set a model for responding to difficult situations as an occasion for deep searching about who we are as Friends and what God requires of us. This article contains the guidelines as they were adopted by the meeting, with only a few minor modifications.

In preparing the guidelines, Friends in Portland balanced a wide range of concerns and of points of view. Situations of possible abuse often involve considerable ambiguity. Some in Portland and some on the Pastoral Care Newsletter *committee would put a different emphasis on parts of the guidelines.*

Do the guidelines say early enough and clearly enough that a first priority is to move to protect anyone who is fearful or at risk? This may need to be done before all the facts are known. Should the guidelines more clearly state that someone who is vulnerable should not be asked to meet face to face with a person who may be intimidating to him or her? A fear was expressed that in Friends efforts to being caring to both abuser and abused we may perpetuate the abuse. It is an exacting discipline to be both caring and *clear and firm. As Portland Friends point out, both are required in cases where there has been or may have been abuse.*

Every situation has a unique set of circumstances. If your meeting were faced with a situation of serious conflict or abuse, you might want to take these concerns into account.

What can a meeting do when one member accuses another of abuse? How do we address strong conflicts that draw in other meeting members? These events sorely try those involved and the community in general.

After some difficult situations were addressed by Portland (Maine) Meeting over a period of several years, some within the meeting felt called to reflect on their experience, do research, and then try to draft guidelines that might help the meeting face any future difficulties with strong interpersonal conflicts or allegations of abuse.

The four members who volunteered to undertake this task met on a monthly basis from January through July of 1996, taking turns drafting and redrafting. They brought their work twice to Ministry and Counsel, once to the Pastoral Care Committee, and finally to a joint meeting with redrafting ongoing.

As they proceeded, they considered the incidents that had happened in the past and projected incidents that might come up in the future. They did not explore the complexities involved in responding to abuse of a child. Also, they found that they were not prepared to write a special section addressing cases involving mental illness or character disorder. The guidelines that resulted address situations involving competent adults.

Copies of the proposed guidelines were made available to all members and attenders long before discussions were held during meeting for business in January and February 1997. At the February meeting, Portland Friends adopted the guidelines for an interim period of at least six months, subject to some conditions:

1. The guidelines were as a work in progress, to be amended and improved with time.
2. Ministry and Counsel was to arrange educational sessions to show how the guidelines might help in practice and to seek improvements to them.
3. Ministry and Counsel might suggest to meeting for business an extension of the period of applicability.

Since then, the meeting has sponsored an experiential workshop to demonstrate the processes outlined in the guidelines. This workshop was found to be so helpful by its participants that the meeting has decided to hold it annually. The guidelines have been slightly modified as the meeting has worked with the *Pastoral Care Newsletter* to present them to a wider audience in the hope that other meetings might find them useful.

As you read the guidelines we ask you to keep in mind two things: first that the guidelines were designed to deal with conflict or abuse between two competent adults; and second, that that they are a work in progress. Portland Meeting welcomes your comments and observations.*

* Contact Portland Monthly Meeting at 1837 Forest Ave., Portland, ME 04103.

I. Purpose of Portland Friends Community

We are a spiritual community. We come together to worship, to seek Divine guidance. We are diverse in our individual beliefs and outlooks, but we also hold dear our sense of community and of gathering together. We wish to seek the light and to see our community prosper. These guidelines are set out in furtherance of these goals.

II. Assumptions

A. General Assumptions

Conflict is a fact of life. For each of us the question is how do we deal with it. Quakers, being as fallible as other people, are not immune to antagonistic or hurtful behavior, including abuse of a sexual, physical or emotional nature.

When conflict or abuse occurs, we need in place a process that:

a. seeks clearness about the facts and context of the behavior;
b. always seeks to hold a compassionate regard for those involved, knowing that there is that of God in everyone and that each of us is more than the worst we have done;
c. requires accountability and limit-setting with respect to the behavior of any participant who abuses another;
d. determines at the outset whether anyone is at risk of abuse in the future, and, if so, takes all reasonable steps to minimize that risk and to ensure that person's safety;
e. offers support, whenever that is possible and desired, for each person involved in a case of conflict or abuse;
f. offers mediation or a clearness process to all involved, if and when mediation or a clearness process is appropriate (mediation may not be appropriate in cases of abuse);
g. honors the importance of the prayerful holding of each person in the Light and of an openness to the intervention of the Spirit.

We recognize that without such a process at Portland Friends Meeting when the test case of conflict or abuse occurs, we are likely to experience avoidance, prejudice, gossip, confusion, distrust and more conflict.

Finally, with the adoption of these guidelines, we affirm that Friends have conflict resolution processes that are likely to work, and we accept our duty to utilize them, to seek the truth in love, and to address behaviors which do much to rend our community or harm a member and little to further anyone's life or spiritual well being.

At a minimum this duty asks each of us to consult with the clerk of Meeting, the clerk of Ministry and Counsel, or the clerk of the Pastoral Care Committee if we sense conflict or abuse in our midst, so that it might aptly be addressed.

B. Our Attitude in Confronting Instances of Conflict or Abuse

It may be helpful for us, whenever we are dealing with any difficult instance of conflict or abuse, to adopt the following attitude, individually and collectively.

> Our prayer should be for *humility*, which allows to to look at our possible contribution to the problem, and for *simplicity*, to speak the truth in gentle and straightforward ways. We can pray for *rootedness*, which will allow us to be mindful of the values that bind us together as a community, and for *patience*, remembering that things will not change overnight. And always, we need a sense of humor.
>
> Arlene Kelly, *"Dealing with Difficult Situations,"* (p. 187).

C. Limits of the Meeting

Any case of conflict or abuse can bring an individual or group to its limits. How do we decide, individually or collectively, that we have reached the limits of what we can do in a seemingly unresolvable situation? Have we thought carefully enough about the simplest of needs, those for support, witnessing, prayer and holding in the light? Is the situation not ours to resolve? If not, are we big enough to accept our smallness? Is this a situation where the most loving act is to set limits upon an individual's behavior (perhaps even to ask the individual to withdraw from the community) to protect either that individual, another, or the community? Can we so act while holding all those concerned in our hearts and prayers?

III. How to Deal with Difficult Situations, in General

The section of Portland's guidelines regarding conflict situations where there is not an issue of abuse is Arlene Kelly's article, "Dealing With Difficult Situations," reprinted with permission from the October 1994 issue of *PCN* (see p. 187).

IV. How to Confront a Situation in Which One Friend Has Abused Another

A. Definition of Abuse

While there are many definitions of abuse, we have settled on a fairly simple one. Abuse occurs when one person has cause to know that certain behavior is hurtful, threatening or offensive to another person and yet engages in that behavior with respect to that person.

Cause to know may take any one of several forms, including: the second person having signaled the first, by word or gesture, not to repeat certain conduct because it is unwelcome; a third person having warned the first person that such conduct is being experienced as unwelcome; or the community or society in general having put its members on notice that a particular behavior is typically experienced as unwelcome. If the alleged abuser denies having had cause to know the behavior was experienced as abusive, that excuse is removed as soon as the meeting raises its concern with that person.

We understand that on occasion someone may experience as abusive behavior which most people would find acceptable. In such a case, it is Ministry and Counsel's responsibility to initiate a process to discern whether or not the behavior is in fact hurtful, threatening or offensive.

Abuse may be either emotional, physical or sexual in nature. It may take the form of one person deliberately trying to upset another, an employer harassing an employee, a larger person picking on a smaller person. Most often the abusive behavior occurs because of a real or perceived difference in the relative power or sense of empowerment between the abuser and the abused.

To illustrate abuse, it may be helpful to look at but one of its manifestations: sexual harassment. Sexual harassment is any conduct by one person directed at another person when the first has cause to know that this conduct is experienced by the second person as sexual and unwelcome. The conduct may range from a sexually provocative remark, to seemingly harmless flirting, to unwanted touching, to stalking. The key questions are whether the second person experiences the conduct as sexual and unwelcome, and whether the first person has cause to know that the second so experiences the conduct. Has the second person signaled the first, either by word or gesture, not to repeat certain conduct because it is unwelcome and sexual? Has a third person warned the first person that such conduct is being experienced as sexual or unwelcome? Is it behavior that the community or society in general has defined as typically experienced as sexual or unwelcome?

B. Procedures for Confronting Instances When One Portland Friends Meeting Participant Experiences Abusive Behavior by Another Participant

The following procedures might be implemented when one participant in the meeting, let us say Alpha, feels abused by another, say Beta.

Step 1. If Alpha is willing and feels safe enough to do so, Alpha can approach Beta, explain that Alpha experiences Beta's particular behavior as abusive, and ask Beta not to repeat it. (One variation: Alpha asks a Friend to come as a support person if both of them feel this would help Alpha to convey the message or help Beta to hear it.)

Step 2. If Beta does not agree to stop the behavior or if Beta does not actually stop it, or if Alpha is unwilling or unable to make a direct approach to Beta, then Alpha is encouraged to contact any one of the following: the clerk of the meeting, the clerk of Ministry and Counsel, or the clerk of the Pastoral Care Committee. (It is assumed here and throughout this section that Beta is not one of the three clerks.)

Step 3. Whichever clerk was contacted by Alpha would then inform the other two clerks (no one person being expected to bear such information alone) of Alpha's complaint. The three clerks (or persons designated by the clerks) would then meet with Alpha and listen with compassion and openness to Alpha's account of Beta's behavior and Alpha's experience of it. Then, in consultation with Alpha, the three clerks (or designees) would decide what the next steps should be: those that recognize the need for safety, justice and the health of the community; those that give Beta a full chance to give Beta's account of what has transpired; those that will aid in the halting of any abusive conduct, the discernment of truth, the expression of regret or apology and the beginning of healing.

Possible further step a. If Alpha agrees (see "c" below, if Alpha doesn't agree), the clerks/designees might meet with Beta to hear Beta's story; or a meeting might be arranged with both Alpha and Beta (each to have a support person if desired), wherein both stories are told to the clerks/designees, and Alpha and Beta have agreed to listen carefully and open-heartedly to one another's story.

Possible further step b. A carefully chosen, small committee of members, or an outside specialist specifically invited to address this problem, might facilitate a meeting such as that described in "a" above. Note that an outside specialist might help preserve a wanted confidentiality or bring much needed expertise at this early stage, but also note that the specialist may feel compelled by law or ethical requirements to report any ongoing abuse.

Possible further step c. If Alpha does not agree to representatives of PFM confronting Beta with Alpha's complaint of abusive behavior, then what can PFM do?

- offer to have a support committee formed for Alpha?
- make note of the reported incident in case other incidents involving Beta are reported later?
- seek clarity in prayer?
- advise Alpha to seek help from a professional or an agency?
- clearly inform Alpha of the limits of what PFM can do under these circumstances?

Possible ultimate steps. Steps beyond this point depend entirely upon the outcome of the initial meeting with Beta alone, or of that with Alpha and Beta together.

Clearly, if Alpha and Beta agree to what has happened and Beta acknowledges that the conduct was abusive, or experienced as abusive, apologizes for the conduct, agrees never to repeat it, and attempts to make amends, the further steps are likely to be fairly straightforward and a good outcome probable. If, however, there is either disagreement as to what happened, or as to whether Alpha should or should not have experienced the conduct as abusive or whether Beta should stop the conduct, then the clerks, committee or consultant will be faced with more difficult questions, such as:

- Does PFM have the possibility, skills, time, willingness to address and resolve this situation?
- Do we need outside experts to help us?
- Would any larger Quaker body be of help in some way?
- Does safety or the law require notification of any governmental agency? What are the consequences to Alpha, to Beta and to the community of taking this step? What are the consequences of not taking it?
- Could support committees of three members be formed for Alpha and Beta? Could these two committees be set up so that there is some mechanism of communication between them, maybe through a third person, so that each committee does not work in complete isolation from the other?
- Would a mediation committee or expert be of help? Note that whereas mediation is often helpful in other kinds of conflict, it is less likely to work and we are unlikely to find experts willing to try it in a case of abuse, where it appears that Beta is dishonestly denying what has occurred or refusing to accept that the conduct was abusive, or where there is a fear for safety or a significant difference in the sense of empowerment between Alpha and Beta.

All steps in this process will require deep, prayerful listening to the specifics of the situation. Our aim is to do all in our power to assist the work of the Spirit toward clarity, justice, safety and sanctuary for all in the meeting, and reconciliation, where possible. The need is to focus upon dealing with the *behavior* while holding each *being* in the Light.

We encourage anyone involved in a case of conflict or abuse— Alpha, Beta, and those who meet with them to try to resolve the matter—to read deeply in the literature listed in the resource section.

V. Confidentiality

Difficult questions of confidentiality arise whenever conflict or abuse occurs within the community. Who needs to know what? Who has a right to privacy that should be honored? How do we strike a balance between the need of various individuals or groups for privacy and others' need for disclosure? Most cases of conflict will require an evaluation of these questions, a process which is related to but also beyond the consideration of the conflict itself.

When a question of confidentiality versus disclosure arises, Friends might consider, at a minimum, the following:

1. Is anyone's safety at risk? If so, how is his/her safety best insured— by what degree of confidentiality and what degree of disclosure?
2. Is anyone's psychological well-being at risk? If so, by what degree of confidentiality or disclosure is her/his well-being best protected?
3. What is the need of any individual or part of the community to know certain information? Is that need of greater importance than the need for confidentiality that some other individual or group has?
4. If there is a need for the community as a whole to know something of the matter, how it's being processed, or its ultimate resolution, can publication of what needs to be known be done in a way that respects the individual's need for confidentiality?
5. Is there a need to contact the police, a government agency, an outside psychotherapist, mediator, lawyer or other professional, perhaps because of a legal requirement, a concern for safety, or a felt need for the bringing to bear of professional services from beyond the meeting? If so, and if that outsider might feel compelled by the facts and applicable law to commence legal action against a participant in the meeting or in some way involve outside agencies in the lives of a meeting participant, are we as Friends ready for this step and how do we need to adjust or maintain our Quaker processes in the face of such developments?

VI. Some Proactive Steps Friends Can Take to Avert or Reduce Conflict or Injury to the Community or to Another Friend

A. Whenever a Friend or a Committee is dealing with a conflict between two participants in the meeting, every care should be taken to provide equal support, opportunity for prayer and chance to use Quaker process to each person in the conflict and notify each that such is being offered to all those involved.

B. Friends have a dual obligation—to be as compassionate as is possible toward all parties and to set very clear and firm limits when they are necessary to protect the safety of a person. Experience shows that many of us have trouble with one or both of these obligations. Any workshop or exercise that a meeting holds to reflect upon these obligations and to role play through difficult hypothetical situations may help the meeting meet both obligations when real conflict or abuse arises within the meeting community.

C. If any Friend is considering taking any action, legal or otherwise, that is likely to affect the meeting community or meeting for worship, that Friend is asked to notify the clerk of meeting of that action, preferably before it is taken and in any case as soon as possible thereafter.

D. If any Friend attends any function in a way that is likely to give the appearance that the Friend represents Portland Friends Meeting when she/he is there only in her/his personal capacity, that Friend should strongly consider finding ways to inform those present that she/he is not representing the meeting.

Portland Meeting invites your comments and suggestions: Portland Friends Meeting, 1837 Forest Avenue, Portland, ME 04103.

I Wish My Meeting Would Have Had These Guidelines

Some years ago, when there was less public awareness and fewer resources for victims of abuse, I was being abused by my husband.

He was in many ways a good man with whom I shared similar interests and values. However, when I disagreed about something he wanted me to do, or not do, or even about an abstract idea he would sometimes become very angry and hit me repeatedly. Afterwards he would be sorry, but would blame me for having made him angry. The effects of his unpredictable anger have been long lasting for our children, now adults, as well as for me.

At the time, I had three sources of support: my extended family, my good friends and members of my Friends meeting. I confided in a few in each group about what was going on in my marriage. Although they were sympathetic, no one intervened and told my husband that the violence had to stop.

A family member said she didn't want to be involved because she didn't want to hurt her relationship with my husband. A friend told me she and other friends had talked about my situation and had decided I "didn't mind." A sympathetic older Friend often said, "If thee just tries hard enough, everything will be all right." I did try, but it wasn't enough.

When I asked meeting members why they had never spoken of my marital difficulties, they said, kindly, "We didn't want to interfere."

If the pastoral care committee of my meeting had the guidelines from Portland Meeting and followed them, there could have been great benefit for our family, my husband included. I am glad these guidelines are being distributed more widely and urge Friends to take seriously incidents of abuse among us.

Anonymous

Questions for Reflection

1. How can our meeting immediately protect victims of harassment or abuse?
2. If a someone in the meeting had a concern about an incident of harassment or abuse how would they know whom to contact?
3. What do we need to do to prepare our meeting to respond promptly and appropriately when a concern is raised?
4. What process do we have for being clear and firm with members or attenders who behave inappropriately?
5. What resources are available to the meeting if a situation arises that seems to be beyond our ability to respond adequately?
6. In what ways might the guidelines developed by Portland Friends need to be modified to be appropriate for our meeting?

A Challenge to be Clear and Caring: Child Sexual Abuse

Pastoral Care Newsletter, Vol. 3, No. 4 • June 1996

by Lindley M. Winston

I T IS HARD FOR US, at least for those of us in the older generation, to understand and come to terms with past blindness in regard to sexual violation of young people in schools, in homes and in religious communities. Until recently, such events have been hushed and hidden. The lives of the victims have been scarred and twisted. The perpetrators have in many cases gone on for years insinuating themselves into situations of opportunity.

The liberating days of the '60s can be given credit for making the community aware of the power differentials in our society which have made the less powerful subject, first, to being abused, and second, to being silenced or not believed. And the powerful have not been held responsible for their deeds. The focus of this article is on how our meetings can safeguard our children, without losing spontaneity and openness in our relationships with children, as we honestly face the reality of abuses which can occur.

But are these not things which exist in our larger society, separate from us as Friends? Need Friends be concerned about sexual abuse and be concerned about the vulnerability of our young people? Sadly, yes. There have been disturbing revelations over the past several years in various yearly meetings, Friends schools and Friends organizations, and in honesty we need to acknowledge that for each situation we know of, there are still others which have not been revealed.

I believe we need to find open and authentic ways to manifest our caring for our young people, ensuring that they are as safe as we can make them from sexual abuse. We need to manifest caring also for the many adults who work tirelessly with the young people, recognizing the danger of innuendo to their reputations.

Thankfully, we are not dealing with large numbers of abuses, but for those in whose lives the abuses occur, the impact can be devastating. And for meetings which have this concern the challenge to community is significant. What is it which we, as Friends, need to learn?

Facing the Problem

When we, as pastoral caregivers in our meetings, acknowledge the need to address the issue of sexual abuse, the first question we face is: How ready are we to truly deal with it in our meeting? In our self? Undoubtedly for some in our meeting, it will be a subject which arouses deep feelings because of a personal experience of having been sexually abused or wrongfully accused of having mistreated another. For many of us, entertaining the possibility that this could happen in *our* meeting is repugnant. We know that we carry deep feelings within ourselves, yet we long to begin in a place of centeredness. It is too easy to go to the extreme either of denying that such danger exists and thus ignoring useful clues, or overreacting and becoming suspicious, for example, of any enthusiastic offer of a man in the meeting to work with young people. Sensing either extreme, whether in ourself or in our meeting community, should cause us to pause and be cautious, for we know we are not operating from a place of centeredness. Do we have the courage to acknowledge that this is a subject which does stir deep feelings, thus allowing our pastoral care committee to then address the next question: What support do we, as a meeting, need to move forward on this? Can we stop and reflect on how our basic beliefs as Friends can serve us in this quest?

Nurturing a Healthy Atmosphere

Within our meetings it will usually be the parents of our First Day School children and the First Day School committees and teachers who will have been most sensitized to the risks of sexual abuse—both to the risks of its occurrence and to the risks of innuendo and suspicion to which teachers may, in this present climate, be subject. What can the pastoral care committee offer in the way of leadership and support?

Working together, Pastoral Care and the First Day School Committee, could start by considering the whole topic of sexual abuse, giving thought to how that concern applies to the safety of the children and adolescents of the meeting. Undoubtedly, for the vast majority of meetings such a discussion would lead to a sense of confidence in how children are supported and cared for. Certainly a meeting should be pleased that it has a climate of trust and openness. A good next question then can be, how do we nurture that climate? How do we build on it to ensure its continuation in a manner consistent with our practices as Friends?

One approach to be considered is the formulation of screening procedures based on queries and advices developed by the meeting. These would be used in a clearness process with each prospective teacher. Orientation can be provided for teachers and youth workers, including a discussion of what is appropriate and what is not, and constructive ways to foster companionship and trust.

As we come to a place of being comfortable in discussing these things openly in our meeting, then both our children and teachers can be prepared to participate in their own protection: children from abuse wherever it may occur, adults from unwarranted suspicion. Teaching about sexual abuse may be part of the spiritual education of the meeting's children. Teachers may be encouraged to ask for a partner in assuming any responsibility for children when they feel any risk of vulnerability.

Each meeting, according to its size and its composition, needs to reflect on what would work best for it in dealing with the subject of safety for our children and support for the adults who work with young people.

When Concerns Exist and/or Abuse Occurs

It is hard to imagine a more difficult challenge to the intention of pastoral caregivers to be both candid and caring than when the possibility of sexual abuse of a child or teenager becomes a distinct probability, or even worse, a reality in a meeting. For one meeting with which I am familiar, this concern was first raised in the Nominating Committee when a name was brought forward for First Day School teacher. A member of the committee knew something which made him doubt the appropriateness of a person proposed to be working with young people. What to do? In that instance, the person with the concern did speak up and indicated that he could not support the nomination, suggesting that there were issues regarding possible sexual abuse. That act of speaking up set in motion a conflict of significant proportions in the meeting. It opened very strong feelings on the subject of sexual abuse which had never been aired, and caused the meeting to break down into factions. How the meeting courageously faced the issue and how the subsequent healing process strengthened them as a community is an important story too long to be told here. But what can we learn from their experience?

(1) Hard as it is, the fact that suspicion has been raised must be made known to the person in question.

With the benefit of hindsight in the example mentioned, the member of the Nominating Committee might have said, when the name was first proposed, "I'm not prepared to approve that name today. I have some serious hesitations, but I have not spoken directly with [the person nominated] to explore those concerns. I would like another member of the committee to go with me while I seek clearness on the right action."

(2) A basic ground rule is that speaking truth clearly and directly, and seeking clearness, are central to who we are as Friends.

Once the question has been raised regarding the possibility of a person being sexually abusive, then it must be brought to a closure which is respectful of the community and respectful of the person whose actions and/or intentions are in question. Not all allegations turn out to be well founded. Unfortunately, not all situations are black and white. Can we have the courage to be in honest dialogue with the person in question? How does the person respond in a conversation about the allegations? Is he or she (most likely he) able to be candid and either refute the allegations, giving evidence that they are untrue, sharing something about the circumstances leading to the allegations? Would it be appropriate for the person, if continuing in a teaching role, to accept adherence to a "two person rule," maintaining that another adult will always be present "within eyesight or earshot"?

We know that such searching is challenging and difficult. It is important to remember that we are successful if we proceed prayerfully and openly, in a spirit of true searching which is grounded in truthfulness. Such searching may or may not result in finding a resolution which is comfortable for all concerned.

Facing the Hard Questions

Our pastoral care committees are accustomed to being confronted from time to time with matters which are painful and potentially destructive in the lives of members of the meeting community, and which occasionally place at risk the health of the meeting community as a whole. As a meeting forthrightly thinks through together, as a community, the issues raised about sexual abuse, it will find itself face to face with some of the most difficult questions.

(1) How do we come to understand more deeply the difference between holding something (appropriately) in confidence and the destructive dynamic of hiding an ugly secret?

Keeping secrets, whether in the life of a family or a meeting, can be part of a larger dynamic of hiding the truth, a dynamic based in shame, denial or guilt. The decision to reveal the secret should grow out of a process of spiritual discernment, based on a carefully considered sense of what is right. Love and personally felt responsibility may lead Friends to the awareness of their need to talk candidly about issues which are deeply personal, but the committee charged with pastoral care in the meeting needs to consider the right to privacy and the destructiveness of gossip and unfounded innuendo.

(2) If a person with a history as a sexual abuser is a part of our meeting, how do we, as a community, respond?

In such a situation a challenging task and an opportunity is offered to the meeting. It requires first and foremost that the children and young people of the meeting be safe. It is not sufficient, however, to have the Nominating Committee quietly (secretly?) build figurative fences around the person. Someone who has abused others is likely to have been abused himself or herself in childhood, and is likely to be deeply conflicted in his/her desires. She may, at the same time, be looking for opportunities to act upon perverse impulses, while also seeking protection from acting out those impulses by searching for a spiritual home.

(3) How does a meeting come to grips with the reality that sexual abuse, should it occur in the meeting or anywhere else, is a crime?

The meeting must take responsibility for determining local regulations and the responses available from the local child protective agency. That agency's first responsibility will be investigation. The meeting may need to *require* that the offender undertake treatment, since he may minimize both the need for treatment and the likelihood that further abuse will occur. If a report is to be made, appropriate persons must be chosen to do so, perhaps including the alleged abuser.

Once government agencies are involved, the meeting will have little to say about how "the case" is handled from a legal point of view. The meeting will then be challenged with a responsibility for continuing support: seeking healing and reconciliation for the sake of the victim (first of all), and also for the sake of the community and the offender.

Recently a pastoral caregiver from another part of the country shared with me how a small core of trusted Friends in her meeting struggled years ago with these questions. A young girl just moving into puberty had been caressed inappropriately by the male leader on a Young Friends outing. She told her parents, who immediately raised it with a member of the pastoral care committee. The abuser was not a stranger to the meeting, but rather was valued for his spiritual contribution to the meeting and was the father of a young family. A small group of those involved in meeting leadership decided to give careful and on-going attention to his roles in the meeting, seeing that he had no responsibility for children. They suggested that he seek treatment. But (this was twenty years ago) no report to public authorities was made. He may not have followed through on the recommendation that he seek therapy, and the girl and her family were not fully informed of the steps that the meeting had taken. Years later the girl, by then a woman, contacted the meeting and expressed her upset and disappointment that more had not been done.

In the intervening years another sexual violation occurred, perpetrated by the same man with yet another young person. This time the meeting followed through in a fuller and more thorough way. The Friend sharing the story, however, reflected on what the years have taught. If the original incident were to occur today, (1) the wider meeting would have been made aware of what had occurred and would have been given an opportunity to talk openly about the issues raised, (2) there would have been appropriate counseling and other support for the young person, her family and friends, and (3) the local child protective agency would have become involved.

Much more could be said on this topic. We have not even begun to mention, for example, the reality that some meeting children are being sexually abused in their families. While thankfully sexual abuse in our meetings and/or wrongful accusation of adults are relatively rare, this is a topic which warrants our attention.

Lindley M. Winston is a member of Willistown (PA) Meeting. He has served for many years as the consulting psychiatrist of the Friends Counseling Service.

A Quaker Survivor of Sexual Abuse Tells Her Story

I'm an active middle-aged woman and a lifelong Quaker. I work in the nonprofit world with children and their parents. I grew up in what was considered a "good family." But there was a lot of abuse, including sexual abuse. My father repeatedly raped me during my childhood. It's scary to admit, and although my father is deceased I still can hear the threats inside me, saying that I deserved it. I learned early on that my mother would not—could not—protect me. She had her own problems.

I was twelve years old before I realized that the "hitting" I was getting was far different from what happened in most other families. My main focus throughout childhood was to be good, to be invisible. I assumed that when my father abused me it must be my fault.

My father was a prominent person in the town I grew up in. He was active in the meeting, and people respected him for the good things he did. They never saw the other side of my father. Because my father was so well regarded, as a child I felt that nobody would believe me if I were to tell them about the violence. Also, my father threatened me, and I feared that if I told anyone the abuse would get worse.

How could someone like my father, who was apparently an upstanding member of the community, be so abusive? It was a power thing. He needed to keep everything under control, under his power. If my brother and I didn't follow him—or if he thought or imagined that we did something wrong—we got hit. The sexual part of the abuse was not about sex; it was about power. It was my father's way of being stronger, exerting power or control over me. It's like other kinds of abuse, in saying "I can hurt you! You will do as I say!" It was a release for my father's violence and anger, in a way that allowed him to maintain the image of the good citizen.

Years later, as an adult, when I spoke about my abuse for the first time to someone at the meeting where I grew up, I just wanted that person to listen. I needed somebody in the meeting to hear about it, to believe that it happened, to confirm that it is part of reality. Like other survivors, I'm very sensitive to the reaction of others. It took courage for me to talk about it, and I had no intention of hurting the meeting member I was talking to, or making her feel guilty. However, I recognized that what I was saying, and the pain that I still had, scared her, so I stopped talking.

My advice to those involved in pastoral care is that you learn how to listen. Just listening can be OK. Even if you're uncomfortable with what you're hearing, don't be afraid of it; don't let it hurt you. And don't feel that you have to "fix" it. **Then accept what I say as true. Accept it even if it flies against everything you think you know about the person who abused me. Realize that sexual abuse of children can happen, that Quakers aren't immune. Then, later, don't share what I say with others until you've asked my permission.**

Going to meeting has been important to me all of my life. It has shown me that, in contrast to the ways of my family, there are peaceful ways. Quakerism shows that there is goodness, even when things feel so awful. It teaches me that there is goodness in me, though for many years I thought I was a bad person. And there is God in all.

The meeting where I am a member is a safe place. It's OK to cry in meeting. Problems can be discussed openly. People are there if I need to talk about something. My yearly meeting has sponsored several support groups for Quakers who have been sexually abused. There have been supportive activities for survivors of sexual abuse at the FGC Annual Gathering, and *Friends Journal* has published articles.

This openness can help Quakers get past the concept "not in our meeting" or "not in our town." It can help Friends get past their need to believe that "that type of person just wouldn't do that." I personally know two more people from established Quaker families who experienced sexual abuse, and no doubt there are many others that I don't know about. Quakers need to remember that we're not perfect.

Questions for Reflection

1. How ready are we to deal with the issue of potential sexual abuse within our meeting? Do we have the courage to acknowledge that the issue of sexual abuse does stir deep feelings?
2. What support do we, as a meeting, need so that we can move forward on this issue? Can we stop and reflect on how our basic beliefs as Friends can serve us in this quest?
3. How does our meeting decide on people to work with our children and young people? What orientation do we give them? What resources are available if they have problems?
4. What is the legal obligation, in our county and state, to report incidents of possible child abuse, sexual or physical? Are we prepared to report, to support reporters, and to see the case pass out of our control and into the law enforcement realm?

PASTORAL CARE FOR PERSONS WITH MENTAL ILLNESS

HELPING FRIENDS SEEK PROFESSIONAL HELP

PASTORAL CARE FOR PERSONS
WITH MENTAL ILLNESS

DEPRESSION: THE INVISIBLE PROBLEM

ALCOHOLISM IN THE MEETING

Helping Friends Seek Professional Help

Pastoral Care Newsletter, Vol. 5, No. 1 • September 1997

by Barbara T. Snipes

WE ARE ENCOURAGED AS FRIENDS to "keep in loving fellowship with those who are growing in a living experimental faith in God, and be available also for individual consultation with members and with seekers facing religious problems."[1]

As Friends, we know that living faith can be nurtured and fed in the depths of a centered meeting for worship and enlivened into service by the loving faith community. We also know that almost all problems or questions are religious or spiritual at heart and that, often, an individual consultation with an experienced Friend can ease a situation or point toward solutions.

But what about those among us who seem constantly stressed and anxious? What about the older Friend who lives alone, becomes handicapped, and can't afford a Friends retirement facility? What about the family whose teenage son is in trouble with drugs or alcohol or the law? What about the Friend who is excessively angry and becomes disruptive during worship, or the one who is withdrawn and may be considering suicide? What about the person who is just irritating and needy and with whom we experience a gut reaction that something is wrong? What about the married couple in trouble? The unmarried couple in trouble? The children of divorced parents who are angry and disruptive?

Our pastoral caregivers are increasingly inundated with human problems, reflecting the problems of the larger, stressed community. We have to be prudent in acknowledging our limitations, personally and as a committee, and be aware of when we are beyond our capacities. We have to be prepared and ready to facilitate a member's access to professional assistance.

[1] Philadelphia Yearly Meeting, *Faith and Practice*, 1972, p. 144.

But how do we go about getting additional help? When and how do we call on professional help? What is professional help anyway?

A person in the helping professions—doctor, nurse, lawyer, teacher, counselor, geriatric social worker, body work therapist, rescue worker, firefighter, police person—has done extra study and is trained for the work she or he does. These professionals also have daily experience with the problems they deal with and can refer to someone with more expertise in the field when needed. If the person is also a practicing Friend, active in a meeting and nurturing a personal spiritual life, we can usually consult him or her with the expectation that they will understand the concerns of Friends.

Identifying the Need

When a person is in emotional distress or exhibiting unusual behavior, meeting members are usually aware of it on some level. Those who sit near her in meeting or are with him during social hour or on committees often know that something is wrong. Reaching out to the person in a spirit of love, and without judgment, can be a first step. If someone can spend a little time over coffee after meeting with a person, ways may be found in which the meeting may be helpful. Simply asking the question "Do you see ways that we in the meeting might be helpful to you?" may open the way to explore with the pastoral care committee the advisability of calling on professional help.

On one Sunday, a young man wrote furiously during meeting and then tried to read his material to the group at announcement time. When he was asked to sit down, he became angry and walked out. A Friend followed him out, discovered he wanted help with his alcohol problem. The Friend felt free to recommend Alcoholics Anonymous. He found out where and when the local group met and went with the young man to the first meeting. He then went to the meeting's pastoral care committee with his concern that there were additional problems that needed addressing. The young man had severe periods of depression and thoughts of suicide. Pastoral care provided him with the telephone numbers of several alcohol treatment centers in the area and offered to talk with the man's parents about financial help from the meeting. The young man decided to take advantage of all that was offered and is in recovery now. He needed a residential program, medication and individual counseling.

Sometimes it is better to first take the concern to pastoral care. There we can receive greater light from the group and learn if there has been a history of outreach to this person. We can ask, "Have others been aware of the problem?" "Have pastoral caregivers tried to meet with that person?" "Do others in the group think that professional help is needed?"

Occasionally there is a Friend who has gone from one sympathetic meeting member to another, using a listening ear as a way to avoid taking positive action to work on the problem at hand. By consulting with the caregiving committee, the concerned Friend creates an opportunity to recognize this pattern. Then the committee can develop a coordinated approach for helping the person move forward. Professional support is often needed in helping such persons face up to the issues and address them.

Discernment, as I understand Friends' use of the word, is a process whereby the larger group can test, focus and hold an individual concern in the light through prayer and discussion. Members of the caregiving committee can help lift up a concern to see if others share it. If Friends feel clear to proceed, someone who knows the person can sit down with him or her, explore the situation, and recommend appropriate professional help.

The pastoral care committee can keep from being overwhelmed by keeping informed about professional resources in their community and by knowing which ones of their number are more comfortable talking with persons in need about addictions, family crises, children, grief, death, loss of jobs, mental illness, depression and so on. One committee member may be able to talk more easily to the Friend who needs immediate attention and take him or her to the hospital. Another may feel able to visit a family in crisis and help to call a neighborhood mediator or a social worker. There are those among us who are familiar with therapists who are trained as addiction counselors and are able to talk sensitively to a troubled person about many of the nearby 12 step programs, including Alcoholics Anonymous, Alanon, Adult Children of Alcoholics, Overeaters Anonymous and many others. Some caregivers know, or could find out about, low cost housing, welfare rights, how the local justice system works and help the person decide if one of these resources would be helpful.

Most communities have Family Service Associations with professional counselors dedicated to strengthen and enrich family life including individual growth and adjustment. Baltimore Yearly Meeting maintains a list of Quaker counselors, and perhaps other yearly meetings do as well. Philadelphia Yearly Meeting sponsors the Friends Counseling Service with counselors available to Friends and consultation available to meetings.

Lawyers can deal with matters of custody, visitation, division of property, child support. They also can quickly obtain from a court a protective order against abuse. Increasingly, lawyers and some family counselors are being trained in mediation and can assist separating or divorcing couples and others with disputes to be less adversarial and to be more supportive.

The medical profession and many insurance providers are moving toward more holistic approaches that treat the whole person instead of just the symptoms. Clinics are available that offer chiropractic, homeopathy, naturopathy and stress management programs. Yoga, meditation, tai chi, shiatsu, massage and many other systems can be very helpful in maintaining bodily, mental and spiritual health.

Meetings can be prepared to provide financial aid or to help with transportation and childcare to facilitate consultation with professional help. It is helpful to be informed about support available from your yearly meeting and other Quaker sources.

What If the Help Is Rejected

The ideal caregiving committee would have developed a deep caring relationship among themselves. They would be able to share success and failures in their own lives. They would be able to hold each other accountable to the light within, which makes it easier to call on professional help when needed. Pastoral caregivers need to worship together, listen to one another, and have fun together, so that they can have the group stability to reach out to others. Being attentive to one another's feelings and concerns can help us to be aware of those difficulties that lie beyond the scope of caring Friends. When we feel supported ourselves, it is much easier to approach someone needing help in a relaxed natural way, without fear of rejection.

Now, supposing I am the one delegated by the caregiving committee to be in touch with a member or family in distress. I'm ready to recommend and help make the phone call to arrange the appointment for help in their situation. But I'm afraid that instead of accepting my help they will become furious, accuse me of meddling and being intrusive, and reject any offers to set up appointments. What happens then?

These ideal caregivers would listen well to me and validate me as a person, as well as my gifts and skills. They may advise me that I'm off track in my suggested intervention. Committee members need to be able to say "No, you are not the one," or "This is not the time to help these people seek a professional." We need to be flexible and abide by the sense of the meeting.

Or they might select another committee member to accompany me or to support me behind the scenes. We could remind ourselves to concentrate on the person's pain and point out how the professional can make things easier. The best way is probably to listen well ourselves, to pay full attention to the person needing outside help, and to take the person and the problem very, very seriously.

Pastoral caregivers making these visits will need encouragement and help to realize that it is all right to fail.

Reluctance to Seek Counseling

Friends are often reluctant to seek counseling. They may fear stigma attached to seeing a counselor or an implication of mental illness. We can help by sharing good experiences in counseling. We can normalize the experience of counseling by sharing personal stories of growth and transformation resulting from counseling. Only a small proportion of people who need or seek counseling are mentally ill. Often short term therapy is all that's needed to help a person sort out the issue that is distressing them.

When our son Howard and his wife Susan were killed in a snow storm in Wyoming on their honeymoon, our family was in crisis. When Friends asked what they could do to help, we asked for a few Friends to come each evening for a week or so to meet with us in worship. As family members and meeting Friends gathered in our Quaker ritual of worship, we found we could weep together, or rail in anger and distress, and feel supported by the intimate group. We felt the true meaning of the phrase "under the care of the meeting."

I was led to seek professional help in my profound misery. I found that by repeating the story of their deaths over and over in the presence of a skilled counselor who helped me express my feelings of anger and despair, I could be eased into my long grief process (7 years) with more hope. I feel now that my meeting and professional help, along with loving husband and children, were essential in my healing—a growing and transforming process. I am convinced that a "deepening" can follow a major loss, debilitating accident or illness and that greater compassion for others and a more profound capacity for joy can be the result. Somehow the terrible wounding of a tragedy or illness makes more room within for God's light and love.

The Loving Community

If we could spend more time together with our meeting family, our faith community, it would deepen our relationships. Then we could be more clear and direct when we need help in asking for a professional. It would be easier to say, "I'm constantly depressed," or "My daughter won't go to school, do you know where I could get help?" It would be easier to say "Would you feel comfortable in taking this concern to the pastoral care committee? They have lists of professionals who can offer a variety of assistance."

Small groups are a good way to foster deeper relationships. Committee meetings needn't be all business. They could start with sharing meaningful events in our lives, followed by worship, then business, and ending with (short) hopes and dreams for ourselves and the meeting. A format that gets us sharing on a deeper, more personal level can lead to more openness and more joyful committee meetings, and can make it more natural to ask for and suggest outside help when needed.

The religious community implies that we are all part of one another. For those among us who are in crisis or whose lives are confused or painful, Friends may find times when it is helpful to call on professionals as a way to "keep in loving fellowship with those who are growing in a living experimental faith in God."

Barbara T. Snipes was a lifelong Friend and longtime member of Falls Meeting in Bucks County, PA. She served on Friends Counseling Service and as a spiritual nurturer. She died in 2001.

Where to Turn When Caregivers Need Professional Support

Start at home. Often by networking within the meeting it is possible to get information that will lead you to the resources you need.

Call your Yearly Meeting Office or Yearly Meeting Committee on Ministry and Counsel. They can inform you of resources within the yearly meeting. Even yearly meetings with little or no staff sometimes have volunteer consultants available to help meetings find resources. They may also be able to refer you to another meeting in the yearly meeting which has faced a similar issue who might have excellent information based on their experience.

Consult your local council of churches about resources utilized by other churches for counselors, attorneys, housing services and other emergencies.

Call a community referral service. Most communities have an information and referral service run by the county government or by the United Way. These services have wide ranging listings for emergency hotlines, social services, housing, legal aid, protective services. They are useful in identifying low cost or free services.

Questions for Reflection

1. In what ways do we cultivate a climate that makes it easy for Friends to talk about their needs and for the meeting's caregivers to acknowledge their limitations?
2. How do we, individually and as a committee, recognize when we are reaching our limits?
3. How do we discern when to recommend to members that they seek professional assistance from outside the meeting?
4. What do we do to create a sense of loving community within the pastoral caregiving committee?
5. What supports do we provide to a committee member who is charged with conveying the committee's recommendation that a member seek professional help?
6. What preparation have we made for identifying appropriate professional referrals when needed? What additional preparations would be useful?

Pastoral Care for Persons with Mental Illness

Pastoral Care Newsletter, Vol. 4, No. 2 • January 1997

by Joseph Rogers

In this essay we present two perspectives on Friends' response to persons with mental illness. The first is by Joseph Rogers, an international consultant on mental health consumer advocacy. He looks at pastoral care from the point of view of an active Friend who struggles with long term mental illness. The second section provides concrete suggestions for pastoral caregivers from an experienced Friend and mental health consultant, Lee Junker.

> I'm sitting in Quaker meeting at age 19, hoping to connect with God and with other people; but my state of mind is making both of these goals nearly impossible to attain. Lately, I have been finding the world increasingly difficult to deal with and don't have a clue about how to begin to relate to the people around me, let alone to God. In fact, I'm in a state of panic about making it through the day.

This is what it was like for me 25 years ago, when I was trying to participate in a small meeting in Orlando, Florida. Most of the members were older and were baffled about how to deal with the relatively recent influx of young, disheveled, hippie-looking kids. Luckily there were a few members who had the inclination and expertise to reach out to a troubled youth.

Today I am both a person who uses mental health services and deputy executive director of a large mental health organization. In my work I have been able to learn about the needs and desires of many others who are coping with a wide range of mental and emotional issues.

My pastoral needs are similar to most people's. I look to a Quaker community to provide a place for worship where I can engage in a dialogue with God and find support in my spiritual seeking. I also see my Quaker meeting as a place to make contacts with other seekers and to get involved in a community. Like most folks with mental illness I have lots of trouble-free times. The ways in which people can assist me in my quest to connect with the community are not very different from the ways in which you would help anyone.

There are times, though, when my mental disability interferes with my participation in the meeting community. At those times, engaging fully in the Friends community has been a challenge, both for myself and for the leadership and members of the meeting.

It is most difficult when I'm in the throes of what I like to consider not just an acute manic episode but a spiritual crisis. When I'm "highest" spiritually may also be when my mind is racing 100 miles a minute and my ability to communicate with people from Planet Earth is limited. But, over the years, I have found that the response I get from people in Quaker meetings can be very helpful—in my spiritual quest and my quest to connect with Earthlings.

When my state of mind is most confused, I have found it helpful to have people reach out and express their concern. Unfortunately, people often react to someone with emotional problems by looking the other way.

When a person is experiencing emotional turmoil within the context of a worship community, there's a tendency to ignore the elephant in the living room. A friend of mine who was in a church leadership position recalls that when he was in a state of severe crisis, no one in his religious community wanted to deal with his obviously bizarre behavior. It's a form of denial—maybe if we ignore it, it will go away.

Also, if we don't know a person particularly well or if we know them in the context of when they're "doing well" or if they have a leadership role, we may feel that an expression of concern is too intrusive.

We have to respect people's privacy to some degree—but not at the cost of helping. So I recommend reaching out to someone in distress. This does not mean to provide mental health treatment. The meeting is not there to substitute for the very extensive mental health system. We're there as a spiritual community, and our primary mission should be to support people in their spiritual quest.

Reaching out can have an enormous impact. Once, in the throes of what the doctors would call a manic episode, I showed up at Quaker meeting at 8 in the morning and decided to begin preaching the gospel to the community at large. Shortly after I began to noisily broadcast my message, several police cars arrived. Since an emergency number was posted on the door of the meeting, a member of the pastoral care committee was called. She felt she could handle the situation and convinced the police that she could deal with me. She then took me to her home for breakfast, and later to meeting.

This simple act of kindness made a significant difference in my life. Obviously, it kept me out of trouble with the police but, more importantly, it showed me someone cared.

Not everyone can do what this Friend did. Some people are concerned about their own ability to be of help, and are fearful of becoming over-involved with an individual who may be troublesome or overwhelmed by someone who is "intense." In a very few cases, especially if illegal drugs or alcohol are involved, people who are very agitated and upset can strike out and hurt someone. It is important for each of us to acknowledge our limitations. At the same time, however, we can acknowledge the strength of what we know how to do by reaching out to the health in a person. Reaching out to that of God in a troubled person is what we are called to as Friends. We all know how to invite someone to lunch after meeting or make a friendly phone call to say we know that it is a hard time and we are holding them in prayer.

Certain people are better at this than others are, so Pastoral Care and Worship and Ministry might—before the need arises—create a "protocol" for handling people who are experiencing serious emotional problems. However, since we are a spiritual community and not a mental health clinic, these matters should not be assigned to special squads made up only of professionally trained Friends—the ones with Ph.D.s and M.S.W.s, etc. There should be a variety of folks who are interested in reaching out. In fact, some of the best helpers in this context may be those without clinical training. No one comes to Quaker meeting to find a therapist (although appropriate referrals can be useful); they come to be involved in a community. I have found that having friends who are there because they want to be my friends can be much more helpful than having one more person who treats me as an object of clinical interest.

Sometimes it may be helpful to inquire about issues such as: Have you taken your medication? Are you getting treatment? Are you dealing with your mental illness? But it is important not to get bogged down in these issues. As a meeting we should do what we are charged by God to do: to help in a person's healing through practices of our faith. The most effective way in which we can engage people, whether their suffering is physical or mental, may be through prayer.

Often, even in my secular work in the field of mental health, I have found that Quaker practices can be the most effective way of dealing with someone in turmoil. I remember walking onto a forensic unit to interview someone who was brought to me in shackles. When I asked that the shackles be removed, the staff responded that, if they removed the shackles, the person would more than likely physically assault me. I still insisted that the shackles be taken off. And I could feel the expectation in the room: shackles off means violence. I was in a quandary about how to engage the person, because I didn't want to be beaten up. So I called on my training as a Quaker and sat in silence, waiting for Divine guidance.

At first the person was obviously agitated and on the verge of doing what was expected of him. But after about 15 minutes of silence, he took a big breath; I could see his muscles begin to relax and a quiet came over him. In about 20 minutes we were engaged in very productive conversation.

As Quakers, we're taught to seek silent and meditative approaches. When we are dealing with someone who seems very unquiet and disturbed, we can forget that; but sitting in silence, especially one on one, and helping someone center down and become focused can become the most healing opportunity. We usually start with quiet, meditative prayer but, after a while, we can become involved in a mutual dialogue or three-way discussion: myself, the person sitting across from me, and God. I can't tell you how often I have found this prayerful approach useful for working with someone who's highly agitated or disturbed. A silent prayerful presence can also be very helpful when a person is depressed and very withdrawn.

We have some of the most useful and beautiful tools in our training as Quakers for helping people accomplish what they want to in a spiritual search. When someone who has serious emotional problems needs or wants to be supported through pastoral care, these tools should be fully engaged. Our work as ministers of Christ is to reach and seek that of Christ in others. What greater challenge and what more exciting result than to work with individuals who, because of a mental illness, are plagued by demons. To find that quiet place and that quiet time to help soothe those demons is our challenge.

Joseph Rogers has been a leader of the mental health consumer movement, working to give consumers a decisive voice in the design and delivery of mental health services. He has served as executive director of the Mental Health Association of Southeastern Pennsylvania. He is a member of Central Philadelphia Monthly Meeting.

Suggestions for Pastoral Caregivers

BY LEE JUNKER

Remember That People with Mental Illness Are People First

If we are unfamiliar with serious mental illness, we can find it fright-
ening, and this fear can sometimes prevent us from seeing the person as
distinct from his/her illness. It is important that we provide understanding and outreach to our members and recognize that they have wonderful gifts and abilities like everyone else, which can and do greatly enrich
our meeting communities. We also need to look for ways to communicate to these individuals that they are cherished, valued and accepted.

Mental Illness May Not Be What You Think

The term mental illness covers a range of serious disorders which
impact on a person's mental, social and emotional capabilities. Joseph
Rogers describes situations when a person's behavior alerts us to their
situation. Not all are so obvious to the external observer. It is often the
case that we are unaware when one of our members is struggling with
an emotional disability.

Most professionals in the field now recognize that mental illness
does have a biological basis. Fortunately, with the new developments
in pharmacology, its symptoms can generally be managed successfully.
People with schizophrenia or affective disorders (manic depressive illness or severe and persistent depression) are often able to lead productive and satisfying lives with the help of medication, and suffer only
occasional relapses. Some, however, are not helped by medication or
have difficulty with significant side effects.

Creating an Accepting Environment within the Meeting Community

Society at large attaches a terrible stigma to mental illness. People
with this disability often feel ashamed, embarrassed and sometimes
even guilty about their illness. If they feel their meeting shares the perceptions of the larger society, they will be hesitant to ask for help. After
an episode in which they may have acted out in strange ways or had a
psychiatric hospitalization, they may be loath to return to meeting.

For this reason, it is helpful if the meeting's caregivers are educated about mental illness and help the meeting community to become better informed. Meeting libraries should include some resources, and adult education classes can explore this topic. It can be very helpful to ask a meeting member with mental illness to speak with the caregiving committee about his/her experience with this disease or to write an article for the meeting newsletter.

It is helpful for Friends to talk openly and honestly with the person about his/her situation, and in times of illness not to be hesitant to express genuine concern for the person's well being. Looking for ways to express support and care is particularly important when individuals are in the grip of a severe depression and tend to withdraw, both physically and emotionally, from everyone. We should, of course, always ask the individual if he/she wishes information about the illness to remain confidential. However, it is my own personal conviction that we should help our members be open about their disability, reminding them that we are their faith community, and we care about them and support them in good times and bad.

Offering to Form a Support Group

Sometimes individuals with mental illness appreciate having a small support group in which they can discuss issues related to their lives. However, as Joe Rogers says in his article, Friends need not and should not try to be mental health professionals. We can function primarily as caring and supportive F/friends.

One question which might be asked of the individual is what he or she would find helpful at those times when the illness is taking over and he or she may not be aware of it. For example, sometimes people with manic depressive illness may become manic and either not recognize it or, because of the nature of the illness, choose to disregard the symptoms; or a person who suffers from depression may withdraw from the community. Talking about such possibilities in advance of the occurrence gives Friends a strategy about what to do in a problem or crisis situation.

Establishing Boundaries

Although Friends need to create accepting and nurturing environments, it does not mean that we should not take action when a person behaves inappropriately, such as giving disruptive messages in meeting for worship or preventing a committee meeting from accomplishing its work. When such situations occur, Friends should take action both to safeguard the meeting and to try to obtain help for the individual. For example, individuals can be told that they are not permitted to attend worship or committee meetings until they are better. Sometimes the meeting may have to brainstorm strategies to be effective in such situations. In some cases, Friends may need to be in touch with the individual's family or the treating mental health professional to ensure that the individual is getting the necessary help.

As previously mentioned, developing a strategy with the individual in advance of a crisis situation is a good remedy. This may involve having the individual give written consent to his/her doctor for a specified meeting member to be able to talk with the professional about the situation. Unless such a written consent is given, the mental health professional is not permitted to release any information about his/her patient, including the fact that the individual is in treatment.

Seeking Guidance

In all situations, we should seek for the guidance of the Spirit.

Lee Junker is a former clerk of Overseers at Central Philadelphia Monthly Meeting. She is a consultant in the Philadelphia public mental health system.

Questions for Reflection

1. Is our meeting supportive and loving toward persons among us who may be struggling with mental illness?
2. How do we reach out to the health in the person? How do we support the person's spiritual quest?
3. In what ways are we alert to signs of severe emotional distress our members may be experiencing? How can we prepare ourselves to respond appropriately when the need arises?
4. What can we do to create an environment in which the meeting and a member with mental illness work together to find ways to meet the needs of both?
5. If the illness of one among us has unsettling manifestations, how are we able to help others in the meeting to be understanding?
6. How can the pastoral care committee prepare the meeting to be clear and firm when someone's behavior in the meeting community is inappropriate?

DEPRESSION: THE INVISIBLE PROBLEM

Pastoral Care Newsletter, Vol. 5, No. 2 • January 1998

BY NANCY L. BIEBER

The previous article, "Pastoral Care for Persons with Mental Illness" (p. 224), principally addresses the more outward and noticeable forms of mental illness. We felt that it would be helpful to provide a companion article on the less easily recognized, but equally serious, problem of depression.

Depression is sometimes called the invisible problem. It is very common, but its victims often become less noticeable rather than more so. Is it invisibly present in your meeting?

Almost certainly every sizable monthly meeting includes persons who are depressed.* They may be suffering silently, depressed but unable to give a name to their feelings. Some people know they are dealing with depression and may be taking antidepressant medication, but they are quiet and ashamed about it. And then there are those who are open about their struggles and fortunately are not burdened by the uncomfortable sense that they have failed in some vague but important way.

What Is Depression?

A person who is depressed may hear most often from family or friends some variation of "snap out of it." There is nothing a depressed person would like better than to snap out of it, but it doesn't work that way. Our culture as a whole does not understand depression, and therefore is often not helpful to those who are struggling with it.

---

* The term "depression" as used in this article refers to "clinical depression," an ongoing, serious condition. We are not referring to the common use of the word to mean the occasional low day which everyone experiences from time to time.

Degrees of depression can be arranged along a continuum. At one end would be someone with a persistent lowness of spirit. Such a person may have low energy and may not seem to care much about things which used to be important. They may feel confused by the low mood but be unable to shake it off. Life isn't the way it used to be. This is a relatively mild experience of depression.

A more serious depression includes the experience of being burdened with sadness, not necessarily sadness about a particular grief, but a global, heavy grief. Spells of crying are common. As we look toward the severe depression, we see an increasing hopelessness. There is a very real sense that it's no use going on. Usually people struggle on though. Perhaps their responsibility for a child or a spouse or someone else who needs them keeps them going, but not always. Tragically, existence can seem so painful and hopeless that sometimes suicide seems to be the only way out.

It may be useful to think of the degrees of depression as the wearing of an increasingly dark pair of glasses. The worse the experience of depression, the darker the world appears. Sometimes someone can hobble along for years wearing the dark glasses of a mild or moderate depression. Sometimes a depression may lift suddenly and inexplicably. With equal mystery, it may return.

The traditional view has been that there are two kinds of depression, one triggered by life events and the other by body biochemistry. At this time therapists generally feel that life events and body biochemistry interweave to create a depressed state. A life event such as the death of a close family member may trigger a depression which may produce biochemical changes in the body. Sometimes there is no apparent precipitating event; a shift in a person's biochemistry brings on a depressed state without warning.

Depression touches every aspect of the sufferer's life. The effects on one's emotions have already been mentioned: lowness of spirit, sadness, hopelessness, enormous self-doubt. Physically, a depressed person may be tired much of the time, and yet unable to get a good night's sleep. Eating habits may change. Usually it is a loss of appetite, but sometimes a depressed person turns to food for pleasure and comfort and seems to be eating all the time. Mental agility can be slowed down and one's thinking can seem foggy. Socially, a depressed person may not have the energy or the desire to maintain the friendships of happier times.

The Depressed Person within the Meeting Community

Depression can also have a very painful effect on one's spiritual life. God may be lost in a fog, too. One questions the reality of the faith one depended on. Depression does not always create a "dark night of the soul" but it can do so. When it does, it is easy not to bother coming to meeting for worship. Sitting in silence for an hour may feel like drowning in the reality of God's absence.

One reason that we come to meeting for worship rather than worshiping at home is that we need community. It is a basic human need. Community roots us among others who are on similar spiritual journeys into the presence of God. When we come together only for meeting for worship yet have minimal contact with each other the rest of the time, we are not being much of a community for each other. In that kind of distant community, it is easy for someone to become invisible, invisible first while present and then through not being there at all. The better we know each other, the less easy it is for that to happen.

We Quakers are very respectful of each other's spiritual journeys. When someone drops out of community worship and committee involvements, we may assume that person simply needs a break from active participation. Our fear of interfering may prevent us from expressing an appropriate concern about an absence. When no friendly inquiry is made—"I just thought I'd call and see if you were all right"—a depressed person can easily conclude that no one has noticed and no one cares.

The lowered energy and bleak sadness of depression combine to make it very hard for a depressed person to initiate or even accept social contacts. Yet when contacts are initiated by someone reaching out, they can give a real boost to one for whom each day is a struggle. There is a sense that others do care and value this Friend's presence.

How to Help

Helping persons who may be depressed calls for a sensitive awareness and a reaching out. It calls for thoughtfulness and consideration for those who may be on the fringes of the meeting community. Unlike the person who demands attention through inappropriate behavior, a depressed person is not likely to demand attention unless desperate and/or feeling a special closeness to the confidant. Men may be especially unwilling to talk about the dark burden under which they are living until they are desperately unhappy.

When meeting members do reach out, it is important not to expect enthusiastic appreciation and a rapid and eager involvement in meeting activities. It may be all a depressed person can do to attend the committee meeting; taking on responsibility may simply be too hard. However, the meeting needs to continue reaching out. If someone broke a leg and couldn't drive to meeting, we would not stop driving for as long as a ride was needed, not expect one effort at chauffeuring to jump-start a person's driving ability again!

Overcoming depression, or at least bringing it to a manageable state, is usually a slow process. (An exception is the effect of an antidepressant medication which can create positive change within a few weeks.) Someone supporting a depressed Friend needs to encourage small steps. Steps like going for a walk in the evening or coming to a social gathering or cleaning up the kitchen (only the kitchen, not the whole house!) may be big enough challenges for a person whose energy has been sapped by depression.

One of the symptoms of depression is pessimism, the expectation that things will never work out. This shows itself in a "what's the use, why bother?" attitude and in negative statements. Supportive friends can become discouraged when all suggestions and encouragement seem to be rejected. They may gradually drift away from the relationship. Recognizing the negativity as a symptom of depression, not a rejection of friendship, can help to maintain the steady support which is so urgently needed.

It is also possible to counter negativity. "I know it might not be a good program, but I'd like to go with you anyway." Acknowledging someone's feelings while holding out the possibility that there is another way to view the situation is useful. "I see what you mean. If I thought my son didn't care about me, I might not feel like calling him either. But I think he really does care about you, only he's not good at showing it."

A change in a specific life situation may bring a lightening of depression. The flow of winter to spring sometimes lifts mild depression. A move to another working environment when the old one has been stressful and critical may have a similar result. Clearly the meeting cannot make these things happen. But we can help in small ways. What would happen if a depressed person hovering on the fringes of the meeting were to be surrounded by a group of people who obviously cared and showed it continually and clearly by their actions? It would definitely be a health-giving environment with a real potential for healing.

The meeting might form a support group for the depressed person and/or the family in situations involving a chronic, long-term illness or a crisis situation involving hospitalization. Unlike a clearness committee for discernment, it is not focused on a decision-making process. It might consist of two or three persons who regularly visit or it could engage the gifts of six or eight persons who help in a variety of ways. Regular contacts by phone may be as important as formal meetings. The group must be custom designed for the need and the person it will be responding to.

Although every group wants to help by doing, often the most valuable contribution of the group is simply being. Simply being present to another brings comfort and encouragement and alleviates loneliness. It is often easier for supporters to feel useful when they are doing something concrete to alleviate distress. However, sometimes the most useful thing is to say, "I can't do anything but I want you to know I am with you," and then to sit together.

Meeting members working closely with a depressed person may need to encourage him or her to get professional help. Often people are reluctant to seek professional help and even more hesitant to take medication. Our unfortunate cultural bias toward perceiving depression as a personal weakness which should be overcome by positive thinking is very powerful.

It is clear, however, that medication and psychotherapy do help. Antidepressants help the body's biochemistry to return to a normal balance. Psychotherapy helps one to deal with the emotional, mental and social experiences of depression. Through therapy, a person may work on a whole spectrum of troubling areas. Often the emotional and social symptoms of depression stir up unresolved problems of the past or worsen already difficult relationships. Psychotherapy can help to resolve these areas.

What about the Risk of Suicide?

The more serious the depression, the more real is the possibility of suicide. This is the scariest aspect of depression, both to depressed people and to their friends. If a meeting has provided a supportive environment, a depressed person may speak to someone about thoughts and intents before taking action. When a friend hears about suicidal thoughts, it is essential to involve professional help. Options here include a 24-hour phone hotline, a mental health crisis intervention service, a contact phone line, the local mental health association, or, if it is known, the physician, psychiatrist or psychotherapist who has been involved.

Turning to professional help is not magic however. Nothing can guarantee to prevent suicide. But in a loving, caring community, we can provide a nurturing net for especially vulnerable persons. Sometimes friends think that a promise of confidentiality means that one should never speak, even if someone has confided an intent to end his or her life. Confidentiality should not interfere with saving a life. Some think that a person who speaks of suicide will not actually do it. There is no substance to that myth. No depressed person's words about suicide should be taken lightly.

It is true that some depressed persons end their lives with no fore-warning to others. We look back and say, "What should we have seen?" "What should we have done?" It may be that the signs were indeed minimal. Many people keep up a good front while in deep, painful hopelessness within themselves. We may be berating ourselves to no good purpose. Perhaps the only good which can rise from the tragic experience of a suicide within a meeting comes when the meeting community grows more aware of and sensitive to its most vulnerable members, when we learn better how to show our caring for each other.

A meeting can become a caring, supportive community for someone who is depressed. It is important that such an effort be spread among a number of people. If it is an on-going situation with all the support coming from one or two persons, they may well burn out. Those who are giving care need also to be taking care of themselves. Support persons need to recognize and honor their limitations. They need to recognize when a peaceful evening at home is essential for their well-being. Giving to others in any fashion is easier when we are filled up ourselves. Supporters need to take the time to do and be that which keeps them filled. Thus the depressed person, the supporters and the entire meeting community benefit.

At the beginning of this article, depression was called invisible. When we know the clues to look for, we can make it visible. When our awareness and compassion are tuned to other members of our meeting community, we can make it visible. When we know that we can help, we are more likely to be aware of and compassionate toward the depressed person in our midst. We can then be, in the fullest sense of the word, Friends in time of need.

Nancy L. Bieber is a psychologist and a spiritual director. She frequently leads retreats for Quakers and other religious groups. She is a member of Lancaster (PA) Meeting where she has served as clerk.

Questions for Reflection

1. Does your meeting provide a safe environment for sharing painful parts of one's life? How does it do so? How could it do more to provide an environment that nurtures sharing?
2. What efforts is the pastoral care committee making to be aware of persons who may be withdrawn and depressed?
3. How is the committee (and others in the meeting community) actively supporting anyone who is dealing with depression?
4. What are limitations for pastoral caregivers or other supportive group in providing long-term support for a depressed person? How do caregivers in a long-term supportive relationship support themselves?
5. If there has been a suicide within the meeting community, how did the meeting provide support for family and special friends? How did the meeting come to terms with this death? If your meeting has not experienced a suicide in its midst, think about how you would handle it.

ALCOHOLISM IN THE MEETING

Pastoral Care Newsletter, Vol. 6, No. 3 • March 1999

AN INTERVIEW WITH ALEX SCOTT

Alcoholism is not something we often think about concerning our meetings. Could it be that nearly all meetings have active or recovering alcoholics and are unaware of it? In this issue, PCN editor, Patricia McBee, interviews Alex Scott, an experienced pastoral caregiver and alcoholism counselor, about his perspective on how our meetings can support Friends in recognizing and recovering from alcohol abuse. The reflections of this seasoned Friend may be useful in the consideration of other forms of substance abuse as well.

Pat McBee: How do you see alcohol abuse affecting our meetings?

Alex Scott: I think it is present in every meeting to some extent or another. One in 10 people in the general population is having a problem with alcohol. I don't know whether Friends exactly fit that statistic. My sense is that Friends come close to the general population.

P: What constitutes "having a problem" with alcohol?

A: Addictions can be identified if any kind of behavior that we're doing interferes with any significant aspect of our lives—our families, our jobs, our hobbies, our creative activities or our spiritual lives. It is rather a broad definition but I think that it's one that works. A problem drinker, then, is someone whose drinking interferes with other aspects of his or her life.

In a meeting one of the tip-offs might be that someone is not fulfilling his/her responsibilities and is always making excuses. Or a number of things might add up to tell the meeting that something is not right—marital problems, for example, might surface an underlying problem of alcoholism, or someone loses a job or has a problem with gambling or you see a family in crisis; it might manifest itself in a variety of ways.

P: You're saying that a number of things can go wrong in the lives of meeting members, and alcohol abuse may be an underlying cause. What can the meeting do if it becomes concerned about possible alcohol abuse?

A: This is a tough situation, and you're going to find yourself challenged in terms of your skills and your comfort level. The ideal is to intervene at the earliest possible time so that people don't have to hit bottom; they don't have to self-destruct. Even though it may seem intimidating, it is better to address something you're concerned about and to resist the temptation to hide behind a sense that you don't want to intrude.

Friends should start with being in touch with a knowledgeable person or support organization who can give guidance about how best to support a person toward recovery. The local Alcoholics Anonymous (AA) office can tell you about what resources are available in the community or give feedback on whether the particular behaviors people in the meeting have observed are something to be concerned about. AA is usually very helpful and very knowledgeable and keeps information confidential. In Philadelphia Yearly Meeting, the Friends Counseling Service can be of help in considering the best way to proceed.

P: Let's look at a scenario in which one by one a handful of people in the meeting begin to realize that something isn't right with a certain member. And they take it to the pastoral care committee and say, "Things just don't look right here, and we don't know how to reach out." How can the committee respond?

A: A first step would be some exploration of family members if they're available, or friends, or people who know that individual. "Is Charley OK?" "Do you see these kinds of behaviors?" I think there needs to be a gathering of information to try to understand what is really happening. Is the fact that the person is worried about a sick aunt causing the behaviors that have caught meeting members' attention?

If you find that you have reason to be concerned, it is important to talk with the person directly. How pastoral caregivers approach someone largely has to do with the relationship of person to person. It is always best when someone who feels close to or is comfortable with the person can approach her or him in a non-threatening way.

P: What happens if you talk to a person or a spouse who says, "We're fine, mind your own business."

A: Well, that's not uncommon because of the shame, guilt and denial connected with alcoholism. You need to pay attention; if you are correct in your suspicions there will be another opportunity. It is an ongoing situation. But it is important not to support the denial. You can state the behavior you have observed and express concern. You can say, "Charley (or Henrietta), you had a bad patch back there last week, is everything OK?" Or, "You used to do your committee work, but now deadlines come and you don't deliver, and that's not like you. I'm wondering what's happening."

Again, it's the relationship. You work to create relationships in the life of the meeting so that when a problem comes up you can say, "Henrietta, I've known you for years. I see changes, and I'm concerned about you. So don't be surprised if I keep coming around and saying, 'How're you doing?' or 'How's Charley?'"

P: If a spouse comes to the pastoral care committee and says, "I think my partner has a drinking problem, and I'm scared and I don't know what to do." Then how might the meeting respond?

A: Remember that people are often ashamed to admit alcohol abuse within their families, so take care to be accepting, supportive and non-judgmental. Try to find out what kind of help this spouse is really needing when he or she asks for support. Also remember that this isn't something that has been on the scene for just a week or two. The couple more than likely have been round and round about this. What's happening? How long has this been going on? Does he hit you? Does she get into trouble at work? How are the kids doing? Has some kind of crisis precipitated the spouse's approach to the meeting?

The pastoral care committee's goal is to help the spouse address concerns with the alcohol abuser in appropriate way. I would get the spouse in touch with a support organization like Alanon or with a professional knowledgeable about alcoholism. If the addict or a family member is in acute risk of harm, the caregivers will want to assist the spouse in taking immediate action to protect whoever is at risk. If the situation is less acute and the spouse is less clear about what support she or he needs, a clearness committee may be useful to identify issues or see that there are no issues. It can create a setting in which there can be open sharing to weed out what is significant and what can be worked on. The clearness committee should include knowledgeable people, who have observed the behaviors and are trusted by the individuals involved.

P: I have heard that people won't deal with addiction until they hit bottom, but you said earlier that it is best to intervene early so that an alcoholic doesn't have to hit bottom.

A: Most early intervention programs deal with education and try and help a person to understand that they can get help and what it is that they're really dealing with. I think a lot of it is ignorance, that people really don't know

P: They don't know they're addicted?

A: They don't know they're addicted. There are all these things: "I'm married, I have a family, I work, I bring home a check, I go to meeting, I do this, I do that. So I have three or four drinks at night before I go to bed, but I go to work." They are just not aware. But the wife would say, "Charley, you don't do anything with the kids. When was the last time we were out? You come home, you sit in a chair and you drink. That's what you do." Sometimes you see people who are obviously hurting and you may not know why. And sometimes you may need to help them see that they're hurting—help them identify their behaviors.

P: OK, so now let's say that the pastoral care committee is pretty clear that there is a problem. Perhaps the spouse or other family member has asked for the meeting's support. Approaching the person who may be addicted would be pretty tricky.

A: What you're talking about is the potential of denial. At some point the individual needs to be spoken with clearly and directly about the behavior and its effects on others. It is often best if more than one person meets with the individual, not one person alone. It could be members of the family who are supported by the meeting or a counselor. It could be someone trusted by the person and knowledgeable about alcoholism, perhaps a meeting member who is in AA. The goal is to get the person into treatment and to get support for the family.

There is a formal procedure, done under professional guidance, called an "intervention." People who care deeply about this person are called together, and the individual in question is present, and people share openly what they have been observing and how they have been affected by the person's behavior. There is a whole agenda for how an intervention takes place. It is really confronting the individual, in a loving, caring, and limit setting way, to get the person to take a step, to get him or her to acknowledge the problem.

The usual procedure is to have already made arrangements to have the person go from that meeting directly to a treatment center. The goal of the intervention is to have the person accept those arrangements. A meeting could be a good place to have a formal intervention. Hopefully, we can do it in a positive, caring way. The folks in that group need to be prepared ahead of time so they know what to do and what not to do. It is very likely that they are going to be confronted with anger, manipulation; all the skills that individual has used to maintain the addiction may be brought to bear in this group. The group needs to be prepared to know how to handle it.

P: What is the spiritual dimension of all this?

A: An addiction is a disease of the body, the mind and the spirit. As I have listened to people's stories, what I hear is that the spiritual side of their lives is really bankrupt. What happens in an addict's life is that they serve the addiction. The primary goal in their life becomes serving the addiction. It's that compelling. It's that demanding. That's what they have left, the addiction. Addiction has become the organizing principle of the person's life. If you're serving something that profoundly, there's not much room for spiritual life. As an addict begins to give up the addiction, there is space to welcome spirituality back into his or her life.

Getting in touch with spirituality can be part of the recovery process. The realization that you're bankrupt and you've got to start somewhere can be a spiritual opening—"let go, let God." If someone is going to effect a healthy recovery, they're going to have to address the spiritual component as well as the body and the mind.

It is very helpful if the Friends who are the support for a person and family recovering from addiction are grounded in their own spiritual life. Even if there is not an opening at first to talk about their beliefs, they can act out love and faithfulness grounded in the Spirit, and that can create a further opening. Friends can hold the person and the family in the light. And, when the person is ready, the meeting can welcome them back in the worship life and spiritual activities of the meeting.

P: Say more about the meeting's role when the person has stopped drinking and is in recovery—either someone the meeting has seen through the hard time or someone who comes to the meeting when they are in recovery.

A: The meeting can treat the recovering person as someone on a spiritual journey. Honor the courage and struggle that has led to this stage in the journey. Embrace him or her in the life of the meeting. And ask what kind of support would be most welcome.

A support system which reinforces the healthy, constructive part of oneself is a key in recovery. The more supports a person has—spouse, family, job, neighbors, AA and the meeting—the greater the likelihood that they're going to be successful.

We should talk about relapse. Recovery from addiction is a long-term process and relapse is not unusual. A person might say, "Well, I haven't had a drink in two years. I'll have one or two and stop." It is not the end of the world. Hopefully that will be a learning process: "I can't do that. I thought I could, but I can't." Sometimes it is good to get it out of the road. "That's behind you now, what have you learned from it?" It can be a constructive experience.

Recovery is life long. I know people who have been in AA 20 years or more. They still have a sponsor; they may be a sponsor, but they still have a sponsor. They talk about "keeping it green"—staying aware of what an addiction is like both intellectually and emotionally.

P: I know of a situation in which a meeting was supporting a member who never overcame his alcohol addiction. Sooner or later the meeting members stopped being present to him because it was discouraging, then they felt guilty about it.

A: It is important to remember that not all situations have this unhappy outcome. Many turn out well, and we should enter the process with hope.

Sadly, some people will never get over the addiction. It has very little to do with the would-be helper. It has to do with some x-factor in that individual who is addicted. So, if at some point you see Henrietta who is self-destructing after all these years, you may need to set very clear limits on the meeting's involvement or even back out. Alcoholism is a chronically progressive deteriorating disease that can lead to death. That is why it is important for Friends to provide loving support to those who *are* working on their recovery.

P: How can we sum this up? What advice would you give your meeting if it were faced with a situation of alcoholism?

A: I would tell them that dealing with alcoholism is a difficult and long-term process:

- Remember that addiction is a disease that is overlaid with guilt and shame that make it difficult to seek and accept help.
- Remember, too, that recovery is an uneven process. Those supporting the recovery can't control the situation and can't make the person better.
- Provide support that is accepting and forgiving. At the same time, be clear about setting and maintaining limits.
- Reach out to the family and help them to find support for their recovery as well.
- Seek support from a knowledgeable resource person who knows about the patterns and progress of addiction and can give guidance about how best to support a person toward recovery.
- When a meeting member is in recovery there may be an opening to do an educational session for the meeting about addiction and recovery.
- Most importantly keep in mind the meeting's special role in the spiritual dimension of recovery. Remain grounded and centered and act in the spirit of love and compassion.

Alex Scott is a social worker who has worked as the director of a drug and alcohol program. He is a member of Radnor (PA) Meeting and has served as a pastoral caregiver and as clerk of that meeting. Alex is a former member of the Family Relations Committee and the Friends Counseling Service.

One Meeting's Experience

On a recent Sunday morning after meeting for worship at Willistown Friends Meeting in Chester County, Pennsylvania, three members were talking. One woman talked of her brother who got drunk one night and threatened to jump off the roof of the house. A man related that he was going to fewer support group meetings and that drinking was starting to look good to him again. The other woman related that the decision not to visit her daughter over the holidays because of her daughter's drinking had strengthened the relationship between mother and daughter.

Although somewhat unusual in most circles, this type of conversation is fairly regular at Willistown. A group of around twelve members and attenders has been getting together for three years sharing their experiences, hopes and sorrows in a supportive and community building way. By talking together they have worked out alternatives to many crisis situations that can accompany abusive alcohol and drug use. In doing this they have built and strengthened the sense of community in the meeting.

While attitudes toward addictive behavior still carry a social stigma, this group of Friends work to actively deter prejudice and social shunning, whether actively hostile or patronizing, with clear statements based on love, understanding and compassion for all. It was therefore an important event for the greater spiritual community when the Meeting for Worship for Business at Willistown acknowledged this ministry in a minuted letter.

Gatherings of this ever-changing group have taken different forms over the years, but center on:

- A regular worship-sharing group that attracts Friends and members of area 12-Step groups. The simple format of inspirational reading relating to meditation and/or addiction followed by speaking from the silence has been enriching for many. It has also attracted several attenders to the meeting for worship on Sunday morning.
- An eight week course, Nurturing the Spirit in Recovery, designed to focus on ways that meditation and the Light within can influence the difficulties of living with addictive behavior, ones own or that of a family member or friend. Along with practicing stress reduction and centering prayer techniques, ample time is given to discuss how spirituality is affected by addictive behavior.
- Meeting for healing to pray over a specific event or situation. We have gathered to pray for the healing in a family where the son was addicted to gambling and to pray for all those affected by drinking during the holiday season.
- Telephone calls play an important role in helping all of us stay in touch with one another. Having someone to talk with can save a day or just put it back on track.

Richard Squailia, Willistown Meeting, PA

Questions for Reflection

1. How does our meeting build relationships within our community so that we are able to reach out in a time of crisis such as a concern about alcohol or other substance abuse?
2. Are we prepared practically and spiritually to intervene when there is a concern, or do we hold back out of a fear of intruding?
3. What resources are available to the meeting for informing ourselves before intervening in a case of possible alcoholism? Is there a resource person within the meeting? Do we know how to contact a local chapter of Alcoholics Anonymous or Alanon? Are these numbers posted where have access to them?
4. Are we prepared to handle sensitive matters with confidentiality and discretion?
5. How does the pastoral care committee support one another in setting and maintaining appropriate limits, particularly in situations when there may be denial and manipulation?
6. How do we maintain clarity about the appropriate role of the meeting as it relates to the roles of the individual, the family, the counselor and others involved?
7. What has been the meeting's experience of providing support over a long period of time? How do we provide consistent support without unduly burdening a few Friends?
8. How do members of the pastoral care committee nourish the spiritual lives of pastoral caregivers so that our caring reflects love and faithfulness grounded in the Spirit?

THE WELFARE
OF EACH MEMBER

NURTURING CHILDREN AND
FAMILIES IN MEETING

NURTURING QUAKER PARENTING

SUPPORTING FAMILIES IN TIMES OF TROUBLE

REACHING OUT TO SINGLES IN OUR MEETINGS

PASTORAL CARE OF MEN IN OUR MEETINGS

DEALING WITH AGING

MINISTRY TO OLDER PEOPLE
EXPERIENCING DISABILITIES

Nurturing Children and Families in Meeting

Pastoral Care Newsletter, Vol. 2, No. 3 • March 1995

By Marty Smith and Carolyn Terrell

> And they were bringing children to him, that he might touch them; and the disciples rebuked them. But when Jesus saw it he was indignant, and said unto them, "Let the children come to me, do not hinder them; for to such belongs the kingdom of God." — *RSV Mark 10:13*

Perhaps a disciple asked, "Don't you know children are restless and noisy?" And perhaps Jesus explained that he valued children's openness to life; children are tender, forgiving, trusting, honest, fun loving and eager to learn. Dr. Benjamin Spock writes, "The capacity of idealism, creativity and spirituality is latent in every child." Children have spiritual awareness. They have questions about creation, the nature of God and why bad things happen to good people. They have an urge to learn by experience. They need help in using the silence in meeting for worship (as do adults). Can our pastoral care committee nurture these qualities and help children share with everyone in the meeting their joy of living?

Many Friends can identify with both the disciples and with Jesus. When the behavior of children is disruptive, adults may feel like rebuking them. Yet we all know what Jesus meant. The focus of this newsletter is on the pastoral care role of nurturing the spiritual lives of children and their families and for finding solutions when the needs of adults and children are in conflict.

Traditionally, pastoral care committees are concerned with clearness for marriage, memorial services and helping members and attenders who are ill or in distress. The 1972 PYM *Faith and Practice* broadens the responsibility of pastoral caregivers to include children and young people by suggesting

> be aware of and foster influences that develop the religious life of the children and young people of the meeting, whether members or non-members, and should assist in giving them an understanding of the

principles and practices of Friends. Overseers should seek to strengthen the work of the Committee on Religious Education or other committees seeking similar ends. Young people desire and need to have a creative part in the life of the meeting; older Friends should recognize the contribution that young people can make.[1]

The Meeting as Extended Family

There was a time when the religious education of children took place in the home, around a Bible each evening, during prayers before meals and at bedtime. Many families attended meeting for worship every Sunday which meant a common experience of shared faith. Now, many families look to the meeting for religious education for their children. However, there is often less than an hour on Sunday for education in the Bible, Quakerism and other topics relating to Quaker testimonies.

Friends once lived in rural settings with grandparents, aunts and uncles or cousins nearby. Now when their children (now parents) need advice or a reassuring hug or when grandchildren want an older confidant or grandparent to listen to them, relatives are often too far away. Parents look more frequently to the meeting for support. When meetings respond to that need, the number of young families with children is likely to increase dramatically.

Preparation for Worship

The length of time children are expected to sit in meeting for worship has decreased; parents new to Quakerism will not have experienced what it is like for children to sit quietly in meeting. Just getting children to meeting can be a chore. However, we must avoid thinking of meeting as an endurance contest. Parents bring to meeting anxieties and worries about what Friends will think about their child's behavior. They wonder if Friends will think they are bad parents if their child cannot sit quietly in meeting. One child may be able to sit quietly in worship while another of the same age may not be able to.

Pastoral caregivers can take initiative in preparing children for meeting for worship. Sharing with children their own experience with worship as children and having older Friends tell of prayers that were meaningful to them as children are two of the ways in which this can be approached. Such sharing helps children learn that meeting for

[1] Philadelphia Yearly Meeting, *Faith and Practice*, 1972, p. 151.

worship is a time to be in the presence of God. Also, it's important to remember that children need encouragement to speak in meeting, when led. Other ways to prepare children for worship include developing prayer cards that are illustrated by children and taken to meeting, and making soft fabric books or toys for the same purpose. The making of these things can be done as an intergenerational project. Adults in one meeting delight in being a "lap buddy" to a particular child so that when a child gets restless during meeting, he or she can walk over quietly and sit on an older Friend's lap. Some meetings have found that a quiet room with books and puzzles, near the worship room and supervised by an adult, is a refuge to which children can go and return as needed during worship.

Supporting Parents and Children

Taking the lead in organizing a parent group to support parents trying to raise their children with Friends values can be a real gift of pastoral caregivers to meeting families. More seasoned Friends can bring experience and leavening to such a group and can be valued organizers or contributors. Several meetings have organized discussion groups where there is opportunity to reflect on situations which children face: violence, materialism, competition and conflict. Ensuring that the library includes books of interest to new parents can be important. Quaker Books of Friends General Conference includes an excellent assortment. In some meetings new babies are introduced at the end of worship with someone giving family history, introducing relatives and holding the baby up for celebration. Still other meetings have taken introduction of new children one step further by holding meetings for dedication during regular worship time or at another time. Some meetings recognize children with a card or gift when they reach milestones like entering school or graduating. One meeting holds a meeting for worship for graduating high school youth. In many meetings children or youth are given a personally inscribed Bible or *Faith and Practice* at an appropriate age.

When Needs of Children and Adults Are in Conflict

Involving young people more effectively in the life of our meetings will occasionally involve conflict between the needs of children and the needs of adults. Have any of these situations occurred in your meeting?

1. A very young baby is making baby noises in meeting for worship; an adult rises to speak, with genuine regret, saying that the baby noises are disturbing his worship. He asks the meeting for help. The young mother is devastated; she stays away from meeting for many weeks.
2. A small group of adults are sitting in a circle for a committee meeting. Small children are running around the circle, with loud laughter. The adults cannot hear each other. The parents say nothing; the nonparents are reluctant to suggest another activity for the children.
3. During an intergenerational game where adults and children are holding hands in a circle, a few older children delay the game by pulling the circle in and out. The parents say nothing; the children ignore other adults who try to speak to them.
4. Children are included in an invitation to see a slide show. It turns out to be of little interest to them and takes longer than they can sit still.
5. After meeting for worship, during social time, children are running around spilling food or drink. Older adults fear they may be knocked over. Parents are engrossed in conversation and do not stop their children.

All these situations involve differences in needs and interests of children and adults. Some meetings have found solutions as follows: When specific individuals were involved, one meeting provided an opportunity for them to express their feelings in a safe environment. The individuals felt much better, even though the problem wasn't solved immediately. Family worship has been initiated in some meetings. Stories, songs, drama, guided meditation and short quiet times have provided a setting for adults and children to worship together. Child care during committee meetings, business meetings, and social events is offered in many meetings. A children's corner has been established in some social rooms where small tables and chairs, books, puzzles and art materials can be used by children when adults are busy talking.

We need to recognize that parents differ in their expectations for children' s behavior. Parents are not usually receptive to unsolicited advice on child-rearing. With facilitation the meeting community can come to agreement on expectations for behavior. In one meeting, for example, some members of Ministry and Worship met with parents and children to set up guidelines for behavior during social hour. Involving children and parents in setting and following through with behavioral expectations is far more constructive than talking negatively or gossiping about either the children or their parents.

Often the pastoral care committee is able to serve as catalysts in finding workable answers when the needs of children and adults are in conflict. The manner in which the solutions are found can serve as a model to children and youth who look to their "elders" to set a good example.

Children with Special Needs

Effectively including a child with special needs is another area of pastoral care in which particular sensitivity is required. One meeting experienced a child in First Day School who continually interrupted the teacher, calling out, and not being able to sit still. She could not recall what the teacher said just ten minutes earlier. The teacher wanted to include the child in the class activities, but others were not able to follow the lesson because of the disturbance. In another meeting, a mentally challenged young adult wanted to learn about his Quaker faith in a middle school class and quietly asked for extra help with instructions or details during the class. The teacher, however, did not have enough time to meet his needs as well as the rest of the exuberant adolescents.

Situations like these need extra loving care from everyone in the meeting. Volunteers, for example, can take turns accompanying the child to First Day School to help with projects, to interpret the lesson, to bring calm when the environment becomes too stimulating or to take the child out of the room for individual attention when needed.

Helping the entire meeting be more sensitive to the needs of children and families who are coping with special challenges is a contribution which the pastoral care committee can make. We can be helpful to families by finding out what the parents want the meeting to know about their child with special needs. For example, "Would you like to tell me about your child?" rather than "What's wrong with your child?" The committee can facilitate the organization of a group for parents in the quarter who have special needs children.

Pastoral caregivers need to be alert to the possibility of serious problems in the lives of meeting children. Often meeting members are unaware that a member is depressed, drinking in excess or is abusive to spouse or children. If concern arises about serious problems in the life of a meeting child, it is essential that the pastoral care committee prayerfully consider how to speak with the family and, if necessary, make connection with a respected professional counselors who is attuned to values important to Quakers.

Differences among Adults in Meetings

There are broad issues which affect Friends in the meeting community. One potentially divisive issue involves what is taught in First Day School. A faithful attender may offer to teach First Day School every Sunday for the whole year. The offer is gratefully accepted. It may be months before Friends discover that they are very uncomfortable with what is being taught. A pastoral care member in one meeting faced this concern by first speaking with the clerk of the Religious Education Committee to see if they were aware of the situation. When the clerk of pastoral care found that the Religious Education Committee had tried without success to satisfy the members' concern, she decided to call a threshing session involving parents, teachers and committees involved with what should be taught. There, general agreement was reached and the recommendations were referred to Religious Education for implementation. Often such problems can be averted by more careful discussion at the time of the offer being made. Clear understandings can help to avoid the hurt feelings which arise when someone has given energy to something only to discover that others are disapproving.

Another issue needing attention in some meetings involves the right time for children to come into meeting for worship, at the beginning or the end? Should First Day School be held before, during or after worship? Should business meeting be held on a weekday evening or on Sunday? Our pastoral care committees can provide opportunities for prayerful discussion of these questions involving Friends from meeting committees with direct experience with the concern.

Intergenerational Activities

Solutions to all the problems described previously will be easier if members and attenders, including children, have opportunities to know each other better.

The pastoral care committee can take initiative in planning intergenerational activities. It is a challenge to find activities that are enjoyed by both children and adults. These questions need to be considered: Why do we want children involved in this event? Will both children and adults play important parts in the game or are the children just there for "show"? Are the directions for the game clear for all ages?

Activities that meetings have tried with success include: name tags for everyone; an album with pictures and names of members and attenders; games, square dances, work or service projects; a display of baby pictures with a prize for the person who can guess the most names; dramatics; camping trips; and an evening where hobbies are presented and displayed.

We hope the experiences of meetings, given above, will be helpful as Friends look for ways to include children, youth and adults in the life of the meeting. We hope that Quaker children will have opportunities to share their insights and openness.

Marty Smith has given long service as director of the Religious Education Committee of Philadelphia Yearly Meeting. She is a member of Moorestown (NJ) Monthly Meeting.

Carolyn Terrell has interacted with children in nursery school, First Day School and in her extended family for many years. She belongs to Mount Holly (NJ) Meeting.

Listening to the Young People

"Be Teachable." In an attempt to live into the spirit of that admonition from the Advices of Philadelphia Yearly Meeting, Phil Anthony and Ruth Cameron, who work with young people at Chestnut Hill Meeting, arranged for Helene Pollock, the co-editor of this newsletter, to meet with three young Friends, to hear their ideas about ways in which pastoral care committees can help meetings be more responsive to the needs of the youth. Participants included Patti Anthony (11), Joe Doolin Richardson (17), and Ben Newlin (18).

When the starting point of the discussion was left to the young people, worship was the place they chose to begin. Each recognized worship as being central to his or her life as a Friend, although interestingly what they credited as having been most important to their growing appreciation of unprogrammed worship was their participation in Young Friends programs at the yearly meeting level.

When asked what they would find helpful, their advice to adults is simple. "Treat us like you'd like to be treated. Treat us with respect," says Ben, "and don't just make chit-chat. I've got views on just about any issue, and I like people who actually can talk about things." Youth want to have significant relationships with meeting adults. Joe says, "There's a man in the meeting who's really cool. If I'm having a problem that is typical to teenagers—sex, drugs, whatever—and I talk to him about it, he'll recognize that the problem has to do with my being a teenager, but he's also able to be respectful of who I am. He hasn't forgotten what it's like to be a teenager. And he's very open. You could almost say he's 'parental' but he's more like an uncle-type of figure. He's like my former First Day School teacher, who has a quality of listening that has something to do with the Inward Teacher."

Patti encourages adults to move beyond their stereotypes about young people. "Some people seem to not get past the fact that I'm only eleven. Then there are people who just think of me as 'my dad's daughter.' It feels really horrible. It feels like they don't really try to get to know me. And I know a few people who think I'm really really really really sweet. But if they got to know me, they would see that I don't like to live up to that. It really drives me nuts. I don't think that most of the adults really know me. But some of them do; I can feel it." Patti continues: "I think one reason why adults don't try to get to know the kids in the meeting that well is because they're scared of us. Don't ask me why. And when they get scared it intimidates the kids and also makes the kids a little shyer. For a kid, when an adult comes up and doesn't even really try to get to know you, it sort of hurts sometimes. But not a lot."

Joe, who became a member of the meeting last year, tells of one meeting member who was able to move beyond first impressions. "When I had my 'Yea!-you're-a-Quaker-now' party, one of the adult members told me how the first time I came to meeting, when he saw how I was dressed, he thought I was just another punk. But later, after hearing me speak in meeting, he changed his mind, and he said, 'Wow, I've gotta get to know this kid.'"

At Chestnut Hill Meeting, a special forum about young people's concerns was organized by Overseers and Worship and Ministry. For Ben, the forum was "the first time that anybody in the meeting ever listened to what I thought. It was really great. Before that no one really knew me." Ben also serves on a yearly meeting committee, an experience which he says has helped him to become more comfortable in relating to older persons. He says, "I've felt very respected and cared for through them."

Young people have a lot to say, and meetings need to find new and creative ways for them to be heard. As Joe reminds us, "Teens can be very intensely spiritual people." But are we adults open to receiving what they have to give?

Questions for Reflection

1. What part do we, as pastoral caregivers, play in welcoming and valuing children and their parents into the meeting community?
2. What changes in our physical plant and in our meeting's procedures would benefit children and their parents?
3. Do we consider the needs of children and parents in our regular pastoral care committee meetings?
4. Do we feel satisfied with the way in which we integrate young people into the life of our meeting? Are there any ways in which we would like to strengthen our efforts in this regard?

Nurturing Quaker Parenting

Pastoral Care Newsletter, Vol. 4, No. 1 • September 1996

by Harriet E. Heath

How can pastoral care committees support parents as they seek to integrate Friends' beliefs, practices, and values into their family life? Quakers search for truth and for how to live by that truth in everyday life. Parenting is part of that search as parents seek to follow Quaker principles in living with and guiding their children. Viewing parenting as part of our search for truth offers another opportunity to support the spiritual journey of members of their meeting.

Our meetings are drawing attenders who are unfamiliar with Friends ways. Among these new members and attenders are parents with young children. Many were raised in a very authoritarian manner. In their searching they are asking "What is the Quaker way of child rearing?"

Even those who grew up in Quaker homes have questions. "We learned anger was wrong, not how to deal with it. I still don't know how, and now my children make me so angry, I strike out. It certainly doesn't create the Quaker home we want."

"The child's first teachers are his or her parents. It is in the home that Friends' principles first become practices."[1] Parents ask how to follow Friends' principles when responding to a two-year-old having a temper tantrum or an adolescent cutting a parent off with a sarcastic remark.

What are the implications of Friends believing that "everyone is a child of God"? What does it mean that "all must relate to one another in terms of the Divine Spark within each"?[2]

This article explores ways the pastoral care committee can support parents' search for how to live with and guide their children. A discussion of integrating children into the life of the meeting can be found on page 249. Here we will focus on the everyday situations that parents

1 Philadelphia Yearly Meeting, *Faith and Practice*, 1972, p. 22.
2 Ibid., p. 32.

face. How they face them is what can make an experience of Quaker living.

We will discuss four areas in which a meeting can support parents:

- integrating Quaker faith and practices into family living
- guiding children according to values important to Friends
- supporting parents concerned about a child
- dealing with parents who may be neglecting, abusing or not guiding their child

Integrating Quaker Faith and Practice into Family Life

Integrating our Quaker faith into our everyday life is a challenge for all of us. For parents the leap is great. They ask, "How do you become or stay centered in the midst of hectic family life? Take that five o'clock hour when everyone is tired and hungry, the children are squabbling and the adults are trying to get dinner on the table. How do you deal with that in a Quakerly way?" Or they ask, "How do you see the Inner Light in a child who knows exactly what to say and do to get you so angry?"

Providing parents an opportunity to raise their concerns is a first major step. Many parents feel that they struggle alone. They may feel they are asking questions whose answers are obvious to everyone but themselves. Learning that other families have struggles and questions legitimizes their concerns. This sharing gives many greater courage to face their struggles.

It is also helpful for young parents to hear from members who are farther along in their child rearing, even at the grandparent stage. It is reassuring to discover that some parenting issues are common to every generation. It also gives perspective on those issues that are new and need new solutions.

From this sharing with other Quaker parents can come ways of integrating Friends practices into the struggles of parenting. Parents have offered such strategies as having a quiet time sometime during the day, learning to center during fleeting moments, reflecting on a recurring situation, learning to hold a child in the Light, keeping the way open and following leadings.

There are several ways committees can facilitate sharing among parents. For one-on-one sharing, we can encourage parents to seek out members of the meeting with whom they would like to discuss parenting issues, or they could set up a mentoring program teaming experienced parents with newer ones.

Sharing in a group setting such as a parents' support group or adult forum provides a more formal opportunity for parents to exchange experiences. Thought should be given to what structure would best serve the meeting's parents, a single session or a series of discussions on related topics. A meeting could choose an informal, self-led group, organize a group facilitated by an experienced meeting member, or invite a skilled person from yearly meeting.

Below are suggested themes around which discussions could be organized.

How can parents incorporate specific beliefs in their family life?

What does "that of God in every person" mean? How does that belief relate to children? Where or when do we see that of God in our children? Is that of God there from birth and determining the child's behavior? If so, is there no need for parental guidance? Or is that of God a potential and the child can grow into goodness with the parent as the guide?

What are the Quaker principles on which home life is to be based?

Are they Brinton's "community, harmony, equality and simplicity"? Or are there others such as tolerance? And how are these principles integrated into family life? Does equality mean each person has equal say about how money is spent, the parents and the three-year-old?

How can parents respond to specific situations which concern them?

The following outline may be useful.

- Describe a specific situation.
- List as many ways of dealing with the situation as you can.
- Make a plan by selecting the ways listed which are most in keeping with Quaker principles.

When discussions become this specifically related to current child rearing issues, the facilitator needs to be aware of factors that will affect what can be done in a specific case. These factors include the developmental level of the children, the temperament patterns of all those involved, and each one's needs and feelings.

Guiding Children According to Values Important to Friends

Parents also ask about expecting children to live by Quaker values. Does living nonviolently mean always turning the other cheek? Never protecting oneself? What happens on the school playground if reporting an incident is seen as tattling and frowned on by both teachers and children? And what is simple living: no TV? no computer? organizing one's time to include family time? something else?

For several years now, members of the Zero to Thirteen Subcommittee of the Religious Education Committee of Philadelphia Yearly Meeting have been facilitating discussions at monthly and quarterly meetings searching with the participants for ways to integrate values important to Friends. They have found a series of questions helpful. First is to clarify what is meant by the value. *How do you define _____? What are the behaviors you would expect to see in a person living according to _____?*

Living nonviolently, as an example, is often defined as dealing with conflict by using mediation techniques and discussion instead of fighting or even name calling. Nonviolence implies a respect for the other person. A person equipped to live nonviolently would have mediation techniques, would be respectful of others, would know how to divert a fight into a discussion of issues.

The second question is *What are different situations in which issues arise in attempting to implement this value?* Situations parents might cite could be conflict between children that might occur at home between siblings, on the playground, in the classroom or on the bus.

Then take one situation and let parents see the possibilities of how to handle it by answering the question: *What are all the ways you can think of for handling this situation?* And the next question, of course, is *Which ways of handling the situation would be in congruence with the value and would help the child learn to live by this value?* The leader may add relevant techniques that others have not offered.

The final question is *What are the implications for our children of living according to this value?* Will my child be safe? Will denying her all the toys her friends have make those toys so desirable she will resist choosing to live simply?

These questions can be used in parent discussion groups. The questions provide parents with a guide for integrating their values into family life.

Supporting Parents Concerned about a Child

Parents may come to a member of the pastoral care committee because they are concerned about a child. The child's behavior is uncontrollable. The parents are at their wits' end. Or the school was reporting behavior the parents did not see. What should they do? Or the parents are ashamed or frightened by what the adolescent or young adult is doing: he's joined a cult; she's entering the military; they're on drugs; the significant other is a scary person.

How can pastoral caregivers respond when parents ask for help with concerns like these?

Listening may be the greatest gift a person can give to a parent. Many times parents will resolve the issue themselves just by having an opportunity to voice it. In other situations well placed gentle questions may help the parent. "In what kinds of situations does this behavior occur?" "Does the behavior in school occur constantly or during certain periods or transitions?" And asking the parents, "What are ways you could deal with this situation?" and "What do you want your child to learn from this situation?" can help parents clarify their goals and next steps. The caregiver might ask "What are your fears about the life your child has chosen? How can we support you in the loss you are feeling?"

The pastoral care committee may discover that an issue is beyond their skill and that professional help may be needed. A committee member can help parents sharpen their grasp of the issue, and then help find a counselor with whom they can work effectively. If the parent is not open to professional help, the pastoral care committee can seek professional advice on how to proceed. Some yearly meetings maintain lists of Quaker counselors. Parents may also wish to work through their health insurance plan or local family service.

Dealing with the Child about Whom Pastoral Caregivers Have a Concern: What If You Suspect Neglect or Abuse?

A concern such as this usually arises out of incidents observed within the meeting. Perhaps the child looks neglected or behavior between parent and child at meeting are indicative of neglect. Perhaps you observe indications of abuse (see p. 205). Or, maybe, the child's behavior at meeting is consistently inappropriate. Fortunately such situations are rare, but unfortunately they do exist and should not be ignored.

A pastoral caregiver in another meeting called wanting to explore whether to act, and if so how, in a case of apparent neglect. For over a year she had been concerned about a child, now five, whose parents are active, well-respected members of the meeting. At meeting the child's behavior is frequently out of control. He will grab a toy from another child. He will ride his bike into an area that is understood to be out of bounds. Though his parents may be present, they ignore his behavior. The caregiver has never seen the parents interact with the child except to give him directions such as, "It is time to go now, get in the car." What precipitated the phone call was that at the First Day School picnic the child had fallen and scraped both knees badly. He cried hard, the knees must have burned. His parents totally ignored him, did not even pause in their conversation. Someone else attended to his hurts. The caller felt the child wanted his parents. "Is this neglect?" she asked. "Can we, should we, let it go unmentioned?"

Or the child's behavior is unacceptable. One meeting reported how two brothers would chase each other after meeting, running over the benches which have cloth covered pads. Friends in from another meeting were concerned about a child who talked loudly and did noisy projects during the whole adult meeting. The parent was proud that child stayed for the full forty-five minutes.

These are difficult situations that come to the attention of our caregiving committees. It is delicate to approach parents. They may not be receptive to unsolicited advice on child rearing. And adults differ as to what is acceptable, even when it comes to racing around the meeting room.

When there is consensus within the caregiving committee about their concern, they should give careful, and prayerful, attention to what would be the appropriate response. The task calls for great sensitivity toward the parents' position as well as that of the child. Action could involve a member of the meeting who is close to the parents and/or respected by them approaching them with the concern. The visitor's major goal may be to lead the parent to talking with a professional counselor. Reaching that objective may take several visits of tender looking at the child's behavior and the parents' perspective. But, as with the issue of sexual abuse, can we ignore the cries of help of our young members? Can we ignore when a child seems to be hurting?

Pastoral care committees, concerned with the well being of the members of their meetings, are in a position to support and guide parents' search for answers. To do so means being open to the struggles of parents. It means recognizing that their search to integrate their Quaker faith into their family life and into their nurturance of their children is part of their spiritual journey.

Harriet E. Heath, Ph.D., a member of Radnor (PA) Meeting, is a licensed development psychologist and teacher. She has lead "Parenting Creatively" workshops for Philadelphia Yearly Meeting. She is an experienced parent as mother of three and grandmother of eight and author of *Using Your Values to Raise a Child You Admire as an Adult.*

Questions for Reflection

1. How can we help parents find peace within that will guide them in living with their children? How can we help them to be centered in the midst of family life?
2. Can we evolve queries that would guide parents as they seek to integrate their Quaker faith into their every day lives with their children?
3. Are we sensitive to the needs of parents and their children? Are we supportive to parents when they are going through a period of turmoil with their children? Are we able to recognize the needs of children from their behavior? Are we prepared to help children who have need of our help?
4. Do we give parents opportunities to raise questions and discuss concerns? Does the meeting discuss Quaker values as they apply to family life? Do we impart skills which can enable parents to integrate those values into their families? Do we help parents be realistic about the effect of Quaker values on children?

Supporting Families in Times of Trouble

Pastoral Care Newsletter, Vol. 9, No. 1 • September 2001

by Judith Owens

During the Depression, when my mother was in high school, my grandfather was the sheriff in their rural county in the state of Washington. Since she knew nothing about problems like domestic violence, child-snatching, addictions or infidelity, my mother felt unprepared for the life she found when she moved to the city and began raising a family in the late 30s. But when she talked to her dad about her dismay, he just laughed. "Families all around us had these problems! We just didn't talk about it." Mom often reminded me of this interchange when I spoke with her about how different life seemed when I had children.

Whether the culture really has changed or we're just talking more about family issues, many meetings feel unprepared for the number and severity of problems faced by families under their care. And no wonder! In the past months, I have known of Quaker families struggling with divorce, infidelity, domestic violence, addictions, sexual and physical abuse, acting out children, custody problems, financial difficulties, chronic illness, grief and more. Friends are called on to be helpful in increasingly complex situations that meetings did not openly discuss in the past.

Even the word "family" reflects a wider reality than we may have grown up with. We find in our meetings single parents, remarried families, mixed race families, gay and lesbian couples and families, and various living-together arrangements.

Individuals and caregiving committees often feel overwhelmed and under-prepared for the issues that arise. Yet Friends have many empowering tools available for supporting one another through the challenges that our lives present.

The Power of the Meeting Community

When we are at our best, Quakers are capable of reaching out with love and insight to each other. In our worship, we wait in silence, listening intently for the Spirit's message. We trust that there is a Power listening when we pray. Offering a gift of listening to each other can be an expression of love that connects us spiritually and satisfies us deeply.

When we remember our belief in the Inner Light we can relax more and think better. We can trust the family's internal healing capacity and take a respectful stance toward each person. As caregivers we don't have to "fix" people, but we can provide loving support as they find their way to healing.

Among the most critical of our structures is a caring community. Whenever a concern arises we are better able to respond when we have shared deeply in the past and have developed bonds of love and trust with one another. A member of a small urban meeting spoke during worship recently of her cancer diagnosis. In the fellowship that followed, people asked her about her treatment, her needs, her hope and how the meeting could be helpful. I was moved by the loving concern expressed, and thought of the more polite, distant response she might have received. We may become distant when we fear that a personal question could elicit some embarrassing emotion, or a request for our time or effort that we don't feel able to give. We may be guarding our own fear or grief. Or we may momentarily be forgetting the powerful gift of listening. As we pay attention to our connectedness this distance can disappear, and we can be lovingly present.

When a Family Problem Comes to Your Committee

Concerns may come to our pastoral care committees in a variety of ways. It is easiest for the committee to respond when a family member contacts someone on the committee and asks for support. On those occasions we don't have to worry about being intrusive. However, we often learn of a concern when a committee member observes something troubling or when another meeting member calls the committee's attention to a situation. In those cases the committee must discern what might be the most appropriate response. Though there may be a concern for the family's privacy, it must not prevent us from reaching out with a friendly inquiry. The family may be hurt that no one in the meeting noticed that they were struggling or offered support.

Often a pastoral care committee sends a member who feels at ease with the family to express loving concern and ask how the meeting could be helpful. We may offer a clearness committee to help a family through a difficult decision-making process. Perhaps a small group could meet in the family's home for worship. Regular phone calls could be set up so the family members are reminded that we care and will listen. Maybe meals and rides are needed.

Although I often hear caregivers lament that such gestures and offers feel so insubstantial in the face of tragedy, I regularly hear families express immense gratitude for the sense of community these thoughtful offers can engender. Caregivers may need to recall times when we were "on the receiving end" to know how powerful a message of love can be.

Finding Support beyond the Meeting

It can be tricky to discern what situations can be dealt with by the care and good listening and spiritual support that we can offer, and what situations are beyond out limits. One measure is our own sense of exhaustion and frustration. By sharing in our pastoral care committees when we feel depleted by a family's needs, it may help develop a fuller awareness of the limits to the committee's skills and energies. By keeping ourselves aware of outside supports that may be available we can feel freer to recognize our limitations.

Quarter Care Committees: In very complicated family situations, monthly meetings can be supported in significant ways by their larger communities. Where meetings are near enough to each other to provide practical help, Friends have formed "Quarter Care Committees." In areas where there are no other meetings nearby, other religious congregations in a community might work together in similar ways. More people can mean more hands, so active help like meals and rides can be provided for a longer time. More people can also mean more brains, so difficult decisions like when to involve the police or how to choose nursing care can receive more attention.

More attention to the spiritual needs of a family and the caregivers can significantly support those efforts. The Quarter Care Committee may provide regular worship in a family's home, or a meeting for healing. Even when meetings are widely scattered, more people can hold the suffering family and friends in the Light.

Referring for Professional Help: When a family needs professional support, there is still a role for the meeting. Sometimes the meeting may provide transportation, childcare or funding to actively assist the family to attend therapy. And at times the referral to therapy comes with the help of the pastoral care committee.

In "Helping Friends Seek Professional Help," (see p. 217) Barbara Snipes discusses at length the issue of making a variety of professional referrals. And in the March 1999 issue on alcoholism, Alex Scott gives good, down-to-earth advice that can be helpful in many kinds of difficult situations.

Members of your committee may want to create a listing of professional resources that are available in the community. In some meetings, there may be Friends who have professional expertise as well as a personal understanding of the family's spiritual needs. Yearly meetings may provide lists of resources or other information.

Some meetings make a book of various resources available to the membership. Such a book serves the double purpose of sharing information and encouraging Friends to seek support for problems they may be experiencing. In addition to counselors, the listing may include lawyers, divorce mediators, addictions specialists, doctors, holistic health providers, low-cost housing and welfare rights advocates.

Risks in the Meeting's Caring

We would like our meetings' support of our members to be loving and seamless. Yet we know that our meetings and our pastoral care committees are filled with human beings with fears and flaws and vulnerabilities. By being attentive to our limitations we may be able to sidestep some of the pitfalls and to be forgiving of one another when our efforts fall short of our ideals.

Confidentiality: A true dilemma arises when we consider confidentiality. Many years ago when my family was relatively new to our meeting, I was about to undergo some major surgery. Since our children were young and our parents were ill, I spoke to a meeting elder about some concrete assistance for us. When I got home from the hospital, I was quite surprised when Friends I hardly knew arrived with casseroles and sent cards. "What happened?" I asked a friend.

"Did someone get up after worship and announce I was having a hysterectomy?" I thought I was joking, but my friend said, "Why, yes!"

It took me a while to understand the balance of community and privacy. I try to remember my initial discomfort upon hearing of that announcement, and weigh those opposing needs. We wish to strive for sensitivity to those we are meaning to help. It is best to ask people whether we can share their needs widely in hopes of a wider response or if they would prefer a smaller circle be aware of their situation.

Knowing Where To Turn With A Concern: When a meeting has shown the ability to be sensitive with one family's dilemma, another family will notice the greater safety created in the community and be more ready to ask for help. But how does a person know with whom to speak? Since many meetings have evolving membership, taking care to avoid an "insider" and "outsider" level of information is critical. Members of pastoral care committees can regularly inform Friends about their role and availability. Some meetings post the name of an individual who can be contacted, usually the clerk of the pastoral care committee or the clerk of the meeting. If a problem is potentially shameful, it can be even more difficult for a member to trust a group, and it may help to know that an individual can be approached. In some situations, the discernment available in a group is of enough value to overcome the concern about privacy.

Choosing Sides: Avoiding the common pitfall of choosing sides is of particular concern in dealing with family problems. Despite our well-honored belief that "there is that of God in everyone," we seem to need a "wrong-doer" when a couple breaks up or charges of abuse surface. But when we choose sides, or seem to, the possibility of being helpful dissipates rapidly. The safety is lost that people in turmoil need in order to ask for our assistance. And since ours is a faith community, we have a special role in continuing our love and support in the face of human error.

Why, when it's clearly not helpful, do we feel the pull to pick a side? Getting up close to people in pain is a difficult task in itself. We want to understand just how such a thing could happen, sometimes fearing that our own family could be struck by a similar event. If we or those we love have been divorced, involved in infidelity, remarried, sought custody of children or suffered in an abusive relationship, we probably have unhealed feelings and needs. The process of seeking clarity, of asking others for their help in discerning our involvement, of listening instead of "helping," may help us and our community.

Expectations About Change: Many meetings have found that the more broadly they define "family," the more deeply people connect. By discovering commonalities of experience, we transcend differences and open possibilities of mutual caring. Yet, we can do an injustice by expecting everyone in our community to be able to "transcend differences" at the same pace.

Supporting inclusive attitudes may border on a paradoxical rigidity, where only the current version of the "politically correct" outlook is acceptable. In these situations, those who have less comfort or experience with diversity may be the ones feeling out of place and needing a welcome and patience. Most of us have work to do to be more loving, either in the direction of accepting more diverse members and families, or accepting those who are struggling with inclusivity.

The Meeting's Wounds: When a family within the meeting has sustained a tragedy, our immediate attention and focus is understandably on the family members themselves. But the fabric of the meeting also has been torn. The community can find ways of moving toward healing itself as well. Sometimes when the tragedy involves a death, the memorial service is a transforming and moving experience for the meeting. But when problems involve no comforting ritual, such as a disability, divorce, loss of a job, custody battle or domestic violence, the meeting needs to be creative and sensitive. In our zeal to avoid gossip, we may also avoid opportunities to speak of our own painful feelings. Meetings for healing and other less formal occasions for discussion can be times to recognize our grief and deepen our connections to each other.

Summary

I believe Quakers are in a strong position to be the caring communities we all need when life becomes difficult. Our values of community, listening, respect and inclusion, as well as traditional structures like pastoral care committees, are powerful tools we can use confidently and intentionally when families need help.

Judith Owens, a member of Haddonfield (NJ) Meeting, has worked with meetings and members as a counselor for Friends Counseling Service and with Philadelphia Yearly Meeting's project, "Deepening and Strengthening Our Meetings as Faith Communities." She works as a family therapist.

One Meeting's Experience: Meetings Supporting Families through Tough Times

Instead of our usual story of One Meeting's Experience, in this issue we bring you vignettes of several meetings who are using creativity and caring in responding to the needs of families.

In one small meeting the live-in boyfriend of a single mother with young children left the family and moved out of state. It wasn't a divorce exactly, since they hadn't been married. On the other hand, the emotional and financial consequences for the mother and her children was just as disorienting. The meeting rallied round in support of the family members who remained in the meeting.

A child developed a fear of death that preoccupied her and kept her awake at night. Her parents, unable to reassure her, asked her if she would like to have a clearness committee in the meeting. There was a session in which Friends shared their feelings about death and their techniques for falling asleep when they were preoccupied. Thereafter, the child slept better and there was a sweet sense of closeness between her and the adults who had met with her.

Several meetings have faced the break-up of a same gender couple who had been regarded in the meeting as the same as married. The range of responses was colored by the gifts and limitations of the meetings and the individuals involved. In one case, there was a meeting for divorce in which the couple and the meeting members had an opportunity to grieve the loss of what had been. In another case the partner who left expressed irritation with those who felt that the meeting should have had a role, "We weren't married after all." Nonetheless, the other partner was grieving, and the meeting was perplexed about how to give support to both.

One meeting made very conscious and careful efforts to be loving and supportive to both partners in a marital break-up. Yet each of the partners shared the feeling that the meeting had been more supportive of the other. Members of the meeting continue to stand in steadfast support of both as they find their way, and both partners are still active in the meeting.

In many meetings families with young children have faced the serious illness of one of the parents. One meeting collaborated with another church in bringing in meals for the family on alternating weeks. Members of another meeting did ten loads of laundry each week to support the healthy spouse who was caring for her seriously ill husband. Other families in a meeting invited the children for overnights with their children so that they could have a time away from the stressful situation. Meetings held prayer circles that helped both the family and the meeting members stay open to the Spirit during a time of illness.

Questions for Reflection

1. How do families access help in our meeting?
2. Is there a sense of being known, of safety, in the meeting? How do we encourage a loving exchange of information so that support can be offered?
3. Do we create the time and space to get to know each other, or are we focused on "getting the job done?" Is it time for us to consider a retreat, more social time, some intergenerational fun?
4. How can we support listening to each other as a Spirit-led activity?
5. Are those who offer pastoral care to our meeting supported by each other and the meeting?
6. When families ask for support and help, do we know where to get information about community resources?
7. Could we organize a Quarter Care Committee or collaboration with other churches for complicated and long-term problems?

Reaching Out to Singles in Our Meetings

Pastoral Care Newsletter, Vol. 6, No. 4 • June 1999

By Bonalyn Mosteller

THINK ABOUT THE LAST THREE NON-WORK-RELATED CONVERSATIONS you had with people. What did you talk about? Did you mention recent events with your kids, grandchildren or spouse? Did you refer to recent activities and conversations with such significant others? Think of the last time you met someone you hadn't seen for awhile. Did you immediately ask "what's new" with the person's children or spouse?

What responses do single people have in such situations? There is often an uncomfortable silence while the single person thinks what is "significant" enough to share: "Dare I tell this person I am concerned about my ailing dog? While important to me, my dog pales in comparison to having grandchildren to talk about." These can be stressful, even sad, moments for singles in that they can reinforce how different singles' life circumstances and issues may be.

Of course, some singles have grandchildren and some marrieds don't, so the example is not completely valid. However, the point is to heighten awareness that singles may experience themselves as outside the mainstream of meetings more than we think.

Many single people feel well integrated into the life of their meeting and play active, even leadership, roles. Even those Friends may from time to time feel outside the mainstream. Here we'll explore ideas about how to make meetings more comfortable and accepting for all the single people among us.

Who Are the Singles in Your Meeting?

When you hear the word "singles," which faces in your meeting come to mind? You may picture young, unmarried women and men. The classification of "singles," however, might include never-marrieds of all ages, separated but married people, people recently separated who had been in long-term (but unmarried) relationships, people in same gender relationships or interested in same gender relationships who don't feel comfortable having the nature of their sexual orientation made public, middle aged or older single people, and recent or long-term widows/widowers or divorced people. The singles group at the FGC Gathering has defined itself as being for "those who have never married and those who have lost a partner to separation, death or divorce."

The categories above call attention to middle aged or older singles separately. My experience has been that as single people reach middle/late middle age (or older), their singleness may become "invisible." The assumption may be that if people have been single a long time, they must want it that way and must, therefore, not want others to think of them in the traditional category of "single." This could be a false assumption, in turn leading such people to feel more isolated as they age.

The same could be true for older widows/widowers—especially widows. I learned through years of hospice work and leading grief and bereavement groups that often shortly after an older spouse's death, people stopped referring to the emotional grieving process (although they continued to help problem-solve issues). With younger widows/widowers, it seemed more customary to discuss the emotional loss and inquire about whether the person was seeing anyone new.

Pastoral care committees in our meetings generally reach out quickly to married people who separate. However, when break-ups occur in relationships with less formal commitments, the suffering may be equally great or greater because such relationships may not be taken as seriously by others. Examples might include break-ups in same gender relationships, relationships without traditional marriage contracts, or break-ups of very young couples.

Another special challenge may be for meetings to support both people during separations and divorces (see p. 98). It may seem natural to give more support to the more verbal, extroverted person or to one who has been left or reports abuse within the relationship. It requires intentional effort to offer equal support to both parties. And, of course, divorces can cause as much emotional pain as deaths, or even more.

In addition to thinking about nontraditional categories of singles, pastoral caregivers also might consider the numbers of active versus inactive singles. Obviously, inactive members/attenders are not having their needs met by the meeting. Even active singles who are well integrated into the life of the meeting may have needs that are not being met. How would you know? Some ideas are included below.

Learning about the Singles in Your Meeting

Your committee might want to begin by stepping back to get a big picture overview of the singles in their meeting. How many single people are there? And what proportion of the total meeting do they represent? You might be surprised to identify how high this proportion is. But even if there is only one single person in the meeting, that person warrants the meeting's pastoral consideration.

Would singles in your meeting agree that a substantial number of meeting activities seem to be inclusive of them? A first step for the pastoral care committee could be to consider unintended ways in which singles might feel excluded from activities. For example, the idea of Quaker 8's suggests four couples. What about 7's? When planning meetings and events, do you consider the special challenges of childcare for single parents? Could you rename "family night" to make the event more inclusive of singles (and marrieds without children as well)? Are events held during work hours when most younger singles are not able to attend? If our meetings can become more aware of unintended ways in which singles might feel in a minority outgroup, they can begin to find creative ways to make activities more singles-friendly.

One strategy for the pastoral care committee is to call a meeting of singles and ask them in what ways their needs *are* and *are not* being met by the meeting. Ideally, singles who don't regularly attend the meeting would also be phoned. In this way, a larger proportion of singles' experiences will be represented.

Another strategy is to ask a single member or attender to be responsible for investigating singles resources in the community, particularly local church-related and/or spiritual singles' events and meetings. This person can then share the information quarterly in the monthly meeting newsletter.

Consider ways to ensure that pastoral care reflects on singles' needs and issues. Do you have at least one single person on your pastoral care committee? Ask this person to be a "point person/pulse taker" for singles. This person would be charged with identifying singles' issues and communicating them to the full committee. Of course, it is not valid to assume that one person could adequately represent all singles' perspectives, but it is helpful to have someone charged with keeping singles' concerns in mind.

Each Quaker meeting could devote a major portion of one pastoral care committee meeting to reflection on singles' issues. Ask several singles to attend and have an open discussion. From time to time, reflect on whether singles' needs and interests might have changed over time. If so, are different approaches needed?

If your meeting has an Outreach Committee, it could be asked to come up with a plan for *internal* outreach, which would include a segment devoted to outreach to singles.

Some Practical Suggestions

The best way to welcome single people is to make sure that your meeting has activities that are welcoming regardless of a person's family status—worship sharing and study groups, hymn sings, pot-luck meals, etc.

In scheduling committee meetings and other meeting events consider the needs of single working people and single parents. Are there singles who need help with transportation for evening meetings?

For singles who don't have grown children or families, it would be especially appreciated to be considered at holidays, which can be especially rough. Singles would really appreciate invitations for holiday meals. Something as simple as a sign-up sheet could be arranged for folks wanting to share the holidays with others.

Singles may need focused support at a time of a health or other personal crisis: transportation to medical appointments, someone to bring in prepared food and/or someone to talk with.

One of the most obvious supports, if there are enough singles in the meeting, is to form a singles group. Even if singles don't come forward asking for support to start such groups, meetings can proactively help singles explore the need. A singles group, then, can serve as a natural, organic approach to outreach to single people in the community, without the "proselytizing" connotations that make Friends uncomfortable. If singles do begin a regular group, the pastoral care committee can support them by offering meeting space and perhaps even some funding for special events. It is important, though, that singles be responsible for their group including generating funding themselves. More detail about creating singles groups is presented on page 279.

There has been a Philadelphia Singles organization in existence for well over ten years. At times the membership has reached more than one hundred, with 40–50 people attending monthly meetings at the peak of the organization's activity. The organization is open to all single meeting members/attenders of area meetings and to others regardless of religious affiliation or belief. Radnor Monthly Meeting has served as the home meeting for this organization for at least eight years. Radnor has generously provided space and covered utility costs during this period. Philadelphia Yearly Meeting has also contributed funds to the group.

Participants have felt blessed by the atmosphere of camaraderie that they experienced. The group leaders intentionally try to establish an atmosphere of "people caring about people" rather than the more common dating orientation often associated with singles groups. Occasionally, I would hear people say that they were looking forward to attending in order to reconnect with people for whom they had generated genuine regard. I warmly remember a few meetings where I experienced the aliveness or spirit that I associate with a "gathered meeting." This seemed to occur when we shared at some new, deeper level: when we sang "Amazing Grace" under the stars after a picnic or when we shared personal hobbies/passions that most touched our hearts.

As a byproduct of hosting the singles, Radnor Meeting has been strengthened. People who may never have been inside a meetinghouse came to know where Radnor Meeting was located. A fair number have become very active attenders of the meeting, serving in leadership and committee member capacities.

Not all the ideas suggested in this article will be appropriate for your meeting. My prayer would be that your pastoral care committee will make some time to ponder the issues raised here. And, even more important, I hope that each meeting will find at least one new way to minister to single people in your meeting. The ultimate goal for meetings is to be places where *all* members, including those who are single, experience the depth of caring required to trust that they can voice their needs and expect that responsiveness will result.

Bonalyn Mosteller is a member of Radnor (PA) Meeting where she has served on numerous committees and been clerk of the pastoral care committee. She founded her own consulting company which specializes in organizational development, culture change and assisting companies to enliven people's spirits in the workplace.

As a Single Person

As a single person who is not in a significant relationship, the meeting is the place that I come to be accepted, to share my love and gifts, and to belong.

I have no family nearby so it takes a lot of effort on my part to have my needs met in what feels like a couples-oriented world. In a world where odd numbers at the dinner table are avoided and couples are awkward about going out together with single people, I can feel left out.

In more than 25 adult years of being Quaker—all of them single and unattached—I've been part of two large urban meetings one on the east coast and one on the west coast and now am in a medium-sized meeting in a smaller city. In every meeting I've been very active in committee work and other volunteer activities for the meeting community, and along the way I've gotten to know just about everyone in the meeting each time. In the larger meetings, I found a number of other single women near my age as well as numerous couples I developed close friendships with. As a middle-aged person finding my place in the social life of a smaller meeting has been more of a challenge. There are no other single women my age and couples near my age are tied up with child rearing. I have, however, received generous pastoral care from this meeting. Shortly after I transferred my membership, I was diagnosed with cancer. The meeting asked what support I wanted and then followed through with escorts to chemotherapy and prepared meals.

Even in the larger meetings, finding my social niche hasn't always gone smoothly. Since I have been active in the meeting some people have had the perception that I'm self-sufficient and happy and don't need special care. There have been times when I've been clerk of this or that but no one calls me up for a meal or a movie or a walk—I find I'm treated as a self-sufficient ecosystem. These have been the loneliest times for me. I, and other single people, have a need to be included in the social life of meeting members, to feel valued without being a super-volunteer.

Many singles are not so outgoing as I am. They need to be invited to volunteer, to socialize, and to become part of the community. I encourage pastoral care committees to be considerate of the depth and breadth of single members' support systems within the meeting. I also encourage them to provide evening adult socializing for both couples and singles in addition to asking for their involvement in the life of the meeting through volunteer work.

Nancy Irving, a member of Olympia (WA) Monthly Meeting, has been active as committee member and staff for Friends World Committee for Consultation/Section of the Americas. She has served on and clerked various committees, including Ministry and Oversight, within monthly meetings in Philadelphia, Portland (OR), and Olympia.

Singles Groups: Keys to Success

- Even if your meeting is small, encourage singles to meet together at someone's home, perhaps quarterly. Each person could identify resources she/he has to offer others and then also to ask for types of support needed from others.
- Encourage smaller Quaker singles groups to link to other local, church-related singles groups. Getting larger groups together adds exponentially to the level of fellowship.
- Encourage several meetings which are close geographically to join together to form a singles group.
- Establish a regular meeting place at a centrally located meeting. Occasionally, events will be held at other locations, but having one "home" location is important so that people are not deterred from attending because they don't know where the group is meeting this month.
- A monthly newsletter is extremely useful, perhaps essential. This can be as simple as a flier with reminders about upcoming meetings. It is key to advertise group activities two to three months ahead of time to pique interest and to get dates on people's calendars.
- Groups need several leaders, not just one. Steering committees work best. If only one person comes forward to lead, encourage this person to identify others to create a steering committee. Having a strong, upbeat, organized leader and steering committee can be crucial to the group's success.
- Another criterion for success is that the atmosphere of the meetings needs to be one of camaraderie and creation of friendships—not one of finding a date. This tone is best set by the

attitudes and personal behaviors of the steering committee members as well as by the types of monthly programs. As a way to generate this atmosphere, make sure that the steering committee members are equally welcoming of both genders and all types/ages/races of single people.

- Time needs to be spent on introductions at each meeting. This can be accomplished using different questions each month to generate energy and provide new ways to get acquainted. Examples are asking people to introduce themselves by sharing something they are concerned about in the world or something they view as positive happening in the world or in their lives. A variation is to ask people first to answer the "introduction" questions in pairs or quartets and then to share a partner's response with the larger group.

- Singles meetings need to have a variety of programs/activities. Some successful examples are singing accompanied by guitar or piano, picnics, sports (volleyball is especially popular), speakers, square dancing and occasional weekend two-day outings. Speakers are useful, if their topics relate to singles. Some successful topics have been parenting, dating and advantages of being single. An example of a creative activity is asking everyone to bring something that reflects a keen interest or hobby. Give each person a few minutes to share his/her "passion."

- Regular meetings need to be interactive. Having a speaker who answers questions from one person at a time doesn't meet this criterion very well. Meetings are more successful when group exercises are employed which ensure that everyone gets to talk. For example, after a speaker, small groups can first share thoughts on a couple of predetermined questions and then share thoughts in the larger group. In this way, everyone has a voice. Another variation would be having discussion topics where people share their personal examples/challenges related to a speaker's points.

- When planning meetings, it is helpful if steering committee members think about creative ways to get more people involved. The principle here is that involvement builds commitment and enhanced valuing of the group. An example of a low-risk way to get people more involved is to recruit new people to be greeters at each meeting.

- Time also needs to be devoted to "advertising" upcoming events. Often, future attendance depends upon the enthusiasm of the person explaining the events. Recruit good "salespeople" for this role.
- Always remember to acknowledge any and all people who have made contributions to the group. As people feel appreciated, they usually become even more committed.

Questions for Reflection

1. Who are the singles in our meeting? At what life stages are they? Who among them are active in the life of the meeting and who are not?
2. What could we do to learn from the single people in our meeting whether they have needs and desires of the meeting that are not being fulfilled?
3. Are our meeting activities "singles friendly" or do we set up barriers that make single people feel outside the normative group?
4. How could we support singles and others in the meeting in sharing holiday meals?
5. What resources do we have to be responsive to the needs of single persons for practical and emotional support when there is a health crisis?
6. How could we support the development of a singles group within our meeting or our quarter?
7. Who on our committee can take responsibility for giving attention to identifying singles issues and bringing them to the attention of the full committee from time to time?

Pastoral Care of Men
in Our Meetings

Pastoral Care Newsletter, Vol. 4, No. 4 • June 1997

Is there anything meetings can or should do specifically for the pastoral care of the men in our communities? The needs of men tend not to be discussed separately from generic discussions of women and men together. Yet men's groups are developing in many meetings, and some seem to be tapping into a need for men to look at their life in the meeting as men.

Since perspectives on men's spiritual and pastoral needs seem to be as varied as men themselves, PCN has asked several men to write about their experience.

Mike Hayes, Westfield (NJ) Meeting

The standards for masculinity and the criteria for "success" as a human male are changing, and quickly. Some of us have been caught between our culture's expectations that a man maintain the appearance of strength and our internal thirst for spiritual connection.

For me, the concept of a spiritual path made little sense until I was ready for it. A busy life, full of family and career and diversion, seemed to leave little time or energy for the spiritual.

It seems that many spiritual journeys, like mine, begin with acknowledgment of a feeling that there is something missing from our lives. This may become a deep, growing desire for a way to make sense of things, to relieve feelings of dissociation and powerlessness. This step often involves a great deal of confusion and pain. This can be a lonely process, especially for one conditioned to hide these perceived "deficiencies." With or without support, we make our best guess, put one foot in front of the other and stumble off down a path.

These experiences in my case took many years and a fair amount of discomfort. My own propensities prevented me from seeking support, and kept me from seeking to share my experiences with others. On the occasions when someone would offer support, I would deny any such need; I was ashamed of being found out. Whenever I felt led to offer support, I was met with similar defenses. I didn't want to intrude on their processes. Ironically, I now see that the most productive sharing between men often results from expressed concern over a friend's condition. It would be wonderful if we could teach spiritual navigation skills the way we teach sports skills and attract more travelers.

Having an individual guide or a functional men's group can be of great help as we seek to learn these spiritual navigation skills. Knowing that a respected male can meet weaknesses honestly in order to overcome them can encourage other men in their own challenges. Our meeting has had several exemplary individuals who would have been wonderful mentors, and I regret that I didn't spend more quality time in their company. They had much to say that I want to hear now that they are not around.

There seems to be an element of guidance in the timing of spiritual sharing between men. Each leg of a spiritual journey, each cycle of growth seems to need time to come to a point of readiness for tempering by discussion. Spiritual experiences are subject to adulteration by attempts to express them before their time.

There are those times of mutual trust, respect, and ripeness, however, that leave no doubt about Providence. At those times, an experience can be recounted to a depth which enlightens even the one who experienced it. Freely expressed feelings solidify respect and trust and lead to deeper sharing.

Crossing the gender boundary can be helpful under the right circumstances. There are more women among my informal mentors than men. The binocular perspective of male-female discussion can be an effective means of spiritual discovery.

I would dearly love to be able to provide our meetings' caregivers with a handbook on how to support this. Not all men desire to embark on a spiritual path and no cookbook nurturing system will serve all the men who do.

As pastoral care committees give attention to the needs of individual men in the meeting they can consider establishing mentoring relationships between a man who is known to be struggling with a certain issue and another who is known to have dealt successfully with a similar issue—such as the needs of fathers of young children or health issues or balancing career demands with other dimensions of life. If there are men in the meeting who wish to establish a men's group, the pastoral care committee can provide sponsorship and logistical support.

First Day School presents further opportunities to begin to practice those spiritual navigation skills, to help our young men be comfortable with the concept of seeking in the company of other males. Sponsoring a men's camping trip, work day or sporting event can help to build community among the men of the meeting.

A healthy, growing spiritual condition is a priceless treasure. I believe we need to work harder at exploring ways to help our men envision and realize it. Our meetings need to explore and experiment with greater awareness and zeal.

Douglas Campbell, Moorestown, NJ

As I look into the eyes of the men gathered for our weekly meeting, I am always amazed that such a meeting is actually taking place. The type of meeting I am speaking of is not just the gathering of a group of men, but the extraordinary sense of being present to one another, seeing past the usual armor, roles and defenses and glimpsing the essential man. What was once a rare event that happened only with my best friend or with my wife, has become a way of life. Thanks to the time spent in this men's group I have begun to see all men as potential brothers. This perspective is a tremendous blessing that all of us deserve.

I am a member of a men's group that has been meeting once a week for nearly three years to talk, listen, discuss and debate the major and minor issues of our lives and times. The issues run the gamut of joys, frustrations and rage, dreams, hopes and fears, sorrows, sex and shame, fathers, mothers and siblings, perception, reception and deception, yesterday, today and tomorrow. Though we feel only marginally affiliated with anything resembling the men's movement, we share with men's groups all over the country the desires and yearnings of finding our own paths.

We are a leaderless group that rotates the role of facilitator each week. In the beginning our meetings operated very much in the twelve-step model. No comments were allowed during our check-in to the group about our previous week's experiences. We had space to speak and men willing to just listen to our words. Eventually there was modification to allow feedback, but no advice or criticism—only words of support.

So much feedback was shuttling back and forth that it got to be that no one could distinguish between where well meaning comments became advice. The boundaries got messy and fluid, and we were talking to one another! We were actively, emotionally, intensely, spontaneously, genuinely, compassionately engaging each other! When the smoke cleared, the only casualties were the inhibitions we had outgrown, and the victor was the man in each of us who had only dreamed that he could express it all and still love the men who share his weaknesses.

One of our greatest gifts to one another is that we can see changes in others that they haven't yet noticed in themselves. We can see them in their fullness and beauty and encourage and honor their development. We all grow strong by blessing one another's growth.

The final point is closure. We take some time and make it a practice to give attention to leaving each other. We close our eyes, link hand-over-hand in the center of our circle, and remain silent for a few minutes. Each man can give thanks in his own way. We end with the same eye contact that started our meeting.

Anonymous

To my knowledge, three of the active members of my small meeting have joined men's groups; in fact, three different men's groups.

All of us have been affected by social changes in sex roles: we are the first generation of males to be faced with anything approaching equality for women. The liberation of sexual minorities has also shaken our social foundations. The roles we learned as children and adolescents are useless for today's relationships. We find ourselves strong, successful and bewildered.

Our fathers were strong and successful, and if they were bewildered they never let us see it. A few untrue stereotypes, an effects-only view of the world (either you did right or you did wrong), seemed to represent their knowledge of masculinity. These did not prepare us for the dynamics of truly close relationships, especially those with strong, successful women.

We turn to each other for release from bewilderment. One of us goes off into the woods and becomes a he-man with adventures and good talk. Another goes off into Freudian and other psychologies, explores the "real" self, finds wonderful mouth-filling words to describe and thus to understand his states of mind. I attach myself to a guru whose spiritual journey has sent him around the world and who has garnered a world full of spiritual exercise. He guides the group into an openness. The warm, loving, sincerity of the group engendered by him leads me to find within myself some of my own answers.

The group gives self-help, not therapy. I came to the group needing therapy, and found strength in the group to go to therapy. But it also gives me a time to explore my life as a male human being, to take my maleness out of me and look at it , not as I alone see it, but also as the rest of the group sees it. It allays the bewilderment and some of the panic the bewilderment can create. It does this through loving where those warm common, everyday words of everyday experiences come from: working out a meaning for everyday life.

We had one guy who didn't make it. He was rather different from the rest of us because he wasn't too verbal. I bet a he-man group would have done wonders for him. I guess the message here is not to give up if your first men's group experience doesn't work.

The only pitfall I can think of is the possibility of a breach of confidentiality, but to my knowledge this has not occurred within our group.

Nate Terrell, Clementon, NJ

Four years ago, I decided to start a men's group since I longed for the opportunity to share my fears, hopes, etc. with a group of men in a trusting, noncompetitive forum. Consequently, I asked all the men I knew about their interest in such a group and eventually collected five men who appeared to share my vision. We agreed to meet on a monthly basis and began to discuss what we were trying to accomplish.

It took us three years to figure this out. Along the way, we have survived (1) endless discussions about whether we should focus on our own problems, on projects such as mentoring "at risk" youth, on achieving our personal goals or on what seem in retrospect to be about a hundred other ideas; (2) personality and stylistic differences among group members which caused group tension; and (3) anger on the part of some group members about others missing meetings and subsequent discussions about the level of commitment each member should have toward the group.

Although I have no doubt this group will continue to evolve over time, we have finally reached a level of stability that most of us thought was impossible in the midst of our intense search to define ourselves. The group member who has been given the leadership role for that meeting leads the group in a discussion on whatever topic he wants. Recent topics have included what we feel good about ourselves as men, how the story of the prodigal son is relevant to our lives and our relationships with our fathers.

Rather than give advice or feedback if a member brings up a personal problem, we usually simply "hear the person out" and ask questions which might help him view his situation more clearly. Just as in a meeting for worship, common themes often emerge which speak to all of our conditions.

I almost always leave our meetings feeling strengthened and renewed by the deep connection I feel with my fellow group members and the support I receive from them. In fact, I get something completely unique from this group. Perhaps it is simply the sense that I have been bathed in positive male energy.

One of our long-term goals is to provide mentoring to "at risk" youth through outdoor education or fun activities such as canoe trips. In the meantime, we have chosen to sponsor a couple of scholarships to a Quaker summer camp in South Jersey which will be utilized by kids who would not otherwise have had the opportunity to gain the benefits of a camp experience.

I believe that men can gain a great deal of meaning and fulfillment by participating in a men's group. Since all the men's groups I know are a bit different in both focus and purpose, I would encourage interested men to shop around to find the right one or start their own if they can't find what they are looking for.

Nate Terrell conducts workshops on men's issues as well as other topics for social service agencies, schools, etc.

Starting a Men's Group in Your Meeting

The ultimate success of a men's group is dependent on there being a core group of men with enthusiasm and resilience to stick with a group as it finds its way. To begin the process and identify men who may be interested in a group, the pastoral care committee might schedule a one-time event for men, perhaps with a speaker. If there is interest in an ongoing group the committee can offer publicity and support.

PCN spoke with participants in men's groups and gathered the following list of issues to be addressed as a group is being formed:

Purpose: Is it worship? mutual support on personal issues? problem solving? projects? (or a hundred other ideas?) Two groups report that they had to struggle at first with questions of purpose. After a while the groups found a focus, and some participants left to find or create another group that better fit their needs.

Open vs. closed group: In an open group, the time and place are announced and whoever shows up for a given meeting is the group. There is no requirement that an individual attend all of the sessions, but it is essential that a core group attend regularly to provide stability. In a closed group, participants make a commitment to attend regularly for a fixed period (six months, a year); new members are only admitted at those fixed intervals. One group cited a commitment to regular attendance as essential to the success of their group. Another has prospered as an open group for over five years.

Size of the group: A men's group can thrive with five or six men committed to regular attendance. Some find a group larger than eight to ten begins to crowd the sharing time and to complicate questions of safety. On the other hand, an open group in a large meeting frequently has 12–15 in attendance.

Frequency of meeting: Groups meet as frequently as weekly or as infrequently as monthly. Sometimes instead of a regular men's group, men in the meeting will schedule special event for men once or twice a year. Most men's groups find it helpful to meet on a regular, predictable schedule. More frequent meetings, such as once a week, contribute to greater depth of sharing.

Location: Will the group meet at the meetinghouse or consistently in another location or will it rotate in member's homes or other locations? A consistent location is helpful in an open group so that occasional attenders can easily find the meeting. Meeting in members' homes can contribute to a greater sense of closeness.

Issues of safety have had to be dealt with in all of the groups we spoke with. Participants may have concerns about how deeply they can share and whether they will be treated with respect if they reveal issues with which they are struggling. A closed group can contribute to a greater sense of safety as participants come to know and have confidence in each other.

Various kinds of structures and norms can be established to enhance a sense of safety: some have found safety in a worship-sharing format with no feedback, others have structured feedback in mutually agreed upon ways, others require participants to speak only from one's own personal perspective avoiding discussing and interpreting the other men's experience. A commitment to confidentiality is an important ingredient in trust building.

Structure: Several of the groups we talked with said that they started with a "check-in." That is a time when members report anything significant that has happened to them in the past week or raise an issue or question with which they are wrestling. After the check-in some groups proceed to informal sharing or they pick up on an issue that has been raised in the check-in and discuss it. One group rotates the leadership, and after the check-in the group member who has been given the leadership role for that meeting leads the group in a discussion on whatever topic he chooses.

Issues of power and leadership seem to shift over the life of a group. Most of the men's groups in meetings do not have a formal leader. Some rotate leadership from meeting to meeting. Others evolve a set of "elders" who embody and live out the norms of the apparently leaderless group. Conflict and competitiveness over power and leadership need to be addressed directly to establish the degree of safety necessary for the group to flourish.

Duration: Open groups can go on and on as long as there are people participating. Closed groups that have required a commitment to regular attendance usually have a stopping point at least annually when those who are finding it difficult to attend regularly can leave the group and perhaps others can join.

Questions for Reflection

1. What activities can pastoral care committees encourage to bring men in the meeting together?
2. Are there meeting opportunities—First Day School classes, forums, discussion evenings—specifically for men who want to expand their spiritual contacts and personal resources?
3. How can men in the meeting be made aware of opportunities within the meeting and at the quarterly and yearly meeting level for men to share with one another as men?
4. What can the pastoral care committee do to determine the level of interest in the meeting for forming and maintaining a men's group?

Dealing With Aging

Pastoral Care Newsletter, Vol. 3, No. 3 • March 1996

by Phyllis A. Sanders

Those of us who are involved in pastoral care in Friends meetings and churches need to begin to talk about the process of growing older. Many Friends want their meeting to be a place where they can share their concerns about aging. It is important for pastoral caregivers to seek opportunities to initiate such conversations.

In my years of working with issues of aging on radio and television, I often ended my shows with two short phrases that were like a theme song: "If we're lucky, we'll grow older. So if we're smart, we'll plan for it." It can be helpful to emphasize that we are, in fact, able to have an effect on what our growing older is going to be like (although of course there are some things over which we have no control).

Having a good older age begins now. It begins as we look into ourselves and ask, "Is this the kind of person that I want to be, and continue on that way?" That's what I think we need to say to young people. As my mother used to say, "What you are today is what you're going to be tomorrow." You've heard the saying that your face will be the map of your life. My mother used to say that too, and I would say, "Yes, sure, Mother." But I didn't really understand back then.

Some Things Change; Some Things Stay the Same

People can be reassured when they realize that the aging process involves a continuation of what is familiar and known. When we grow older, we don't come to the top of a mountain and suddenly go falling off the other side. We don't become a different person. But people imagine that "the other side of the mountain"—or "old"—will be some different place, and they say "I don't want to get there. I'm happy where I am now; I don't want to be looking to that time when I'm going to get there." For many people part of this also involves a fear of dying.

There's a tendency to be afraid of change. We want things the way we always had them, living in the place we like, with the people we like to be with. But when we get older, we may no longer be in the place we like, with the people we like, doing what we like to do. But there's something comforting that I have discovered, and that is that even if all these unwelcome changes take place, they'll only be changes on the outside. The important things don't change; they're on the inside.

Older people often have problems getting around; we may be physically limited in what we can do. But even so, since each of us really is the same person we were when we were younger, we can recognize that we are carrying the person who experienced the most exciting time in our life, at age 16, 30, 55, 65 or whenever. We claim that young person as part of our identity. But then we take a long look in the mirror, and say "Oops! Is this me?"

What It Means to Be a Particular Age

It might be interesting to have a discussion in the meeting about what it means to each of us to be the age we are. I've been struck by the fact that every time a person moves or meets a new group of people, he or she has the experience of being only partially known, based on his or her age at that particular time. When I moved to Chappaqua, New York, I was in my 50s. I would say to myself, "What people see is a woman in her 50s, but I'm more than that. At one time I was a 30-year-old woman, and a 35-year-old woman. But all that people see is this outer shell." We all want people to see beyond the outer shell.

The older you get, the harder it is to climb back over the years that you've passed. In other words, if we start meeting people at age 65, 75 or 85, how in the world can we cover all the years of living in a new friendship or in anything else? So we often find that the friends we make in our older years don't have the same depth as the earlier relationships did. Even so, these new friendships provide an opportunity to start out on the basis of shared interests. It's not that my children know yours, but that we know each other, and we're in the same general situation.

All of us are affected by the myths and stereotypes about aging in our culture. We look at older people with their wrinkles and physical problems, and at some unconscious level we may think, "They are where we might be some day." We're not sure that that is what we really want to be, so we feel uncertain. Pastoral care committees need to find ways to help Friends overcome this uncertainty.

When I was doing my television show and interviewing older people about growing older, I would ask them, "Would you like to be 22 again? Or 25?" "Oh no, no," they would reply. Yet there is an image that somehow older people are just longing to become a wonderful young person. This is just a myth, an illusion. When we remember the things that didn't go right in our 20s, we recognize that there are some good things about being at a different stage.

Discrimination

Our society is rife with discrimination—race discrimination, sex discrimination, and age discrimination as well. An example of sex discrimination is a situation in which I, as a woman, am talking to some people, and I make a contribution that I think is worthwhile. But nobody says anything. Then a minute later somebody else—a man—says the same thing I said, and everybody says "Gee, that's a great idea!" And I think, "Wait a minute. Where were they when I said the same thing?" This subtle, unconscious discrimination is something that at some point we women began to be very aware of. What it really meant was that nobody listened to us as women.

The same thing can happen to older people. People can be very polite, just as they are with women. They're listening but they aren't listening. What they don't realize is that older people are really not stupid (although people think that when you get older you get stupid, but they miss the boat). Older folks say to themselves, "Ah, I get the message. It's not what I wanted to hear, but I can see what's happening here."

It helps when an older person is a very visible part of the meeting. In my situation, the fact that I was doing something very public in my broadcasting work made it a lot easier for me to gain people's attention when I said something. But very few older people are so visible. There are some older people you can hardly see. They just sort of move in and out. It's the older people who seem to be disappearing into the woodwork that meetings need to be most concerned about.

The Importance of a Sense of Community

An interesting aspect of my broadcasting work was the opportunity to interview three professors of gerontology who conducted a long term research project about aging in different cultures. The goal of the research was to find out what makes for a satisfactory old age.

What they concluded was that older people are happiest when they are surrounded by people and places they know, and when they are in a setting in which they are known. Then if they become less active, people around them remember when they used to be active, and that gives them a sense of belonging and a feeling of being remembered.

Friends meetings provide something vitally important when they create a sense of continuity with the earlier stages of one's life. People in our meeting are "the people who knew me when."

Some Practical Suggestions

I have come to recognize that as people grow older, they may have good reason to fear that the time may come when nobody will remember them, or what they have done. When you can't walk as fast, and you can't do as many things as you once could, you say to yourself, "Yes, but I once was. I would hope people would remember that I once was."

It's essential that Friends think of ways to affirm older members, being sensitive to the particular individual. People react differently to public acknowledgments. Some Friends would love to be asked to tell stories about the projects and activities of the meeting through the years; others simply want to know that they are remembered. What matters is that the older Friends recognize that we are thinking of them, and that we value what they have done. What is being said to each individual is: "We value you. You are still in our mind. You are still that person who has done all those things."

I know of meetings that have invited older people to come in and talk about their special interests. Everybody has some kind of interest. Give the person an opportunity to share it, and then be sure that it is acknowledged. Some people don't talk; they just "do." It is especially important to acknowledge these behind-the-scenes contributions like flower arranging, cooking or property maintenance. People whose gifts are more artistic or mechanical often don't get much recognition.

I'm thinking of an older Friend in my meeting who is limited now, but was once very active. I remember one time when I went to visit her and her husband, and she brought out their wedding album. We had a delightful time. It isn't always easy to know how to affirm a person who is very limited physically, and no longer active. Don't underestimate the importance of sitting with the older Friend and talking to him or her about the past, with updates on what is currently going on in the meeting.

There's no one approach that always works in visiting older people. The important thing is to provide a friendly, warm environment where the person can feel comfortable sharing. It helps to know the person's family and to seek ways to involve the family in any problem-solving that needs to be done, if that seems comfortable to the older person.

I am really very fortunate; at age 76, I don't have any trouble with my sight or hearing, and I don't have Alzheimer's Disease. I use a cane and I use a scooter; I can live with that. I know of many other people who have a whole range of problems, including problems with hearing, eyesight and remembering. I have a very good friend here at Medford Leas, and I'll say "Let's have dinner together here, tomorrow night," and she says "Phyllis, you know I'll forget it."

Two of the most common problems of aging are problems with hearing and seeing. If people don't hear well they feel left out of conversations, and if they don't see well they miss some of the things that others can see.

Be sure that people can hear you. If they don't hear you, they may not want to say they don't, because they don't want to look stupid. They may worry that if they say "What?" people will talk too loudly, or yell. Unfortunately, some people do yell when they are with someone who is hard of hearing, but that's not the right approach. What you should do is lean forward and speak slowly, and look them straight in the face. Those are little techniques that ought to be passed on to meeting members.

It seems to me that transportation, which becomes an increasing problem for older people, should be the business of the meeting. Transportation assistance could be a larger buddy system for checking on older Friends. Many meetings have a "Friendly contact" system to remain in touch not only with older members, but with members and attenders of all ages.

Special activities for older people can be planned (figure out a way to assist with transportation). We forget that in the olden days it was the sewing, quilting and cooking groups that tied women together. And men had their ties as well.

All types of intergenerational programs are also possible. People who are homebound or living in nursing homes can be visited by kindergartners, elementary and junior high school kids. Programs involving dialogue between young and old are a good idea. Younger people can ask, "What was it like when you were growing up?" or,

"What did the meeting do then?" Or, "What was society like?" People of all ages can be asked, "What are some of our concerns now?" In our meeting we asked some older members to describe what it feels like to grow older, and to share what they would like to have members of the meeting know about aging. A very simple, broad conversation can be of real value to the entire meeting. The pastoral care committee might also want to invite someone who has experience working with older people to come and talk about aging. But don't overlook the wisdom among your own members—of all ages.

Any type of program that opens up discussion about the process of growing older can be a real benefit to the meeting. It's an important way to build community in a world that too often separates old and young.

Phyllis A. Sanders was active in many meetings as her family moved around the United States and Latin America. She began a career in broadcasting at age 52 and worked as a commentator, producer and host of television programs on aging in New York and Philadelphia. She died in 2001.

One Meeting's Ideas for Supporting Older Members

Several years ago, overseers at Haddonfield Meeting noticed that a few of their older members had stopped attending meeting for worship on a regular basis. Through sensitive conversations, they discovered that the older Friends were staying away because of physical problems. The committee then implemented a series of solutions so that each of the older Friends felt comfortable returning to meeting. Shortly thereafter, attenders at a special Adult First Day School discussion came up with a list of suggestions for ways of supporting older members, which follows in a slightly edited form:

- Pay more attention to the spiritual wisdom of older members, perhaps through systematic sharing of values, beliefs and life histories. Work to eliminate prejudice against older people, particularly the infirm aged.
- Know elders well enough to be able to touch, to know when a hug would be welcome. *Never* talk to an aged person as though she or he were a child! (And reconsider the way we talk to children!) Respect the autonomy and dignity of private people. Consult with elders before doing things to or for them.

- Provide comfortable seating with footstools during meeting for worship. Provide transportation to meeting for worship, committee meetings, social gatherings and quarterly and yearly meeting events. (A taxi fund may be needed if no one is conveniently situated to drive).
- Use larger type for the newsletter and meeting list. Also, improve the quality of information shared about meeting events and meeting people, in light of the specific needs of older people.
- Keep in touch with those who are homebound through cards, notes, phone calls and visits. Offer homebound persons the opportunity to worship in their homes with a small group. Hold committee meetings and some social gatherings in the homes of the homebound. (This may involve help with preparing a room or refreshments.)
- Consider various kinds of practical support. Help with the task of clearing out a house, especially before moving. Provide coordination of gifts of food during periods of illness or bereavement, taking dietary restrictions into account. Provide readers for those with limited eyesight. Speak clearly when visiting with those who have hearing problems. Develop a list of services needed by older members, and a list of meeting people who can do specific simple home repairs or other services. Offer to set up clearness committees for those who are trying to decide whether or where to move.
- Support those called to minister to the aged in whatever ways are necessary. These Friends might be released from committee work, given financial compensation for travel, provided with emotional and spiritual support and public recognition.

Some Additional Ideas Offered by Members of the Family Relations Committee

- Younger people need to recognize that older people have fears—fear of developing Alzheimer's Disease or some other incapacitating condition, fear of being dependent on children or other loved ones. As an older Friend put it, "If younger people are going to know us, they need to recognize that we have fears."
- Meetings should emphasize not only the importance of having a valid will, but also the importance of making one's wishes known regarding life support systems, organ donation, what to do with

one's remains and preferences about a memorial service. The meeting and the children or other next of kin should have copies of instructions.

- The pastoral care committee can help when children are estranged from, or angry with, aging relatives, or when relatives disagree with each other (and possibly with the older person's wishes) about what is best.

Questions for Reflection

1. How can we become more open in talking about issues of aging that we face as individuals and as a meeting?
2. What are we doing to help older members feel acknowledged and remembered?
3. How can we reach out to those whose poor hearing affects their participation in worship? What aids have we provided for hearing impaired Friends?
4. What provisions have we made for the special needs of people who have mobility problems? Are handrails, ramps and straight-backed chairs readily available?

Ministry to Older People Experiencing Disabilities

Pastoral Care Newsletter, Vol. 7, No. 1 • September 1999

by Rose Ketterer

I AM NOT YET OLD, having just turned 57 this spring. My background in aging comes from academic study, internships in two nursing homes, and participation in the care of several aged relatives. I have experienced temporary disability, both physical and cognitive, for about eighteen months. I could barely walk, was in constant pain and suffered severe short-term memory disruption. The hardest part of my recuperation was my inability to live as an active Friend. My ministry shriveled and, at times, I wondered whether I really was a Quaker any more. What helped most was encouragement to attend a retreat for which one Friend made all financial and transportation arrangements, and the faithful calls, week after week, from a member of Worship and Ministry, offering rides to meeting. Most disappointing was a small "care circle" that met only once. My remarks rise from this background.

When I began to attend Friends worship, I was struck by the many quite old people who were extremely active in organizing and facilitating the life of the meeting. Since then, I've heard other convinced Friends describe their surprise and delight in the radical leadership of white-haired Friends. It is reassuring to know that none of us will ever be considered unfit for spiritual or social ministry simply by reason of age.

Although many people retain health and strength into their eighties and beyond, sometimes until the very end of their lives, others are not so fortunate. Old age afflicts many with decreased energy, less acute vision and impaired hearing, as well as various chronic health problems. Disability activists sometimes refer to the able-bodied as "temporarily able-bodied," a caution that those of us who live long will probably encounter limitations on our mobility and sensory losses at some time in our lives.

My first experience with the changing needs of an aged person came when I was eleven years old. My grandmother, a strong and determined character, had asked me to accompany her to a social event. After the gathering, we climbed into a trolley car for the journey home. When the trolley started, Grandmom staggered and stumbled across the aisle, bumping her head on a pole. The conductor scolded me, "Why aren't you taking better care of your grandmother, a big girl like you?" My grandmother was tiny, less than five feet tall and slightly built, but I had never thought of her as needing anyone's care, certainly not mine. Shocked and apologetic, it didn't occur to me even then that she had asked me to come along, not as a child to a treat or a companion on an outing, but as an escort. I knew her eyesight was deteriorating because of cataracts. No one knew of the cancer that would incapacitate her soon after that day. She never asked me for help, and I was not sensitive enough to offer any.

The situation reverberates for me today in relation to pastoral care in our Friends meetings. When my grandmother stumbled, I felt helpless. I had no idea how to respond to her weakness. Friends may also hesitate to offer help because of the shame and grief attached to disability in our culture. How often do we act as my grandmother did, hiding our needs, screening our important struggles? How often do we act as I did, failing to recognize problems that may be obvious to strangers? I believe that refusing to ask for help and failing to perceive needs are vital aspects of pastoral care that challenge Friends, especially in regard to disabilities of aged members and those who care for elders.

Building a Supportive Community

Historically, Friends have responded to the needs of aged members by pioneering the development of group residences and by producing a number of publications on aging and old age. The writings tend to be optimistic about the opportunities for continued spiritual development and emotional well-being in late life. The topics of loss and disability are generally cushioned with admonitions that old age is much more than a state of diminishment. There is little that addresses the effects of loss of mobility, limitations on driving, memory disruptions and lessened capacity for work.

No one wants to offend by offering help that isn't needed and no one wants to be a needy person who always asks for help. Most of our doubts about whether to offer or accept assistance are resolved when the people involved know each other well. Friends have an ideal forum for encouraging awareness of the circumstances of others' lives in worship-sharing. A regular program of worship-sharing in small support groups fosters deep listening, respectful attention to the pressures of individual situations, and appreciation of each person's unique gifts and burdens. Sample queries could include: Where am I most stressed in my daily life? What support do I need to lead a happier, more centered life? How could the meeting help me? How could I help the meeting? What is the finest act of ministry ever done for me? Have I ever felt that Friends let me down?

The meeting can educate members in issues of aging and disability through called meetings, adult first day classes, and articles in the newsletter. Committees or an adult class can choose a pamphlet on aging, disability, or pastoral care to read together. After the reading, guided discussion, perhaps relating the material to queries, can help Friends express concerns and suggest action.

If this process of sharing and education reveals that the meeting is not being adequately responsive to the needs of older persons, the meeting's pastoral group may call for those with special sensitivity to the changing needs of members to come forward. Announcements after worship and in the newsletter can help the whole meeting understand what to do and whom to alert in case of need. One strong strategy is to divide the entire membership into small sharing groups with clear lines of communication to the pastoral group.

Pastoral care can reach beyond simple adjustment to changing needs. It can facilitate the developmental tasks of old age by helping aged Friends to reflect on their lives, celebrate their mystical tendencies, summarize their wisdom and find ways to nurture and encourage younger people. For example, one long time First Day teacher who no longer has the energy to work with children holds workshops for inexperienced volunteers and has recorded topics that worked well with her classes.

Accepting and Honoring the Changes
That Come with Disability

Friends have chosen to belong to a religious society that requires a great deal of effort from each member. We value active commitment to spiritual ideals and active involvement in social concerns. One danger in the high valuation Friends place on activity is that we may inadvertently devalue those, including ourselves, who become less active.

Viktor Frankl, existential psychotherapist, survivor of Nazi death camps and author of the inspirational *Man's Search for Meaning*, writes about a nurse who was incapacitated by terminal illness. The woman had derived great satisfaction from caring for and comforting others. Unable to work any longer, she sank into severe depression. Frankl struggled to help the woman find meaning in the final stages of her life but was defeated by her bitter judgment of her own uselessness until he asked whether the patients she had nursed had also been useless. The woman defended her patients fiercely, cherishing the many spiritual and emotional gifts they had given her. Then Frankl asked if she could give the same gift to those who cared for her, blessing their lives by allowing them to minister to her.

When health problems or conflicting obligations cause Friends to become less active in the ministry, they may, like Frankl's nurse, feel less worthy. Low self-esteem and depression can make asking for help almost impossible. Dependency imposed by health limitations is a hard way of life and one that is very different from an active life freely chosen. The humility needed to submit to the care of others is not a skill that is praised or taught in our individualistic culture.

Responding to Individual Needs

A few guidelines will spot most serious problems. Has an individual withdrawn from usual activities? Has movement become more limited? Has driving become difficult? Has there been a strong change in personal style, an assertive person becoming very quiet or an equable person irritable and touchy? Has memory deteriorated markedly, not just the common forgetting of names but troubling lapses that could cause danger or wildly unexpected or frequent lapses? Does someone frequently remark that she/he can't hear or see something when others seem to have no difficulty? Does someone uncharacteristically decline social invitations and requests for service?

Our Quaker tradition of forthright speech can empower honest, caring inquiries whenever a Friend seems overburdened. By asking what is happening and what is desired, the meeting can tailor its response to the needs of each individual.

Meetings can encourage all members to make plans in advance of a time of disability. If a problem should become obvious within the meeting, who should be notified? The next of kin or geographically nearest relative may not be the ideal contact. Do loved ones know what an individual would want? Have long-term care insurance, living wills and powers of attorney been considered? Can an individual's home be modified for mobility limitations? A man once chose a long-term care facility for his mother based on his own preferences: the menu and the beauty of the grounds. Unfortunately, the most important aspect of the mother's daily life was the activities program, which did not meet her needs. Making one's own arrangements in advance may ease the loss of freedom when independent living can not be sustained.

Offers of help should be specific. Vagueness is usually received as lack of interest, so a general "Let us know if there's anything you need" is less useful than a direct offer of comfortable seating or help in using electronic mail. Skilled listeners and problem solvers can facilitate brainstorming with disabled or overstressed members about how to facilitate their full participation and ministry. Friends may discover simple, practical answers to some problems, such as making sure everyone can hear vocal ministry during worship or scheduling activities such as midweek meeting or study groups in elders' homes, if that is their wish.

The meeting need not, and probably cannot, provide all services, but the meeting can help in working with the member's support system and in helping to discover resources within the community. It is crucial, however, not to raise false hopes. One Friend was deeply disappointed by a support group that met twice, raising expectations of sustained and dramatic help that never materialized. The most important support may be simply letting Friends know that someone cares.

Intimacy based on deep knowledge of one another and appreciation for each one's gifts and limitations helps us to arrive at the most appropriate response. Support groups or clearness committees can be formed to help every member of the meeting to name their gifts, and to call forth those who love to minister in various ways. If a Friend's responsibilities have grown too heavy, others can suggest lightening the load, perhaps by reduced committee work or help with transportation. When members suffer changes in their abilities, the pastoral group can search for other means of service that fit their gifts but require less strength and mobility. Thus ministry to elders can offer opportunities for deep and sustained spiritual growth to the whole meeting community.

I find the essence of Quaker community in one of Kenneth Boulding's Naylor Sonnets which opens "Are not my friends built round me like a wall?" Ministering to disabled older members and those who care for elders can help Friends stand together against the ravages of pain and loss. When Friends can rely on the constancy of communal support, we can say, as the sonnet continues:

> We stand together in a firm stockade
> Around the cheerful fire our faith has made,
> Its light reflected from the eyes of all.

Rose Ketterer is a member of Haddonfield (NJ) Meeting. She has served on Worship and Ministry both for Haddonfield Meeting and for Philadelphia Yearly Meeting.

One Meeting's Experience: Senior Concerns Committee at Millville Meeting

Millville Meeting is a small meeting (55 members) in rural north central Pennsylvania. Their pastoral care committee has five members. In the spring of 1997, a few members became concerned about the needs of a growing number of older members. The committee had been addressing these needs on an individual basis, but there was a sense that this care could be given in a more focused way. Thus was born the "Senior Concerns Committee," first on an *ad hoc* basis and now as a standing committee of the meeting.

The committee began by holding small group round table discussions with senior members to hear what were their concerns and what they would hope for from the meeting. This was followed by individual interviews with each of the 10 or so older people in the meeting. The interviews began with what are your concerns today and what are your worries for tomorrow? Those interviews have resulted in a range of responses based on the older member needs and desires from the meeting including: meeting jointly with family members to discuss plans for a possible period of disability; education about resources such as reverse mortgages, long term care facilities, living wills, durable power of attorney for health care; and helping assess the older persons' homes for safety hazards and accessibility.

It has also led to modifications at the meeting to be more responsive. Arrangements are being made for transportation to meeting for worship when needed. There is now a wheelchair available at the meetinghouse and plans are being made for a more accessible bathroom. Older members who can no longer carry full committee work continue on committees bringing the skills and energy they have available. Every older member has a "buddy" who phones every day to check in. Often, two older members are buddies for one another. Every few months there is a special event for older members, often in the home of one of the older members.

The Senior Concerns Committee meets monthly and briefly reviews every senior's situation. A review may be just a 30 second check-in, but it provides an opportunity to be responsive if a special situation has come up. They have developed a "Senior Concerns Inventory," (see p. 306) which has been continually revised to meet the evolving understanding of the committee and the seniors. This questionnaire helps the committee to be attentive to areas of concern. The committee includes a nutritionist, a psychologist, an attorney and a person with skills in financial management so that these skills can be available for seniors planning for their futures.

The work of the committee is delicate and sensitive. At first there was a natural reserve on the part of some older members about sharing personal information and how it would be used. There is also a delicate balance of not usurping the responsibilities of family members. The committee has worked carefully with these concerns. They observe strict confidentiality of their work and their written records. They speak to family members or others only with the authorization of the older person. Over these two years the meeting has come to trust and value the work of the Senior Concerns Committee.

The work with seniors has produced new approaches to caring for younger members of the meeting as well. A new committee is forming to address issues of aging with middle-aged members. Every member, of any age, is encouraged to have emergency medical information on file with the meeting. Pastoral caregivers have begun the process of visiting all meeting families in their homes.

Information for this article was provide by Robert Miller, clerk of Overseers, Millville (PA) Meeting.

Adapting a House or Apartment for an Elderly or Disabled Resident and Good Ideas for Everyone . . .

- Smoke detectors, on a wall where they are accessible to turn off a false alarm and to change batteries
- Warning light on stove and oven to tell when it is on
- Doorbell(s) which can be heard throughout the house
- Audible telephone bell, and phones where person spends time: by bed, by TV, in bathroom, etc.
- Portable phones
- Special phone equipment for hearing or sight impaired
- Important numbers written large and near every phone
- Remove floor hazards—electric cords, slippery rugs, curled edges and corners of rugs, steps
- Bright lights on stairways, outside entrances, garage door
- Large, illuminated outside house numbers
- Light switches that are activated by noise or motion
- One of those long things with a grip to reach things on high shelves or things that fall down out of reach
- Grab bars in tub and shower
- Raised toilet, if person has trouble sitting or rising from sitting position
- Timed thermostat for warmth when getting out of bed
- Remote control TV
- Portable timers, with long-ringing bells, to use as reminder of things cooking, end of washer cycle, time to take pills, appointments
- Labeled, compartmentalized containers for medicine
- Sturdy step stool, with something to hold onto, near pantry and refrigerator, to reach high shelves in kitchen, basement, etc. One for each place
- Magnifying glasses near phone book, near pantry and refrigerator for reading food labels and cooking instructions, in bathroom for medicine directions
- Reorganize storage to avoid lifting and bending
- Large, readable outdoor thermometer
- More chairs with arms, raiseable (electric) seats on chairs
- Combination storm/screens, at least on windows the person will open frequently

Senior Concerns Inventory

Below is a summary of the questionnaire used by the Senior Concerns Committee of Millville (PA) Meeting. For an explanation of how it is used, see the "One Meeting's Experience" on page 303.

I. Background information

Name, address, phone number, birth date
Emergency contact, physician contact
Household members
Immediate family and close friends' address and phone
Millville Meeting buddy's name and phone
Persons to be notified in case of illness
Persons who have access to your house

II. Visit information

Date, names of visitors
Names of family or friends in attendance

III. Senior concerns

These topics are explored with the person being visited. On Millville Meeting's form there are lines after each item for writing information and evaluation.

A. Daily routines
B. Transportation
C. Household safety and maintenance
D. Medical needs: medications, primary and other physicians
E. Mental health
F. Health habits and nutrition
G. Spiritual needs
H. Social life
I. Recreational and avocational interests
J. Financial and legal
　　Will—executor, date, location
　　Living will—date and location
　　Durable health care agent—name, date, location
　　Power of attorney—name, date, location
　　Durable power of attorney—name, date, location
　　Location of information regarding financial institutions and
　　　account numbers

K. Insurance
   Health insurance—type & policy number
   Long term care insurance, other
L. Death Requests
   Role of Millville Meeting in making arrangements
   Family members to be in contact with
   Wishes regarding memorial service
   Wishes regarding burial or cremation.

IV. Summary

Present status
Recommendations and solutions
Concerns for the future

Questions for Reflection

1. How do Friends feel when faced with illness or incapacity in ourselves or others? How do these feelings color our work in pastoral care?
2. How can Friends be encouraged to share their feelings and articulate their needs to others in the meeting?
3. What procedures are in place to assist Friends laboring under disabling circumstances?
4. Given our limitations, what reasonable expectations can we have for ministry to older members and members who care for disabled elders? If unsatisfied with our response, how can we achieve a more welcome answer?
5. Is everyone in the meeting equally likely to receive support in adversity? What personal characteristics do we most value and therefore respond to most readily? How can we be more receptive to the need of those to whom we are less drawn?
6. How can vocal ministry be more available to those with hearing impairments: voice projection training for the general membership, use of a sound system, recording a summary of verbal ministry or other methods?

RESOURCES

Sources of Support for Your Meeting

Yearly Meeting Ministry and Counsel Committee. A sometimes overlooked resource for meetings is the Ministry and Counsel Committee at the yearly meeting level who are often available to assist meetings in considering pastoral care questions. Consult your yearly meeting directory.

Friends General Conference Traveling Ministries Program. The Traveling Ministries Program can help meetings find seasoned Friends who will visit the meeting to help in addressing specific concerns that have arisen or simply for the richness of worshiping and talking together. Seasoned Friends might visit for a period of one to several days depending on the needs of the meeting and the availability of the traveling Friend. Contact the Traveling Ministries Coordinator 215-561-1700 or email friends@fgcquaker.org.

Pendle Hill On the Road arranges facilitators for retreats at your meeting or quarterly meeting including such topics as Inquirers' Weekends and pastoral care. Contact the Outreach Coordinator at Pendle Hill, 800-742-3150, extension 137.

Philadelphia Yearly Meeting Friends Counseling Service is available to meetings in Philadelphia Yearly Meeting to consult on pastoral care and counseling. Contact the Counseling Service Coordinator, 215-248-0489.

The Deepening and Strengthening Our Meetings as Faith Communities Project provides facilitators to meetings in Philadelphia Yearly Meeting to look at their spiritual grounding, the business of the meeting and the meeting community. Contact Arlene Kelly, 215-241-7018 or email arlenekel@aol.com.

Many of the resources listed below are stocked by QuakerBooks of FGC and can be ordered by: calling 800-966-4556, e-mailing bookstore@fgcquaker.org or on the web at www.quakerbooks.org. Except for magazine articles and extracts, materials listed which are not in stock can usually be specially ordered even if they are out of print.

Many of these materials are also available from the Henry J. Cadbury Library of Philadelphia Yearly Meeting, 215-241-7220. Friends outside Philadelphia Yearly Meeting can subscribe to the library.

The Role of Pastoral Caregive (pp. 1–40)

Britain Yearly Meeting. *Caring for One Another: Notes for Overseers in the Society of Friends.* London: Quaker Home Service, 1978.

Britain Yearly Meeting. *Corporate Eldership and Oversight.* London: Quaker Home Service, 1990.

Britain Yearly Meeting Committee on Eldership and Oversight. *Patterns of Eldership and Oversight.* London: Quaker Home Service, 1997.

Britain Yearly Meeting Committee on Eldership and Oversight. *Spiritual Reviews.* London: Quaker Home Service, 1999.

Bownas, Samuel. *A Description of the Qualifications Necessary to a Gospel Minister: Advice to Ministers and Elders Among the People Called Quakers, 1750.* Wallingford, PA: Pendle Hill, 1989.

Cambridge Friends Meeting. *CFM Ministry and Counsel Eldership Resources.* Cambridge, MA: Cambridge Friends Meeting, February, 2000.

Edwards, Tilden. *Spiritual Friend: Reclaiming the Gift of Spiritual Direction.* New York: Paulist Press, 1980.

Greene, Jan, and Marty Walton, editors. *Fostering Vital Friends Meeting: A Handbook for Working with Quaker Meetings.* Philadelphia, PA: Quaker Press of Friends General Conference, 1999.

Greene, Jan, and Marty Walton, editors. *Fostering Vital Friends Meetings (Part Two): Resources for Working with Quaker Meetings.* Philadelphia, PA: Quaker Press of Friends General Conference, 1999. This entire collections of resources can be accessed at www.fgcquaker.org.

Grundy, Martha Paxson. *Tall Poppies: Supporting Gifts of Ministry and Eldering in the Monthly Meeting.* Wallingford, PA: Pendle Hill Pamphlet #347, 2000.

Hoffman, Jan. "Experiences of the Relationship of Minister & Elders" in *Growing in Faith: The Collected Writings of Jan Hoffman.* Available from QuakerBooks of FGC, 2000.

Kelley, Arlene. "Strengthening Our Meeting As a Caring Community." *Friends Journal,* October, 1984.

Loring, Patricia. *Listening Spirituality, Vol. II: Corporate Spiritual Practice Among Friends* (chapter 7). Washington Grove, MD: Openings Press, 1999.

Ratliff, Bill. *Out of the Silence: Quaker Perspectives on Pastoral Care and Counseling.* Wallingford, PA: Pendle Hill, 2001.

Wilson, Lloyd Lee. *Essays on the Quaker Vision of Gospel Order.* Philadelphia, PA: Quaker Press of Friends General Conference, 2002.

Membership in Our Meetings (pp. 41–69)

Books of Faith and Practice. The best resource on membership is your yearly meeting's *Faith and Practice.* Because of a diversity of views on membership you might find it helpful to consult other yearly meetings as well.

Britain Yearly Meeting Committee on Eldership and Oversight. *Moving into Membership.* London: Quaker Home Service, 2001.

Gillman, Harvey, ed. *Reaching Out: On Membership.* London: Quaker Home Service, 1996.

Heron, Alastair. *Caring, Conviction, Commitment: Dilemmas of Quaker Membership Today.* London: Quaker Home Service, 1992.

Heron, Alastair. *On Being a Quaker: Membership—Past, Present, Future.* Kelso, Scotland: Curlew, 2000.

Hoffman, Jan. "Clearness in Double Discernment: Membership and Marriage," in *Companions Along the Way.* Florence Ruth Kline and Marty Grundy, eds. Philadelphia, PA: Philadelphia Yearly Meeting, 2000.

Loring, Patricia. *Listening Spirituality Volume II: Corporate Spiritual Practice Among Friends* (especially chapter 2). Washington Grove, MD: Openings Press, 1999.

Pastoral Care for Marriage and Divorce (pp. 71–105)

Britain Yearly Meeting. *When the Wind Changes: Young Peoples' Experience of Divorce and Changing Family Patterns.* London: Quaker Home Service, 2001.

Britain Yearly Meeting Committee on Eldership and Oversight. *Committed Relationships.* London: Quaker Home Service, 2001.

Hill, Leslie. *Marriage: A Spiritual Leading for Lesbian, Gay, and Straight Couples.* Wallingford, PA: Pendle Hill, reprint 1995.

Hoffman, Jan. "Clearness in Double Discernment: Membership and Marriage," in *Companions Along the Way.* Florence Ruth Kline and Marty Grundy, eds. Philadelphia, PA: Philadelphia Yearly Meeting, 2000.

Hoffman, Jan. "On Marriage: No Safe Dallying with Truth." *Friends Bulletin,* October, 1989. The article also appears in *Growing in Faith: Collected Writings of Jan Hoffman.* March, 2000.

Kelly, Arlene. "Separation and Divorce: The Meeting's Role," *Friends Journal,* February 1991.

Love Makes a Family: Lesbian and Gay Families in the Religious Society of Friends. FLGC, 1992. Video.

Markman, Howard, et al. *Fighting for Your Marriage: Positive Steps for Preventing Divorce and Preserving a Lasting Love.* Jossey Bass, 2001.

"A Minute on Marriage." *The Friend,* March 1, 1996.

New England Yearly Meeting. *Living with Oneself and Others: Working Papers on Aspects of Family Life.* New England Yearly Meeting, revised edition 2002.

Ohio Valley Yearly Meeting Committee on Sexuality. *Guide for Discussions on Sexuality: A Menu Plan for Nourishing Discussions in Monthly Meetings,* 1991.

Olson, David and Amy Olson. *Empowering Couples.* St. Paul, MN: Life Innovations, Inc., 1999.

Philadelphia Yearly Meeting Family Relations Committee. *"In the Presence of God and These Our Friends . . .": A Quaker Marriage.* Philadelphia, PA: Philadelphia Yearly Meeting, rev. 1988.

Philadelphia Yearly Meeting Family Relations Committee. *A Resource Guide to Be Used by a Same-Sex Couples.* Philadelphia, PA: Philadelphia Yearly Meeting, 1988.

Spring, J. *After the Affair.* New York: Harper, 1996.

Watson, Elizabeth. *Marriage in the Light: Reflections on Commitment and the Clearness Process.* Philadelphia, PA: Philadelphia Yearly Meeting Family Relations Committee, 1993.

Sources of Support for Couples and Marriage

Friends General Conference Couple Enrichment Program. Trained couple enrichment facilitators are available throughout North America to lead retreats for couples in your meeting or to help in establishing an ongoing couples support group. Contact the leader couple in your yearly meeting, call Friends General Conference, 215-561-1700 or look at www.fgcquaker.org under programs see Couple Enrichment.

On Homosexuality, Not Specifically on Marriage

Barnett, Walter. *Homosexuality and the Bible: An Interpretation.* Wallingford, PA: Pendle Hill Pamphlet #226, 1979.

Both My Moms' Names are Judy. Lesbian and Gay Parents Association. Video.

"Christians and Homosexuality: A Discussion of Biblical and Ethical Issues." *The Other Side Magazine*, Philadelphia, PA, 1990.

Each of Us Is Inevitable: Some Keynote Addresses given at Annual Midwinter (and other) Gatherings, 1977–1989. Friends for Lesbian and Gay Concerns, 1989.

Fager, Chuck, editor. *The Bible, the Church and the Future of Friends: Papers from the Quaker Issues Roundtable.* Wallingford, PA: Pendle Hill, 1996.

Furnish, Victor Paul. *The Moral Teaching of Paul: Selected Issues.* Nashville, TN: Abingdon Press, 1983.

Sources of Support for Lesbian and Gay Friends

Friends for Lesbian and Gay Concerns (FLGC). For contact information and to receive the FLGC newsletter see the website at www.quaker.org/flgc.

Gay, Lesbian and Straight Education Network (GLSEN), 212 W. 27th Street, New York, NY 10001. (212) 727-1035 or see their website at www.glsen.org.

Parents, Families and Friends of Lesbians and Gays (PFLAG), P.O. Box 34792, Washington, DC 20043-4792. (202) 638-4200.

Care of the Meeting Community (pp. 107–154)

On Nurturing Community (pp. 109–115)

Cronk, Sandra. *Gospel Order: A Quaker Understanding of Faithful Church Community.* Wallingford, PA: Pendle Hill Pamphlet #297, 1991.

Loring, Patricia. *Listening Spirituality, Vol. II: Corporate Spiritual Practice Among Friends.* Washington Grove, MD: Openings Press, 1999.

O'Shea, Ursula Janey. *Living the Way: Quaker Spirituality and Community.* Backhouse Lecture #28. North Hobart, Tasmania: Australia Yearly Meeting, 1993.

Orleck, Terry. *The Second Cooperative Sports and Games Book.* New York: Pantheon Press, 1982.

Peck, M. Scott. *The Different Drum: Community Making and Peace.* New York: Simon & Schuster, 1987.

Shaffer, Carolyn R., and Kristin Anundsen. *Creating Community Anywhere.* New York: Putnam, 1993.

Snoek, Diedrich. *Hunger for Community.* Wallingford, PA: Pendle Hill Pamphlet #188.

Steinke, Peter. *The Healthy Congregation.* Bethesda, MD: Alban Institute, 1996.

Steinke, Peter. *How Your Church Family Works.* Bethesda, MD: Alban Institute, 1993.

Taber, William and Frances. *Building the Life of the Meeting.* Melbourne Beach, FL: Southeastern Yearly Meeting, 1994.

Tromans, Lynne-Marie. *Commands & Invitations: Sharing Our Experiences of Hearing, Responding to and Living out God's Call.* London: Quaker Home Service and Woodbrooke College, 1995.

Wilson, Lloyd Lee. *Essays on the Quaker Vision of Gospel Order.* Philadelphia, PA: Quaker Press of Friends General Conference, 2002.

On Race (pp. 116–128)

Anderson, Jervis. *Bayard Rustin: The Troubles I've Seen.* New York: Harper Collins, 1977.

Brandt, Joseph. *Dismantling Racism: The Continuing Challenge to White America.* Minneapolis: Augsburg Fortress, 1991.

Cadbury, Henry J. "Negro Membership in the Society of Friends." *The Journal of Negro History*, Vol. XXI, No. 2, April 1936.

Davies, E. and P. T. Hennessee. *Ending Racism in the Church*. Cleveland, OH: United Church Press, 1998.

Fletcher, Jim and C. Mabee. *A Quaker Speaks from the Black Experience: The Life and Selected Writings of Barrington Dunbar*. New York: New York Yearly Meeting, 1979.

Harrison, E. C. *For Emancipation & Education: Some Black & Quaker Efforts 1680–1900*. Pennsylvania: Awbury Arboretum Association, 1997.

Hirabayashi, Gordon. *Good Times, Bad Times: Idealism Is Realism*. Argenta, BC: Argenta Friends Press, 1985.

Gonzalez, Juan. *Harvest of Empire: A History of Latinos in America*. New York: Viking, 2000.

"Japanese American Internment: A Retrospective." A series of articles in *Friends Journal*. November, 1992.

Kivel, Paul. *Uprooting Racism: How White People Can Work for Racial Justice*. Gabriola Island, BC: New Society Publishers, 1996.

Selleck, Linda. *Gentle Invaders*. Richmond, IN: Friends United Press, 1995.

Soderlund, Jean R. *Quakers and Slavery: A Divided Spirit*. Princeton, NJ: Princeton University, 1985.

Swatzler, David. *A Friend among the Senecas: The Quaker Mission to Cornplanter's People*. Mechanicsburg, PA: Stackpole Books, 2000.

Takaki, Ron. *Strangers from a Different Shore: A History of Asian Americans*. New York: Little, Brown & Company, 1998.

Tatum, Beverly D. *Why Are All the Black Kids Sitting Together in the Cafeteria?* New York: Basic Books, 1997.

Woolrych, Lilamani. *Communicating Across Cultures*. Joseph Rowntree Quaker Fellow Report 1992/93. England: Joseph Rowntree Charitable Trust, 1998.

Sources of Support for Friends of Color and for Working on Race and Racism

Fellowship of Friends of African Descent, 1515 Cherry Street, Philadelphia, PA 19102, 215-627-6665. Website: www.quaker.org/ffad

Friends General Conference Committee for Ministry on Racism, 215-561-1700, Website: www.fgcquaker.org.

On Meetinghouses (pp. 129–138)

Ives, Kenneth. *A Friendly Meeting Place: Visitors Increase When You Have Your Own Meeting*. Progressiv, 1988.

Lynch, Michael. *How to Care for Religious Properties*. Preservation League of New York State, 1982.

Mennonite Conciliation Service. *Mediation and Facilitation Training Manual*. See especially chapter 6, "Conflict in Groups." Akron, PA: Mennonite Central Committee, 1995.

Philadelphia Electric Company. *Reducing Energy Costs in Religious Buildings: A Workbook for Congregational Leaders*. Philadelphia, PA: Philadelphia Electric Company, 1992.

Springer, Margaret. *A Meeting Home*. Canadian Quaker Pamphlet 31. Argenta, BC: Argenta Friends Press, 1989.

On Clearness Processes (pp. 139–147)

Canadian Yearly Meeting. *Organization and Procedure of Canadian Yearly Meeting.* See chapter X, "Clearness Committees, Committees of Care, and Oversight Committees.

Central Philadelphia Monthly Meeting. *Responding to Calls to Ministry.* Philadelphia, PA: Central Philadelphia Monthly Meeting, 1995.

Farnham, Suzanne G., et. al. *Listening Hearts: Discerning Call in Community.* Harrisburg, PA: Morehouse, 1991.

Friends Consultation on Discernment. Quaker Hill Conference Center, 1985.

Hoffman, Jan. *Clearness Committees and Their Use in Personal Discernment.* Philadelphia, PA: Quaker Press of Friends General Conference, revised 1996.

Kline, Florence Ruth, and Martha Paxson Grundy, editors. *Companions Along the Way: Spiritual Formation within the Quaker Tradition.* Philadelphia, PA: Philadelphia Yearly Meeting, 2000.

Loring, Patricia. *Spiritual Discernment: The Context and Goal of Clearness Committees.* Wallingford, PA: Pendle Hill Pamphlet #305, 1992.

Pacific Yearly Meeting. *Faith and Practice of Pacific Yearly Meeting.* San Francisco, CA: Pacific Yearly Meeting, 1985.

Paine, Ruth Hyde. *How Do I Know It's a Calling?* Michener Memorial Lecture, 1992. Melbourne Beach, FL: Southeastern Yearly Meeting, 1992.

On Stands of Conscience (pp. 148–154)

Avery, Chel. *Peace and Taxes—God and Country: A Guide for Seeking Clearness on War Tax Concerns.* Philadelphia, PA: Philadelphia Yearly Meeting, 1990.

Benn, Ruth and Ed Hedemann, eds. *War Tax Resistance: A Guide to Withholding Your Support from the Military.* Philadelphia, PA: New Society Publishers and New York: War Resisters League, 1992.

Caldwell, Barbara, and Dorothy Reichardt. *Growing in the Light: Units for All Ages.* Philadelphia, PA: Philadelphia Yearly Meeting, revised 1998.

Central Philadelphia Monthly Meeting. *Responding to Calls to Ministry.* Philadelphia, PA: Central Philadelphia Monthly Meeting, 1995.

Corbett, Jim. *Leadings.* 1994 J. Barnard Walton Lecture. Melbourne Beach, FL: Southeastern Yearly Meeting, 1995.

Craudereuff, Elaine. *War Taxes: Experiences of Philadelphia Yearly Meeting Quakers through the American Revolution.* Wallingford, PA: Pendle Hill Pamphlet #286.

Handbook on Military Taxes and Conscience. Friends Committee on War Tax Concerns, 1988.

Olmstead, Sterling. *Motions of Love: Woolman As Mystic and Activist.* Wallingford, PA: Pendle Hill Pamphlet #312, 1993.

Prutzman, Priscilla, et al. *Friendly Classroom for a Small Planet: A Handbook on Creative Approaches to Living and Problem Solving for Children.* Gabriola Island, BC: New Society Publishers, 1988.

Randall, Stuart, editor. *Meeting Needs: A Handbook for Quaker Groups and Meetings.* London: Quaker Home Service, 1992.

Pastoral Care for Illness and Death (pp. 155–183)

Backstrom, Kirsten. *In Beauty: A Quaker Approach to End-of-Life Care.* Wallingford, PA: Pendle Hill Pamphlet #355, 2001.

Bell, Sherry M. *Visiting Mom: An Unexpected Gift.* Sedona, AZ: Elder Press, 2000.

Caposella, Cappy, and Sheila Warnock. *Share the Care: How to Organize a Group to Care for Someone Who Is Dying*. New York: Simon & Schuster, 1995.

Dickens, Monica. *Miracles of Courage: How Families Meet the Challenge of a Child's Critical Illness*. New York: Dodd, Mead, 1985.

Lampen, Diana. *Facing Death*. London: Quaker Home Service, 1979.

Levine, Stephen. *Meetings at the Edge: Dialogues with the Grieving and the Dying, the Healing and the Healed*. New York, NY: Anchor-Doubleday, 1984.

McIver, Lucy Screechfield. *A Song of Death, Our Spiritual Birth: A Quaker Way of Dying*. Wallingford, PA: Pendle Hill Pamphlet #34 , 1998.

McLeod, Beth Witrogen. *Caregiving: The Spiritual Journey of Love, Loss and Renewal*. New York: John Wiley and Sons, 1999.

Morgan, Ernest. *Dealing Creatively with Death: A Manual of Death Education and Simple Burial*. 14th ed. Hinesburg, VT : Upper Access, Inc., 2001.

Noeld, Elizabeth Parker. *Seven Choices: Taking Steps to New Life after Losing Someone You Love*. Houston, TX: Centerpoint Press, 1997.

Planning Ahead: Meeting Our Responsibilities When Death Occurs. Honolulu Friends Meeting Final Affairs Committee, 1990.

Shannon, Thomas A. *Let Them Go Free: A Family Prayer Service to Assist in the Withdrawal of Life Support*. Kansas City, MO: Sheed and Ward, 1987.

Smith, Bradford. *Dear Gift of Life*. Wallingford, PA: Pendle Hill Pamphlet #142, 1965.

Taylor, Phyllis. *A Quaker Look at Living with Death and Dying*. Philadelphia, PA: Philadelphia Yearly Meeting Family Relations Committee, 1989.

Watson, Elizabeth. *Guests of My Life*. Philadelphia, PA: Quaker Press of Friends General Conference, 1996.

Morris, Virginia. *Talking about Death Won't Kill You*. New York: Workman, 2001.

Facing Conflict in the Meeting (pp. 185–213)

Britain Yearly Meeting Committee on Eldership and Oversight. *Conflict in Meetings*. London: Quaker Home Service, 2000.

Mennonite Conciliation Service. *Mediation and Facilitation Training Manual*. See especially chapter 6, "Conflict in Groups." Akron, PA: Mennonite Central Committee, 1995.

New England Yearly Meeting. *Addressing Sexual Abuse in Friends Meetings*. Worcester, MA: New England Yearly Meeting, 1994.

Proceedings of the 1982 Friends Consultation on Eldering. Quaker Hill Conference Center.

The Wounded Meeting: Dealing with Difficult Behavior in Meeting for Worship. Philadelphia, PA: Quaker Press of Friends General Conference, 1993.

Pastoral Care for Persons with Mental Illness (pp. 215–246)

Alcoholics Anonymous. *Twelve Steps and Twelve Traditions*. Dallas, TX: Alcoholics Anonymous World Service, 1981.

Beattie, Melody. *Codependent No More/Beyond Codependency*. New York: MJF, 1997.

Cronk, Sandra. *Dark Night Journey: Inward Repatterning Toward a Life Centered in God*. Wallingford, PA: Pendle Hill, 1991.

"I am a Quaker and I am an Alcoholic." Philadelphia, PA: *Friends Journal*, August, 1989.

Fields, Richard. *Drugs in Perspective*. New York: McGraw Hill, 2001.

Jamison, Kay Redfield. *An Unquiet Mind*. New York: Random House, 1995.

Kaysen, Susanna. *Girl, Interrupted*. New York: Random House, 1993.

Klein, Donald F., M.D., and Paul H. Wender. *Understanding Depression*. New York: Oxford University Press, 1993.

Kurtz, Ernest and Katherine Ketcham. *The Spirituality of Imperfection: Story Telling and the Journey to Wholeness*. New York: Bantam Books, 1994.

Mihalas, Dmitri. *Depression and Spiritual Growth*. Wallingford, PA: Pendle Hill Pamphlet, 1996.

Sheehan, Susan. *Is There No Place on Earth for Me?* New York: Random House, 1983.

Styron, William. *Darkness Visible*. New York: Random House, 1991.

The Wounded Meeting: Dealing with Difficult Behavior in Meeting for Worship. Philadelphia, PA: Quaker Press of Friends General Conference, 1993.

The Welfare of Each Member (pp. 247–307)

On Children and Families (pp. 249–272)

Asselin, Judy and Denis. *Simple Riches: Reflections on the Work of the Quaker Parent*. 25th Annual Michener Lecture. Tallahassee, FL: Southeastern Yearly Meeting, 1995.

Boulding, Elise. *One Small Plot of Heaven: Reflections on Family Life by a Quaker Sociologist*. Wallingford, PA: Pendle Hill, 1989.

Britain Yearly Meeting Committee on Eldership and Oversight. *Pastoral Care of Children and Young People*. London: Quaker Home Service, 2001.

Coles, Robert. *Spiritual Life of Children*. New York: Houghton Mifflin Co., 1990.

Curran, Dolores. *Stress and the Family: How Healthy Families Control the Ten Most Common Stresses*. Minneapolis, MN: Winston Press, 1985.

Heath, Harriet. *Answering That of God in Our Children*. Wallingford, PA: Pendle Hill, Pamphlet #315, 1994.

Heath, Harriet. *Parents Planning: A Manual*. Haverford, PA: Conrow Publishing Company, 1983.

Living with Oneself and Others: Working Papers on Aspects of Family Life. Worcester, MA: New England Yearly Meeting, revised edition 2002.

Murdock, Maureen. *Spinning Inward: Using Guided Imagery with Children for Learning, Creativity, and Relaxation*. Boston, MA: Shambhala, 1987.

Orleck, Terry. *Second Cooperative Sports and Games Book*. New York: Vintage Books, 1982.

Pollack, S. and J. Vaughn. *Politics of the Heart: A Lesbian Parenting Anthology*. Ithaca, NY: Firebrand, 1987.

Rutter, M. *A Measure of Our Values: Goals and Dilemmas in the Upbringing of Children*. London: Quaker Home Service, 1984.

Taffel, Ron and Melinda Blau. *Parenting by Heart*. Upper Saddle River, NJ: Addison Wesley, 1993.

On Singles (pp. 273–281)

Anton, Linda Hunt. *Never to Be a Mother: A Guide For All Women Who Didn't—Or Couldn't—Have Children.* San Francisco, CA: Harper, 1992.

Fagerstrom, Douglas L. *Baker Handbook of Single Adult Ministry.* Grand Rapids, MI: Baker Books, 1997.

Hendrix, Harville. *Keeping the Love You Find: A Guide for Singles.* New York: Pocket Books, 1992.

Shellenberger, Susie, and Michael Ross. *Adventures in Singlehood: A Map for Singles.* Grand Rapids, MI: Zondervan Publishing House, 1996.

Smith, Harold Ivan. *51 Good Thing to Do While You're Waiting for the Right One to Come Along: A Guide for Being Single.* Nashville, TN: Broadman & Holman, 1994.

On Men (pp. 282–289)

Hazelden Foundation. *Touchstones: A Book of Daily Meditations for Men.* New York: Harper and Row, 1986.

Jastrab, Joseph. *Sacred Manhood, Sacred Earth: A Vision Quest into the Wilderness of a Man's Heart.* New York: Harper Collins, 1994.

Meade, Michael. *Men and the Water of Life: Initiation and the Tempering of Men.* San Francisco, CA: Harper, 1993.

Osherson, Samuel. *Finding Our Fathers: The Unfinished Business of Manhood.* Chicago, IL: Contemporary Books, 2001.

Thompson, Keith, ed. *To Be a Man: In Search of the Deep Masculine.* Los Angeles: Jeremy Tarcher, 1991.

On Aging (pp. 290–307)

Ansello, Edward F., and Nancy N. Eustis. *Aging and Disabilities: Seeking Common Ground.* Amityville, NY: Baywood Publishing, 1992.

Gentzler, Richard H., and Donald F. Clinger. *Aging: God's Challenge to Church and Synagogue.* Nashville, TN: Discipleship Resources, 1996.

Jacobs, Ruth Harriet. *Be An Outrageous Older Woman.* New York: Harper Perennial, Division of Harper Collins, 1997.

Morris, Virginia. *How to Care for Aging Parents.* New York: Workman, 1996.

Morrison, Mary C. *Let Evening Come: Reflections on Aging.* New York: Doubleday, 1998. (This is an expanded version of *Without Nightfall Upon the Spirit*, Wallingford, PA: Pendle Hill Pamphlet #311, 1993.)

Myerhoff, Barbara. *Number Our Days.* New York: Simon and Schuster, Touchstone Books, 1980.

Quadagno, Jill S. *Aging and the Life Course: An Introduction to Social Gerontology.* New York: McGraw, 1998.

Ram, Dass. *Still Here: Embracing Aging, Changing and Death.* New York: Riverhead Books, 2000.

Scott-Maxwell, Florida. *The Measure of My Days.* New York: Penguin, 1979.

Yungblut, John. *On Hallowing One's Diminishments.* Wallingford, PA: Pendle Hill Pamphlet #292, 1990.

Subject Index

This index will assist in locating the page where an article relating to the listed subject begins.